Transdisciplinarity Revealed

Transdisciplinarity Revealed

What Librarians Need to Know

Victoria Martin

Foreword by Alfonso Montuori

LIBRARIES UNLIMITED™

An Imprint of ABC-CLIO, LLC

Santa Barbara, California • Denver, Colorado

Library of Congress Cataloging in Publication Control Number: 2016058429

ISBN: 978-1-4408-4347-1
EISBN: 978-1-4408-4348-8

21 20 19 18 17   1 2 3 4 5

This book is also available as an eBook.

Libraries Unlimited
An Imprint of ABC-CLIO, LLC

ABC-CLIO, LLC
130 Cremona Drive, P.O. Box 1911
Santa Barbara, California 93116-1911
www.abc-clio.com

This book is printed on acid-free paper ∞

Manufactured in the United States of America

We will never solve problems by using the same level of consciousness we used when we created them.

—Albert Einstein

Contents

Foreword

Alfonso Montuori

Victoria Martin's volume on transdisciplinarity is a very welcome and much needed addition for those of us already immersed in transdisciplinary research, for individuals wishing to learn more about this fast-growing approach to inquiry, and of course for her target audience, librarians. Transdisciplinarity reflects a new approach to, and relationship with, knowledge in which librarians are a vital nexus. They will play a key role because the organization of knowledge is at the heart of transdisciplinarity.

The term "transdisciplinarity" is certainly a mouthful. Initially, it may seem like yet another arcane transatlantic academic fad with all the appropriate neologisms and impenetrable jargon, soon to be buried in the mysterious place of forgetting where intellectual elephants go to die. But even if it does occasionally tip over into excessively polysyllabic terminology, transdisciplinarity's fundamental aim is radical and even revolutionary, and its goal is actually very practical. Transdisciplinarity has developed to make sense of an increasingly complex, interconnected world with the goal of actually doing something about the overwhelming problems facing humanity in ways that have escaped traditional disciplinary research.

Transdisciplinarity is radical and revolutionary because it goes to the roots of the way we organize knowledge and the way we think. Transdisciplinarity does not reject disciplinary research and disciplinary specialization. It proposes that the present emphasis on disciplinary hyper-specialization is limited and limiting. The way we currently think about knowledge and organize knowledge is insufficient. As human beings historically accumulated more and more knowledge about specific topics, new disciplines spun off from mother philosophy, which initially encompassed all love of knowledge. With increased knowledge came specialization, and with specialization came a division of labor. At a certain point, it became necessary to specialize in one particular field because it reflected the researcher's interest but also because there was more and more research and writing being done in the new field that specialization was becoming necessary to keep up with all the new developments.

Disciplinary specialization was a natural result of the increasingly systematic study of the world, with the development of universities, and attempts at organizing knowledge. The organization of knowledge in academic departments reflected the Cartesian/Newtonian worldview, which saw the world as being made up of closed, mostly noncommunicating parts. In order to understand these parts one had to dig deeper and deeper inside the part. Maintaining clarity and coherence required a strict Aristotelian logic: something was either A or B, but could not be both A *and* B. The organization of knowledge separated disciplines into "clear and distinct" spaces, increasingly smaller disciplines and subdisciplines, with increasingly sharper demarcation from everything around them.

This paralleled the way Descartes had argued for the value of clear and distinct ideas in our thinking. Simplicity was the order of the day, and complexity was merely a reflection of the fact that our knowledge had not properly understood the subject. At the turn of the century, when psychology was not yet a fully developed discipline, figures like William James explored both psychology and philosophy. As psychology's disciplinary identity developed, it became more and more of a closed system, like all other disciplines. Boundaries became more rigid. Systems closed. Turf was established. One was either a sociologist or a psychologist. A psychologist or a philosopher. It was either/or.

Specialization, which started earlier in the natural sciences than in the human or social sciences, was initially useful and revolutionary and the source of great scientific advances, indeed the engine of progress. Now, it is increasingly becoming the source of the very problems we are attempting to address. And if those problems are caused by a specific way of thinking and organizing knowing and knowledge, then we can't use that same way of thinking of knowing to address our problems.

Once upon a time, it was said that men like Aristotle knew just about all human beings knew about the world. Pico Della Mirandola, who died in 1494, is often cited as an example of the last men to have such truly comprehensive, encyclopedic knowledge; he knew all there was to know, all human beings had categorized and systematized, at least in Europe. Pico Della Mirandola himself though was probably aware of his limitations, because he knew that in Europe there were many strands of knowledge, many diverse secret traditions, many forms of esotericism, as well as knowledge women shared among themselves but not with men, and for which they were later punished in the cruelest ways. This raises the question, who defines what does and does not constitute knowledge? A timely question that transdisciplinarians are forced to address.

In the second half of the 20th century, Buckminster Fuller and a few other maverick "thinkers," mostly informed by general system theory, have argued for the importance of "comprehensivist" or "integrative" approaches, critiquing disciplinary fragmentation and the inability of reductionist perspectives to understand wholes and interconnected systems and interesting, *life*. Newtonian physics had been considered the most important and powerful science. Its approach had been emulated by the social sciences, and it should come as no surprise that the founder of general system theory, the Austrian Ludwig von Bertalanffy, was a biologist. Following the fruitful connection of general system theory, cybernetics, and information theory, most notably at the Macy conferences of 1946 to 1953 (Bateson 2004; Heims 1993), but also at Arthur Koestler's later Alpbach Symposium of 1968 entitled "Beyond Reductionism" (Koestler and Smythies 1972), much of the key impetus in the most interesting strands of Transdisciplinarity has been informed by scholars steeped in the systems sciences, with Erich Jantsch, Jean Piaget, Edgar Morin, and later Anthony Wilden and Basarab Nicolescu.

Despite some countertrends, there is no doubt that ours has overwhelmingly been a time of hyperspecialization, with enormous amounts of new information generated across a wide variety of disciplines. What we now need, and what has been sorely lacking, is a way to bring that information together and apply it to the enormously pressing issues we are all facing today. Our problems are increasingly of a global nature, yet our knowledge is increasingly hyper-specialized, and in the process we lose sight of the larger whole and of fundamental interconnection and interdependence. Any number of exciting developments in the sciences are shedding light of phenomena in startling new ways. The success of neuroscience in capturing the popular imagination is just one example. But how many books can we read about the neuroscience of love or creativity, illustrating the remarkable goings on in the brain when we fall in love or have an insight, without beginning to wonder if it wouldn't have been helpful if the authors had familiarized themselves with the decades of existing research on those subjects in other disciplines?

My intention here is certainly not to dismiss neuroscience, which is a fascinating and important area of research and new insights. What I do find problematic is the tendency among some popularizers and even some specialists to reduce the phenomenon they are studying to the insights of one particular disciplinary perspective, and in the process, wittingly or unwittingly, also dismiss what has gone before. Never mind all that "soft" qualitative stuff, all that talking to people about their "subjective" opinions, now we can see the brain light up when they get an idea! Neuroscience is by no means the only guilty party here, of course. The problem is precisely that all too often we find that disciplines operate like silos, oblivious to the work being done on the same subject in the universes next door, in other disciplines. Different disciplinary perspectives are either ignored or dismissed. Knowledge is reduced, in space (the boundaries of one discipline) and in time (only research within the last five years is considered).

The philosopher Bruce Wilshire's underappreciated classic *The Moral Collapse of the University* went to great lengths to show the historical processes of disciplinary "purification" in academia (Wilshire 1990). Wilshire documented how junior faculty were told very clearly to stay within the limits of their discipline, never venture outside, and shed any traces of attachment to other disciplines. There are any number of reasons why this purification occurred, ranging from the difficulty of getting funding from research that crossed disciplines to the feeling that dabbling in more than one discipline is ultimately amateurish and leads to superficiality at best.

Today this disciplinary territoriality still exists, even as there is an emerging realization that in order to be relevant and address the complexity of the issues we are facing, we need new approaches, transdisciplinary approaches. Transdisciplinarity does not mean knowing everything about everything. It draws on what the French philosopher Edgar Morin calls "pertinent" knowledge. Knowledge, in other words, that emerges from an assessment of situations, and is not imposed and limited by the boundaries of disciplines. This does not mean the end of specialization, but rather specialization in areas rather than disciplines. It also calls for a different form of education, different forms of inquiry, and different approaches to developing "pertinent knowledge." It requires a special form of discernment, of knowing what we need to know as well as a reflection on how we know what we know.

All too often disciplinary science does not challenge its underlying assumptions, the way it constructs its understanding of the way and its notions of how to engage the world.

Transdisciplinarity is radical because it takes us back into these (often implicit) fundamental assumptions, into the philosophy of social science, into questions about the way in which knowledge is constructed, what is foreground and what is background, how people and events are connected in time and space, issues of fundamental ontology and epistemology. This is not done in an abstract sense, but with the very clear purpose of understanding the many ways in which we organize our knowledge, construct our understanding of a phenomenon, and deal with a plurality of perspectives on the same issue. This epistemological reflection is not engaged as a performance for the entertainment of other academics at an intellectual circus. It is engaged precisely because knowledge shapes our understanding of a situation and informs action in the world.

For students and researchers engaged in transdisciplinary research, how to develop a thorough knowledge base in their chosen area of inquiry becomes a complex issue. My own research on creativity led me initially to what I call the Dominant Disciplinary Discourse of creativity (Montuori 2005). This is essentially the place where most of the action is, most of the research, the journals, and so on. In the 1980s in the United States, and in the case of creativity, this was unquestionably psychology. But it soon became clear that sociology and cultural anthropology also contributed important perspectives on creativity, and by the time the 1990s rolled around, the management literature was beginning to make substantial contributions. Now creativity and innovation are huge topics in that discipline. So how does the unsuspecting student with ambitions of transdisciplinarity even begin to get a sense of all this literature, to realize that it's out there, to see what the different underlying assumptions are? Psychologists have focused almost exclusively on the individual creator, largely ignoring the role of relationships and society. Sociologists and anthropologists focused on social and cultural factors and ignored the individual. What does this all mean? And on top of everything, the terminology the different disciplines used was a little different. Psychologists talked about creativity, in management it was creativity and innovation, but in philosophy the term "imagination" covered much the same ground.

During my graduate studies, a visit to my university library was a fairly primitive affair. Card catalogs were still in use, and there was nothing like the access to information we have today. Developing a broad knowledge base and then diving deeply into the specifics of a topic that was relatively new to me was an enormously time-consuming task. It was not unusual for me to browse through bookstacks and suddenly come across a book in a discipline that I wasn't familiar with only to see that they were addressing some of the specific issues I was interested in, and that nobody in the psychology of creativity even seemed to be aware of. (Or if they were aware of it, they weren't telling.)

Access to information when I was a student (admittedly in the days when some people still used slide rules) was a key issue. Today, my students don't complain about the difficulties they have getting access to journals and books. If anything, they're overwhelmed by the enormous amount of information that's available. They don't know how to make sense of the information glut, where to begin their research, what's useful and what isn't, and how to develop a solid knowledge base in a number of different areas. Even more troubling, they don't know that they don't know, because it all appears so easy, so accessible, so right there on the fingertips and on the screen. They're not alone facing that challenge, of course.

As far as I can tell, students at least initially feel that the Internet and the ability to Google information or more generally look for information online is unequivocally good and true and a natural birthright. Most of the faculty colleagues I speak to find the Internet both a blessing and a curse, a much more complex phenomenon. We all hear stories about students who Google a topic and often settle on the first definition or article or book they come across. Many arguments have been made about the reliability of Wikipedia, but I'll never forget the student who came up to me rather sheepishly one day and asked me why I had published an article in *Human Relations*, a well-established British social science journal published by the Tavistock Institute in London (Montuori 2003). He had read on Wikipedia that the Tavistock Institute was involved in a dastardly plan for world domination involving the use of LSD and mind control. How could I be involved with these people, he wondered? We decided to look over the offending Wikipedia page together, and the references to LSD and world domination were gone. They had been removed because they were clearly untrue, inserted by a British conspiracy theorist who believes the world is run by lizards (which may be true, although I suspect more metaphorically than literally). My student had landed on the page during the few minutes the page had remained uncorrected by the Wikipedia patrol.

I mention this rather extreme example to point to the many difficulties facing students who are exploring new areas, the temptation of having "information" at one's fingertips, and the importance of guidance and new forms of critical thinking, discernment and awareness in dealing with this immense availability of information. Recent news reports have discussed how students struggle to assess online content credibility, and in an allegedly "post-truth," "post-fact" world, a different relationship with knowledge is required.

Transdisciplinarity requires the development of both a critical and a creative approach to the integration of knowledge, and to the organization of knowledge. Once we decide to move across disciplines and into uncharted territory, and increasingly even within our own areas of specialization, whether disciplinary or transdisciplinary, we need to be able to step back and study the information we come across, avoid superficial connections and definition, and find ways to assess both the integrity of the individual works we read and how they fit in to the larger context of our inquiry. Once we begin to connect the disparate threads that can shed light on an issue, it is essential to contextualize our work, to develop a sense of the larger historical, theoretical, and methodological frames that inform the work we are using. It is essential to become aware of the possibilities of connections but also of the dangers of shotgun weddings between ideas and research findings that don't really belong together. Transdisciplinary research requires, therefore, the ability to take a *meta* position that is constantly questioning underlying frameworks and the way that knowledge is constructed. Transdisciplinarity itself is a creative process, and one that also views the works it integrates as creative products and the results of creative process by our colleagues.

Victoria Martin's thoughtful and comprehensive book provides us with an important survey of transdisciplinarity that will be of an invaluable reference for researchers as well as librarians. It is itself a transdisciplinary work that provides us with much needed historical background, illustrating how and why transdisciplinarity arose, giving the reader a useful review of the key figures and the main current directions. It also helpfully points out many practical dimensions that are often overlooked, from the role of communication to the need for funding and the way transdisciplinary work can be evaluated. Martin shows us the way in which transdisciplinarity is making explicit the need for changes in the university, as well as how it emerged from the need to address concrete problems and bigger questions that got lost in fragmentation of disciplinary specialization. She also stresses the importance of creativity and collaboration, two topics that require far more attention in education. Martin cites interdisciplinary scholar Bill Newell's remark that universities are slow to change, and this is sadly true. At the same time, a historical perspective shows us the degree to which the university is really constituted by modernity's foundational principles of organization, and we can see there is an enormous institutional as well as personal investment in these principles. It is also often difficult to envision a new way of approaching things that have been done the same way for as long as we can remember. I'll never forget publishing an article critiquing the notion of the lone genius with a colleague. We argued for the recognition of collaborative creativity, showing among other things that many academic works are coauthored, and that contributors are wrongly penalized for collaborative works, particularly when researchers from different disciplines come together to approach a topic through the integration of several disciplinary perspectives. Soon after the article was published, my colleague's promotion committee sent me a letter asking me exactly what percentage of the article I had written. Only a certain percentage of that paper would count toward my colleague's promotion. It's clear that transdisciplinarity will have to play a role in changing academia's way of thinking about very basic practices, not least of which being how to assess, encourage, and reward collaborative inter- and transdisciplinary research.

Despite our academic sluggishness, I'm delighted to see that faculty, students, and even universities and funding agencies are beginning to recognize the urgency of transdisciplinary work. The challenge of a complex world is reflected in the need for a new way to understand, what constitutes inquiry, pertinent knowledge, and the relationship between knowledge and action. Victoria Martin's clear and succinct work is useful and a particularly valuable resource for anyone wanting a thoughtful understanding of transdisciplinarity. She addresses the practical issues facing transdisciplinary researchers and most of all for librarians. Librarians not only provide invaluable support for students and researchers but help us frame that most important task of understanding what Edgar Morin has called the challenge of complexity, and the knowledge of knowledge. We should all be grateful for their work, and for Victoria Martin's impressive contribution to her field.

Suggested Readings

Bateson, M. C. *Our Own Metaphor: A Personal Account of a Conference on the Effects of Conscious Purpose on Human Adaptation.* Cresskill, NJ: Hampton Press, 2004.

Heims, S. J. *Constructing a Social Science for Postwar America: The Cybernetics Group, 1946–1953.* Cambridge: MIT Press, 1993.

Koestler, A., and J. R. Smythies (eds.). Beyond Reductionism. New Perspectives in the Life Sciences. Proceedings of the Alpbach Symposium, 1968. London: Macmillan, 1972.

Montuori, A. "The Complexity of Improvisation and the Improvisation of Complexity. Social Science, Art, and Creativity." *Human Relations* 56, no. 2 (2003), 237–255.

Montuori, A. "Gregory Bateson and the Challenge of Transdisciplinarity." *Cybernetics and Human Knowing* 12, no. 1–2 (2005), 147–158.

Wilshire, B. (1990). *The Moral Collapse of the University: Professionalism, Purity, and Alienation.* New York: SUNY Press.

Preface

In recent decades, "transdisciplinarity" has become a popular term in discussions about the production and use of knowledge, stirring up a worldwide interest well beyond the academic community. Yet, transdisciplinarity appears to be a "rather elusive concept" (Jahn, Bergmann, and Keil 2012) and still remains a vague or controversial idea for some scholars. The label "transdisciplinarity," undermined by easy generalizations and widespread misinformation, has been applied to other matters such as multi- and interdisciplinary approaches and projects, while the phrase "doing transdisciplinarity" has been used to either describe a wide spectrum of activities that cannot be successfully addressed using a single method, or to signify the broad scope of certain research areas.

This vagueness poses significant challenges to scholars and, even more so, to librarians who work with them. In the lively discourse on transdisciplinarity, the role of libraries is rarely mentioned. Limited references to this topic do exist but they are scattered across a variety of sources. Library science literature focuses more heavily on the implications of interdisciplinarity for library services and, to date, there has been no comprehensive study devoted to the concept of transdisciplinarity in librarianship. In library circles, there is little awareness of this relatively new phenomenon in the knowledge culture and, because of that, there is some mystery surrounding the concept of transdisciplinarity. Many still believe that there is no difference between the concepts of multidisciplinarity, interdisciplinarity, and transdisciplinarity. When it comes to supporting transdisciplinary research conducted by faculty and students, librarians are often at a loss as to how best to address their information needs.

Simply put, transdisciplinarity is a new mode of knowledge production that strives to make academic research more pertinent to the complex problems of the real world (or the "life-world" as some scholars call it) such as those dealing with violence, hunger, poverty, disease, or environmental pollution. Transdisciplinary research seeks to address these societal challenges by engaging different disciplines that do not usually interact with each other and by involving synergistic collaborations with policy makers, educators, practitioners, development agencies, and other stakeholders outside of academia. It also includes the subjects of study and users of scholarly outputs as active participants throughout the research process and as contributors to research framing and project evaluation, and thus it is being carried through *with* them rather than *on* them. Transdisciplinarity challenges the disciplinary silos by bringing disparate, and sometimes conflicting, viewpoints and research methodologies into focus on a complex research problem. By including nonacademic participants in the research process, it links together scholarly and "life-world" knowledge, reflects their mutual dependencies, and leads to an interdependent learning partnership between scholarship and society.

The transdisciplinary research model is becoming increasingly prevalent, as acknowledged by a rather large number of recent scholarly publications, and thus presents a paradigm shift for academic and research libraries that must employ new ways of working with information and with information users. A clear understanding of what transdisciplinarity is and how it impacts library services and collections is becoming crucial for librarians.

These are the main considerations that have led to the writing of this book. With the current expansion of interest in new modes of knowledge production and the shift toward transdisciplinarity that is occurring within the research community, the need for librarians to understand transdisciplinarity and to effectively apply this understanding to their work has never been greater. A better understanding of this new area, which is often associated with innovation and groundbreaking research, will better position librarians within the academic sphere and enable further innovation in their pivotal role—that is, assisting library users in navigating the complexities of the information "resourceome" (Cannata et al. 2005) and ultimately in generating new knowledge.

The main contributions of this book are twofold. On the one hand, this book aspires, as its title suggests, to reveal the "mystery" of transdisciplinarity by providing a strong, yet accessible, overview of this new research model. It defines key terms, explains core ideas, and describes specific transdisciplinary projects and initiatives. This book also clarifies the distinction between the four modes of knowledge production (disciplinary, multidisciplinary, interdisciplinary, and transdisciplinarity) and captures the wisdom of existing scholarly works on the subject. On the other hand, this book strives to illuminate gaps in the library science literature by discussing the impact of transdisciplinarity on libraries and library services and highlighting the new needs of researchers that librarians are not yet well equipped to address. The focus of this book is somewhat more theoretical than pragmatic, although the second part of the book does touch upon concrete suggestions that librarians working with transdisciplinary scholars may wish to follow.

The primary intended audience for this book is academic librarians, particularly those involved in teaching information literacy skills, providing scholarly communication, grant writing and research support services, as well as library administrators, who can add vision, visibility, and impact to these initiatives. The book will also be of value to digital collection and electronic services managers, database designers, indexers and taxonomists who build research collections, as well as to a more global audience—from the general reader to academic scholars. It is to be hoped that this book is the first in a series of works on the subject and that it will spur the librarians' interest in transdisciplinarity and help them recognize the value of this concept for their own work.

Readers without the background knowledge of transdisciplinarity are advised to read the book in a linear fashion, chapter by chapter. For the reader's convenience, the book includes a list of acronyms, a glossary, a list of references, a detailed subject index, as well as a list of suggested readings at the end of each chapter.

Acknowledgments

I wish to extend a heartfelt thank you to those individuals whose enthusiasm, support, and generosity of spirit helped bring this book to fruition:

Lise Dyckman, senior acquisitions editor at Libraries Unlimited, for helping me shape an abstract idea into the successful book proposal

Dr. Alfonso Montuori, professor at the California Institute of Integral Studies, for his brilliantly written Foreword, which I will always treasure

Barbara Ittner, senior acquisitions editor at Libraries Unlimited, for guiding me—patiently and respectfully—through the editing process

Emma Bailey, project editor at Libraries Unlimited, for her prompt helpful responses to my questions

Michelle Scott, production editor at ABC-CLIO, and Gordon Hammy Matchado, senior project manager at Apex CoVantage, for their flawless competence and incredible courtesy during the book production process

My husband James for being my loyal and thoughtful first reader and best friend

I am also deeply indebted to all of the authors cited in this book whose commitment to the vision of transdisciplinarity marked the beginning of my fascination with this innovative approach to knowledge production and whose invisible support inspired the creation of the book you now hold in your hands.

List of Acronyms

AAAS	American Association for the Advancement of Science
AAC&U	Association of American Colleges & Universities
ACRL	Association of College & Research Libraries
AULSF	Association of University Leaders for a Sustainable Future
BCC	Basic Concepts Classification
BE	Biocomplexity in the Environment Initiative
BIC	Broader Impact Criterion
BRAIN	The Brain Research through Advancing Innovative Neurotechnologies
CFAT	Carnegie Foundation for the Advancement of Teaching
CIRET	Centre International de Recherches et Études Transdisciplinaires (The International Center for Transdisciplinary Research)
CMC	computer-mediated communication
COC	citations outside category
CRG	Classification Research Group
CSCW	computer-supported cooperative work
DARPA	Defense Advanced Research Projects Agency
DDS	Dewey Decimal System
DOD	Department of Defense
DOE	Department of Energy
ETH	Eidgenössische Technische Hochschule (The Swiss Federal Institute of Technology)

FDA	Food and Drug Administration
GSS	group support systems
GUT	grand unified theory
HCI	human-computer interaction
HHMI	Howard Hughes Medical Institute
ICT	information communication technology
IDEATE	Institute for Design and Advanced Technology
IHR	Institute of Humanities Research
ILC	Integrative Levels Classification
IOCT	Institute of Creative Technologies
IOM	Institute of Medicine
ISKO	International Society for Knowledge Organization
KOS	knowledge organization system
LCC	Library of Congress Classification
LCSH	Library of Congress Subject Headings
LIS	library and information science
LTER	Long-Term Ecological Research
NAE	National Academy of Engineering
NAS	National Academy of Sciences
NGO	nongovernmental organization
NIH	National Institutes of Health
NNI	National Nanotechnology Initiative
NRC	National Research Council
NSF	National Science Foundation
OA	open access
OECD	Organization for Economic Co-operation and Development
OED	*Oxford English Dictionary*
ORUS	Observatoire International des Réformes Universitaires (The International University Reforms Observatory)
P2P	peer-to-peer
PCAST	President's Council of Advisors on Science and Technology
PI	principal investigator
PLoS	Public Library of Science

SciSIP	Science of Science and Innovation Policy
SOTS	science of team science
SPARC	Scholarly Publishing and Academic Resources Coalition
STEM	science, technology, engineering, and mathematics
TCS	Transdisciplinary Case Study
TD	transdisciplinarity
TOE	theory of everything
TR	transdisciplinary research
TREC	Transdisciplinary Research on Energetics and Cancer
TTURCs	Transdisciplinary Tobacco Use Research Centers
USPTO	United States Patent and Trademark Office
VREs	virtual research environments

PART 1

In Search of Unity: An Introduction to Transdisciplinarity

The point is not what is new or old, what should be replaced or superseded with what, but rather how each perspective is enriched by the presence of others.

—Jann Pasler (1997, 21)

CHAPTER ONE

A Neologism with Ancient Roots: The Challenge of Defining Transdisciplinarity

The term *transdisciplinarity* retains a certain pristine charm, mostly because it has not yet been corrupted by time. It has begun spreading around the globe, popping up in unexpected places, giving voice to a lively new concept that is not yet widely understood.

—Basarab Nicolescu (2002, 1)

Although the term "transdisciplinarity" has been around for over four decades, it still is a subject of terminological confusion. It doesn't yet have dictionary status.[1] At the time of this writing, there is no single authoritative definition of transdisciplinarity in the scholarly literature.

Etymologically speaking, the word "transdisciplinarity" is a hybrid of the prefix "trans" and the word "disciplinarity," both of which are of Latin origin. The prefix "trans," occurring in English words borrowed from Latin, means "across, beyond, on or to the other side, through, into a different state or place" (Fowler, Fowler, and Crystal 2011, 938). Although the prefix "trans" is open to interpretation, it implies movement or change and suggests "something further, greater, more powerful, or more encompassing" (Klein 2000b, 49). Young (2000) provides a vivid description of the meaning of the prefix "trans" as "extending across or through, crossing, going beyond the limits of common thought or ordinary limit, being above and independent of something else, or providing the essential conditions for something else (space and time, for instance, being a priori elements of perception or the nature of the mind conditioning the nature of human knowledge" (126).

The word "discipline" has ancient roots as well. It is derived from the two Latin words "disciplina" (teaching, learning) and "discipulus" (pupil, disciple) (*Merriam-Webster's Collegiate Dictionary* 2004). The *Oxford English Dictionary* (1989) lists nine meanings of the word "disciple," all of which imply training, limitations, or a set of rules imposed on individuals under command or control. The same dictionary notes that the word "discipline" has come to use through the New Testament and was applied to the 12 disciples of Jesus Christ. Gilmore (2000) makes an interesting observation with regard to this:

> It would seem odd that our interest in transdisciplinarity would be rooted in its religious origins. Indeed, the opposite would seem to be implicit in the neologism. Transdisciplinarity is, if anything, heretical, implying a mindset that goes beyond beliefs, orthodoxy, or any particular branch of knowledge. . . . It is necessarily and intimately rooted in the disciplines and beliefs from which it rebels. . . . This may be the most important feature of transdisciplinarity: its inherent aptitude or capacity to assimilate and then go beyond, or transcend, any particular disciplinary worldview. (187)

Transdisciplinarity shares characteristics with some other terms that describe the concept of research that uses methodologies and insights from a wide range of disciplines. For instance, transdisciplinarity is sometimes used as a synonym for knowledge integration, "a major component in knowledge management [which includes] knowledge acquisition, representation, transmission, and use" (Sage 2000, 163), or as a synonym for convergence, which is defined as "an approach to problem solving that integrates expertise from life sciences with physical, mathematical, and computational sciences, medicine, and engineering to form comprehensive synthetic frameworks that merge areas of knowledge from multiple fields to address specific challenges" (Convergence 2014, 17).

The term "transdisciplinarity" itself is a 20th-century word. It is generally believed that this term was introduced at the First International Seminar on Interdisciplinarity held in 1970 at the University of Nice, France. Nicolescu (2002, 2005 attributes the original use of the term to Jean Piaget, a Swiss biologist, philosopher, and psychologist, who is best known for his theory of "genetic epistemology." The term was introduced in order to distinguish transdisciplinarity from multidisciplinarity and interdisciplinarity and "to give expression to a need that was perceived—especially in the area of education—to celebrate the transgression of disciplinary boundaries" (Nicolescu 2002, 1).[2] In his post-seminar essay "The Epistemology of Interdisciplinary Relationships," Piaget described transdisciplinarity as a "higher stage succeeding interdisciplinary relationships . . . which would not only cover interactions or reciprocities between specialized research projects, but would place these relationships within a total system without any firm boundaries between disciplines" (1972, 138). According to other sources, it was Erich Jantsch, an Austrian-born American astrophysicist and systems scientist, who coined the term "transdisciplinarity" at the same seminar (Leavy 2011; Newell 2000; Weingart 2010). In his post-seminar essay "Towards Interdisciplinarity and Transdisciplinarity in Education and Innovation," Jantsch defines transdisciplinarity as "the co-ordination of all disciplines and inter-disciplines in the education/innovation system on the basis of generalized axiomatics (introduced from the purposive level) and an emerging epistemological ("synepistemic") pattern" (1972, 106).

The contemporary use of the term "transdisciplinarity" is still open to broad interpretation. Scholars describe transdisciplinarity (sometimes abbreviated as TD or Td) in a great variety of ways—as a conceptual phenomenon, an original methodology, a new way of thinking, a research paradigm, a unifying principle, a new mode of knowledge production, and a strategy for solving complex problems, among others. The term "transdisciplinarity" is sometimes used as a synonym for integrative knowledge or unity of knowledge. What is more, this term is mistakenly confused with two other terms—"multidisciplinarity" and "interdisciplinarity." The tendency to use these terms interchangeably further heightens the terminological confusion about its meaning.

To picture the full spectrum of definitions of transdisciplinarity is a challenging task. They can vary even among members of the same research team. Shenton and Hay-Gibson (2011) write: "Today, 'transdisciplinarity' is applied so variously that it is not only impossible to isolate a single, generally accepted statement as to what the word means; it is also difficult to identify a coherent strand that runs through the range of definitions that has been offered. In some cases, writers use the term without any elaboration at all, and readers are left to determine for themselves the intended meaning from the context in which it appears" (167).

Klein (2009) points out that "[t]o speak of transdisciplinarity as a meta-methodology, analysis, theory, or system is not to demand allegiance to a single definition" (64). The following sample of definitions by some key champions of transdisciplinarity illustrates her point.

[Transdisciplinarity is] "scientific work done by a group of scientists . . . with the intention of systematically pursuing the problem of how the negative side effects of specialization can be overcome so as to make education (and research) more socially relevant" (Kockelmans 1979, 128).

"Transdisciplinarity is a new form of learning and problem solving involving cooperation among different parts of society" (Häberli et al. 2001, 7).

"[T]ransdisciplinarity concerns that which is at once between the disciplines, across the different disciplines, and beyond all disciplines" (Nicolescu 2002, 1).

"Transdisciplinarity: a higher stage of interaction that entails an overarching framework that organizes knowledge in a new way and, in a new discourse, cooperation of multiple sectors of society and stakeholders in addressing complex problems" (Klein 2009, 65).

"Transdisciplinarity is about the relationship between inquiry and action in the world" (Montuori 2010, 10).

"Transdisciplinarity is a reflexive research approach that addresses societal problems by means of interdisciplinary collaboration as well as the collaboration between researchers and extra-scientific actors. Its aim is to enable mutual learning processes between science and society; integration is the main cognitive challenge of the research process" (Jahn, Bergmann, and Keil 2012, 4).

None of the aforementioned interpretations, which are arranged in chronological order, is intended to indicate the superiority of one over the other, although the last definition by Jahn, Bergmann, and Keil seems to reflect a general consensus among scholars of transdisciplinarity.

The plurality of definitions suggests that transdisciplinarity connotes significant scope and scale. Krimsky (2000) notes the "fluidity" of the term "transdisciplinarity" suggests that "one is not bound by disciplinary canons in any one field" (110). Klein and Macdonald (2000) predict that a definition of transdisciplinarity "will always be under construction . . . will continue to be a metaphor and will resist transformation into a mere simile" (217). Macdonald (2000a) believes that "true transdisciplinarity resists pigeon-holing" and can be defined only "metaphorically" (244).

Indeed, transdisciplinary collaborations and their corresponding research outcomes are often described using metaphors that create powerful insights into the essence of transdisciplinarity. The metaphor of a web (sometimes a three-dimensional web) is invoked most often (Gibbons et al. 1994; Klein 2000a, 2004). In the "web" of transdisciplinary research collaborations, numerous nodes of connection are being spun continuously and "become strung out across the globe in growing density and connectivity" (Klein 2000a, 11). The metaphor of the web suggests that complexity and interconnectedness are key to an understanding of transdisciplinarity.

Other metaphors likewise invoke the ideas of unity, synergy, and interrelatedness that are essential traits distinguishing transdisciplinarity from other approaches to research. Morgan (2000) describes transdisciplinarity as "a switchboard between fragmented knowledge specialties" (38). Young (2000) links transdisciplinarity to "stereoscopic vision" that helped her and her research partner achieve a deep, three-dimensional perception of their project focused on gender and religion. Somerville (2000) compares transdisciplinarity to different colored lenses that form a spectrum of wavelengths.

The botanical term "rhizome" has also been used to describe the rhizomatic nature of transdisciplinarity (Klein 2004; Gibbs 2015; Maguire 2015). The idea of rhizome and rhizomatic thinking was first posited by Deleuze and Guattari (1987) in their wide-ranging philosophical work *A Thousand Plateaus.* The authors summarize the essential characteristics of a rhizome in this extensive but important quote:

> Unlike trees or their roots, the rhizome connects any point to any other point, and its traits are not necessarily linked to traits of the same nature; it brings into play very different regimes of signs, and even nonsign states. The rhizome is reducible neither to the One nor the multiple. It is not the One that becomes Two or even directly three, four, five, etc. It is not a multiple of units but of dimensions, or rather directions in motion. It has neither beginning nor end, but always middle (milieu) from which it grows and which it overspills. It constitutes linear multiplicities with n dimensions having neither subject nor object, which can be laid out on a plane of consistency, and from which the One is always subtracted (n–1). (21)

When applied to transdisciplinarity, the metaphor of rhizome implies a nonhierarchical multiplicity and interconnections between all aspects of knowledge and society whose "order is not a structure of entities but connections" (Klein 2004, 54).

Given this wide range of themes and metaphors, it is hardly surprising that the definition of the term "transdisciplinarity" is still "under construction," to borrow Klein and Macdonald's phrase. It is also hardly surprising that this lack of agreement on definition has contributed to some confusion in the discourse on transdisciplinarity as this term has been applied to a variety of research activities, projects, organizations, and educational programs. This book adopts the following definition (based on

a composite of various references) in order to capture the essential characteristics of transdisciplinarity in an easy-to-understand language. Transdisciplinarity is a new way of conducting research, in which multiple
contributors and stakeholders, both from within and from outside academia, are collaboratively working on identifying specific societal problems and on finding solutions to these problems.

Notes

1. The term "transdisciplinarity" is not included in the *Oxford English Dictionary* (OED) and other dictionaries of common usage. The *Oxford English Dictionary* (1989) defines a related word "transdisciplinary" as "[o]f or pertaining to
more than one discipline or branch of learning; interdisciplinary" and "the
ultimate degree of coordination in the education/innovation system."

2. In his *Manifesto of Transdisciplinarity*, Nicolescu writes that the term "transdisciplinarity" originally appeared "almost simultaneously in the works of such
varied scholars as Jean Piaget, Edgar Morín, and Erich Jantsch" (2002, 1). However, four years later, Nicolescu attributes the term "transdisciplinarity" only to
Piaget and not to others (Nicolescu 2005).

Suggested Reading

Klein, Julie Thompson. "Discourses of Transdisciplinarity: Looking Back to the
    Future." *Futures* 63 (2014): 68–74. doi: 10.1016/j.futures.2014.08.008.

CHAPTER TWO

Transdisciplinarity in Retrospect: Origins and Benchmark Events

> Transdisciplinarity is a theme, which resurfaces time and again. It responds to an underlying need and an inherent belief. The former is the loss to what is felt to have been a former unity of knowledge. The latter is the expectation that transdisciplinarity contributes to a joint problem solving that it is more than juxtaposition; more than laying one discipline alongside another.
>
> —Helga Nowotny (2004, 1)

The epistemological quest for unification of knowledge that lies at the heart of the discourse on transdisciplinarity is not new. This quest descends from many generations of scholarship. Wilson (1998a, 1998b) believes that it can be traced to "Ionian Enlightenment" (also known as "Ionian Enchantment") that transpired during the archaic period in Greece 25 centuries ago. The philosopher-scientists[1] of the "Ionian Enlightenment" believed that the cosmos was an orderly place and thus they were seeking a unified "theory of everything" that would explain both the cosmos and the world around them. Later, in ancient Greece, Plato revisited the question of the unity of knowledge and advocated philosophy as a unified science. His pupil Aristotle argued that a philosopher was the one who was best capable of collecting and organizing all forms of knowledge and who could "know it all," in an encyclopedic sense.

The vision for a unity of knowledge was also present in the medieval *Summae* with its ideas of universal knowledge and in the Renaissance philosophy that made no distinction between arts and sciences. Today, Leonardo da Vinci, who was an artist, engineer, inventor, and anatomist, would be regarded as a transdisciplinary thinker. In the 18th century, French encyclopedists undertook a major effort to bring together different domains of knowledge that culminated in creation of the 17-volume encyclopedia titled *Encyclopédie, ou dictionnaire raisonné des sciences, des arts et des métiers* (*Encyclopedia, or Reasoned Dictionary of the Sciences, Arts, and Trades*), edited by Denis Diderot and Jean Le Rond D'Alembert and produced over a period of 21 years (1751–1772).

Belief in the unity of knowledge persisted in European philosophy and natural sciences from the 16th through the 19th century. Bacon, Descartes, Leibniz, Kant, Hegel, and Comte expressed, each in his own manner, a concern about the fragmentation of knowledge and reflected on the ideal of a unified scientific worldview. Descartes, for example, expressed his ideal of unity as follows: "All philosophy is like a tree; the roots are metaphysics, the trunk is physics, and the branches that have grown out of this trunk are the other Wissenschaften.[2] These latter can be traced to three main disciplines, namely medicine, mechanics, and morals" (Descartes 1647/1954). In the natural sciences, the notion that knowledge must be unified in one way or another is apparent in the ideas of Lorenz Oken, a German naturalist and leader of the Naturphilosophie ("philosophy of nature") movement in Germany in the 19th century. Oken's theory of unified "anatomy" of the world bears witness to his hope for explaining the mysteries of nature by bringing the knowledge of separate disciplines into one unified knowledge base. Later, Charles Darwin's theory of evolution, which resulted in his revolutionary work *On the Origin of Species by Natural Selection*, served as a basis for multiple fields of study, including biology, genetics, geography, and geology.

In the 20th century, several initiatives and movements have attempted to recover a sense of lost unity in the sciences and promoted the vision of synthesized knowledge, most notably the Vienna Circle in Austria with its ambitious project to compile *The International Encyclopedia of Unified Science*, and the Unity of Science campaign in the United States initiated by philosophers of science and natural scientists that was aimed at integrating scientific statements into a common foundation and terminology. The unifying theme is also prevalent in other fields and domains of the 20th century such as in Einstein's theory of relativity, laws of cybernetics, the "grand unified theory" (GUT) and a "theory of everything" (TOE) in physics, von Bertalanffy's general systems theory, and E. O. Wilson's theory of consilience. This idea of the unity of knowledge has also circulated in fields within the social sciences, humanities, and arts that emphasize synergism and linkages. These include, for instance, social innovation research, gender and country studies, Umberto Eco's search for the perfect language, and digital art.

The quest for creating a more reflexive relationship between knowledge production and the "life-world"[3] (which is another imperative of the transdisciplinary approach) has time-honored roots also. French philosophers of the 18th century (Voltaire, Diderot, D'Alembert, Montesquieu, among others) strived to disseminate existing knowledge to the public with the intention of improving society through education and enriching their culture with scientific discoveries. John Locke in his *Of the Conduct of the Understanding* asserted that knowledge, in order to be useful, must connect with the social environment. In the early 20th century, the Annales School of History, led by Marc Bloch, Lucien Febvre, and later Fernand Braudel, used a transdisciplinary approach to build a foundation for their theory of a "global" history (the *synthèse historique*) that emphasized the importance of taking into consideration the intellectual worldview of the common people, or "mentality" (*mentalité*).[4] Although these older ideas and initiatives were employed under different names (unity, coherence, integration, and consilience, among others), they can all be considered the precursors of transdisciplinarity. Their goals were similar in intent. These goals—to create knowledge that transcends traditional disciplinary boundaries and to apply this knowledge to the resolution of concrete societal problems found in the "life-world"—are still being sought today.

The debate surrounding transdisciplinarity as a new conceptual phenomenon of the 20th century was introduced to the world at the First International Seminar on Interdisciplinarity held in 1970 at the University of Nice, France, and jointly sponsored by the Organization of Economic Cooperation and Development (OECD) and the French Ministry of Higher Education (Jahn, Bergmann, and Keil 2012; Klein 2004, 2014; Nicolescu 2002).[5] At this seminar, scholars and educators across multiple disciplines and domains reflected on the epistemological issues of interdisciplinarity, discussed their interdisciplinary activities, and established terminology to clarify a rather vague at that time concept of interdisciplinarity. Also, at this seminar, a number of scientists, including a psychologist and philosopher Jean Piaget, an astrophysicist Erich Jantsch, a physicist and mathematician André Lichnerowicz, and a philosopher Joseph Kockelmans, raised concerns about knowledge production in research, education, and public institutions, the role of academic disciplines, and the issues that divide them. They expanded the concept of interdisciplinarity to encompass transdisciplinarity that was defined as "a common system of axioms for a set of disciplines" that transcends the narrow scope of disciplinary worldviews through an overarching synthesis (Apostel et al. 1972). Piaget (1972) considered transdisciplinarity as a "higher stage succeeding interdisciplinary relationships . . . which would not only cover interactions or reciprocities between specialised research projects, but would place these relationships within a total system without any firm boundaries between disciplines" (138). Lichnerowicz (1972) elaborated on Piaget's insight relating it to set theory and logic. Jantsch (1972) viewed transdisciplinarity as "the coordination of activities at all levels of the education/innovation system towards a common purpose" (114).

This seminar and the resulting conference proceedings *Interdisciplinarity: Problems of Teaching and Research in Universities*, published in 1972, became not only a widely cited authority on interdisciplinarity but also a major event in the history of transdisciplinarity. These proceedings provided a framework for new thinking about teaching and research beyond and across disciplinary boundaries and stressed the need for researchers, and research and educational organizations, to modify their approach to knowledge production.

The concept of transdisciplinarity introduced at that seminar remained largely undeveloped and rarely cited until the early 1990s[6] (Bernstein 2015) when several sociopolitical developments caused a resurgence of interest in the idea of a unification of knowledge and in making knowledge production more socially relevant and valuable. These developments, brought about by significant degrees of social, political, and economic change, led to a greater awareness of global interconnectedness and a renewed concern about ultra-specialization within disciplines and increased disciplinary fragmentation. This "disciplinary big bang," in Nicolescu's (2002, 34) words, resulted in large bodies of specialized knowledge that showed little overlap and thus were unable to address complex, large-scale societal problems such as increased globalization, climate change, and the transition to sustainable energy systems. A new conceptual framework became of primary importance, the framework that would not only "build bridges between isolated disciplines" (Rapport 2000, 135) but would also move beyond traditional academic settings and create synergetic collaborations among the academic, government, and private sectors in order to provide integrated solutions to urgent problems of the life-world. These concerns and sociopolitical changes put a spotlight back on transdisciplinarity as a promising research model for addressing these urgent problems as well as a valuable approach to tackling "wicked problems"[7] in many areas concerning science, technology, policy, and education. Transdisciplinarity gained further popularity through the influential works of Funtowicz and Ravetz on post-normal science (1990, 1991, 1993), in which the authors argued that post-normal science (in contrast to traditional "normal" science) could provide the path to the democratization of science by addressing the aspects of complex issues such as uncertainty and conflicting values that tend to be neglected in more dogmatic scientific practice.

The First World Congress on Transdisciplinarity was held in 1994 in Convento da Arrábida, Portugal. At this Congress, an editorial committee produced the *Charter of Transdisciplinarity*, drafted and signed by an artist Lima de Freitas, a quantum physicist Basarab Nicolescu, and a philosopher and sociologist Edgar Morin. This *Charter* contained 14 articles that described "the fundamental principles of the community of transdisciplinary researchers" and referred to the notions of the multiple levels of reality, the logic of the included middle and the Hidden Third, and the complexity of the world. These notions were later developed in Nicolescu's book titled *Manifesto of Transdisciplinarity* (2002) in which Nicolescu presented a new vision of knowledge organization and inquiry and promoted prescriptive ideas for making revolutionary changes in knowledge creation.[8]

In 1994, the same year the *Charter of Transdisciplinarity* was produced, a different vision of transdisciplinarity gained worldwide attention. In *The New Production of Knowledge* (1994), the authors, Michael Gibbons, Camille Limoges, Helga Nowotny, Simon Schwartzman, Peter Scott, and Martin Trow, who were the experts from different disciplinary fields and domains, argued that besides the traditional disciplinary production of knowledge (which they called Mode 1) that has little need for collaboration with nonscientists, there is another form of knowledge production (which they called Mode 2) that transcends the boundaries between science and society, integrates disciplinary paradigms, and is strongly sensible to societal needs. At that time, the concept of Mode 2 knowledge production was an innovative idea because it emphasized that knowledge production should not be limited to the sciences, technology, and medicine but should also involve experts from government, industry, and the private sector and also extend to the humanities and arts.[9] While a "Nicolescuian" perspective on transdisciplinarity could be seen as more "programmatic and oracular," Gibbons et al. presented a more practical view on transdisciplinarity, although it lacked Nicolescu's "bold visionary insights" (Bernstein 2015).

Another important event in the development of transdisciplinarity was the International Transdisciplinarity Conference held in Zurich, Switzerland, in 2000. This conference presented and popularized a more pragmatic, although not unique, approach to transdisciplinarity, referred to as the Zurich School (Augsburg 2014; Bernstein 2015; McGregor 2015a,

2015b). The Zurich School drew largely upon Gibbons et al.'s (1994) Mode-2 approach to knowledge production. One of the basic premises of the Zurich approach was the assumption that problems that are being addressed by higher education institutions are stemming from the sciences and not from the real world. It emphasized the importance of trans-sectorial collaborations where multiple stakeholders, both within and outside academia, are actively involved in working out solutions to concrete societal problems. As a result of such collaborations, ". . . the knowledge of multiple participants is enhanced, including local knowledge, scientific knowledge and the knowledge of industries, businesses, and NGOs [nongovernmental organizations]. The sum of this knowledge will be greater than the knowledge of any single partner" (Klein et al. 2012, 7). Although the Zurich School did not produce any original methodologies, it made an important contribution by disseminating the principles of transdisciplinary research.[10]

In the ensuing years, a number of scholars with varying viewpoints contributed to the discussion about the concept of transdisciplinarity. Among the most notable contributors to this discussion was Edgar Morin, a French philosopher and sociologist, whose concept of complexity drew upon a plurality of disciplines (or what he calls *pertinent knowledge*) and was discussed in his writings on the evolution of disciplines, including six volumes of *The Method* (1977–2004) and his book *On Complexity* (2008). Other key contributors to this discussion include Julie Thompson Klein (Wayne State University, USA), Gertrude Hirsch Hadorn (University of Konstanz, Germany), Helga Nowotny (European Research Council), Christian Pohl (ETH Zurich, Switzerland), Alfonso Mountuori (California Institute of Integral Studies, USA), Daniel Stokols (University of California, USA), and Atila Ertas (Texas Tech University, USA). Although not arriving at a consensus, this "plurality of transdisciplinary models" (Nicolescu, 2008, 13) shares the centuries-old concern about the fragmentation of knowledge, the difference between scientific and life-world perceptions of complex societal problems, and engaged, socially responsible scientific research. From this standpoint, transdisciplinarity can be seen as "the contemporary version of the historical quest for systematic integration of knowledge" (Klein 2010, 24).

Notes

1. There was no distinction between philosophers and scientists during that period.

2. *Wissenschaften* is a German word that can be translated as "scholarship," "science," "discipline," or "field of study."

3. In phenomenology, the "life-world" (*Lebenswelt* in German) is the world that is experienced directly and immediately by individuals in everyday life. The life-world, meaning the world "as lived," is distinguished from the "world" of the sciences, which employ the methods of abstract representation, or analysis, to specific individual experiences. The concept of the life-world was introduced by Edmund Husserl in his *The Crisis of European Sciences and Transcendental Phenomenology* (1936).

4. Other terms relating to the interaction of academic research and society have emerged in recent decades, including the terms "mandated science" (Salter 1988), "regulatory science" (Jasanoff 1987), "post-normal science" (Funtowicz and Ravetz 1993), "knowledge policy" (Fuller 2002), "Mode-2 science" (Gibbons et al. 1994), "knowledge democracy" (Veld 2010), and "knowledge alliances" (Novy, Habersack, and Schaller 2013). These terms and the corresponding concepts are examples of the overarching trend that emphasizes the importance of more extensive cross-disciplinary linkages and of knowledge production that is more responsive to political and social needs.

5. Miller et al. (2008) traces the origins of the discourse on transdisciplinarity further back to the 1950s when first discussions on the need for cross-disciplinary collaboration for addressing social and environmental issues took place.

6. An exception was a chapter "Why Interdisciplinarity?" (1979) contributed by Joseph Kockelmans to the book *Interdisciplinarity and Higher Education*, which Kockelmans edited (Bernstein 2015). In this chapter, he defined transdisciplinarity as "scientific work done by a group of scientists . . . with the intention of systematically pursuing the problem of how the negative side effects of specialization can be overcome so as to make education (and research) more socially relevant" (Kockelmans 1979, 128).

7. The concept of wicked problems was introduced by Rittel and Weber (1973) in their treatise on a general theory of planning. Based on this treatise, Brown, Harris, and Russell (2015) defined a wicked problem as "a complex issue that defies complete definition, for which there can be no final solution, since any resolution generates further issues, and where solutions are not true or false, or good or bad, but the best that can be done at the time" (4).

8. The notions of the multiple levels of reality, the logic of the included middle and the Hidden Third, and the complexity of the world are discussed in Chapter 3 of this book.

9. Because part of their message concerned the partnership of experts from different disciplinary fields and domains, the fact that their book was a collaborative effort is itself compelling.

10. One of the consequences of the Zurich conference was the creation of the *Network for Transdisciplinarity Research* known as td-net (http://transdis ciplinarity.ch/en/td-net/Aktuell.html). This Swiss-based network serves as a communication and collaboration platform for researchers, educators, and stakeholders in society who advocate the Zurich approach to transdisciplinarity and are involved in inter- and transdisciplinary research and teaching.

Suggested Readings

Funtowicz, Silvio O., and Jerome R. Ravetz. "Science for the Post-Normal Age." *Futures 25*, no. 7 (1993): 739–55.

Gibbons, Michael, Camille Limoges, Helga Nowotny, Simon Schwartzman, Peter Scott, and Martin Trow. *The New Production of Knowledge: The Dynamics of Science and Research in Contemporary Societies*. Los Angeles, CA/London: Sage, 1994.

Kuhn, Thomas S. *The Structure of Scientific Revolutions: 50th-Anniversary Edition*. Chicago, IL: University of Chicago Press, 2012.

Wilson, Edward O. *Consilience: The Unity of Knowledge*. New York: Alfred A. Knopf, 1998.

CHAPTER THREE

Transdisciplinarity: An Elusive Concept

> Transdisciplinarity is not a single form of knowledge but a dialogue of forms.
>
> —Kate Maguire (2015, 168)

The relative novelty of transdisciplinarity and lack of agreement on its definition have contributed to some confusion during discussions about the concept of transdisciplinarity. Transdisciplinarity still remains "a rather elusive concept" (Jahn, Bergmann, and Keil 2012, 1). It is often grasped in different ways, sometimes called by different names, and suggests a certain fluidity that allows for some conceptual experimentation. This elusiveness and fluidity have created some tension between the two "dominant transdisciplinarity camps" (McGregor 2015b, 10), frequently referred to in the literature as Nicolescuian transdisciplinarity and the Zurich School's transdisciplinarity (Augsburg 2014; Bernstein 2015; Jahn, Bergmann, and Keil 2012; Klein 2004; McGregor 2015a, 2015b).

Nicolescuian transdisciplinarity is named after a theoretical physicist Basarab Nicolescu, who is considered one of the major proponents of transdisciplinarity.[1] According to Nicolescuian transdisciplinarity, which was first introduced in the *Charter of Transdisciplinarity* (Freitas, Nicolescu, and Morin 1994) and further developed in Nicolescu's *Manifesto of Transdisciplinarity* (2002) and his later works, transdisciplinarity is not merely a new approach to conducting research but a new methodology in its own right. Nicolescu's vision of transdisciplinarity as a new methodology stems from and is deeply informed by discoveries and insights from quantum physics, living systems theory, and chaos theory. These discoveries and insights, in contrast to the single, one-dimensional reality of classical thought, acknowledge multidimensionality and complexity of the present world and challenge the basic laws of classical physics.

In his *Manifesto of Transdisciplinarity*, Nicolescu states the goal of transdisciplinarity as "the understanding of the present world, of which one of the imperatives is the unity of knowledge" (2002, 44) and encapsulates the methodology of transdisciplinarity into three axioms (or three "pillars"): ontological, logical, and epistemological. These are respectively:

1. *Multiple levels of reality and the Hidden Third.* According to Nicolescu, this ontological axiom replaces the classical Newtonian single-level, one-dimensional reality with a multilevel, multidimensional, and multireferential structure of Reality, or trans-Reality, which is organized along three levels: transdisciplinary Object (comprised of environmental, economic, and cosmic/planetary Realities), transdisciplinary Subject (comprised of political, social, historical, and individual Realities), and, what Nicolescu calls, the Hidden Third, "a zone of non-resistance to our experiences, representations, descriptions, images, and mathematical formulations" that "allows for the unification of the transdisciplinary Subject and the transdisciplinary Object while preserving their difference" (Ibid., 54, 55; capitalization in original).

2. *The logic of the included middle.* This logical axiom challenges one of the fundamental principles of traditional Aristotelian logic indicated by the law of the excluded middle, which is "harmful in complex cases" (Ibid., 12) and introduces a new logic of the included middle that enables the conceptualization of coherence among multiple levels of Reality and of a unity between the subject and object so that the subject and the object can, in Nicolescu's words, "correspond" to each other (Ibid.).

3. *Complexity.* This epistemological axiom highlights the principle of interconnectedness and interdependence of the Universe and emphasizes the idea of complexity that "penetrate[s] each and every field of knowledge" (Ibid., 60).

For Nicolescu, these three "pillars" of transdisciplinarity reveal coherence among the different levels of reality, account for inconsistencies and contradictions, and enable a more comprehensive understanding of complexity. He stresses that the transdisciplinary methodology does not replace disciplinary methodologies, nor does it strive to master multiple disciplines but rather complements and enriches them with "new and indispensable insights" (Nicolescu 2002, 122) and "aims to open all disciplines to that which they share and to that which lies beyond them" (Freitas, Nicolescu, and Morin 1994).

Unlike Nicolescuian transdisciplinarity, the Zurich School's transdisciplinarity, which emerged from the International Transdisciplinarity Conference held in Zurich, Switzerland, in 2000, views transdisciplinarity as a new form of problem solving rather than a new methodology. One of the basic premises of the Zurich approach, which draws largely upon Gibbons et al.'s (1994) Mode-2 approach to knowledge production, is the assumption that problems that are being addressed by higher education institutions are stemming from the sciences and not from the real world, and that knowledge production is being "confined to a close circle of scientific experts, professional journals and academic departments" (Häberli et al. 2001, 18). The Zurich School's transdisciplinarity emphasizes the importance of trans-sectorial collaborations where researchers from different disciplines, multiple stakeholders, and "everyone who has something to say about a particular problem and is willing to participate" (Ibid.) are actively involved in working out solutions to concrete societal problems. As a result of such collaborations, ". . . the knowledge of multiple participants is enhanced, including local knowledge, scientific knowledge and the knowledge of industries, businesses, and NGOs [nongovernmental organizations]. The sum of this knowledge will be greater than the knowledge of any single partner" (Ibid., 19).[2] Based on these premises, the Zurich School identified the following goals of transdisciplinarity:

a) To design and implement solutions to tangible problems found in the life-world

b) To enable the process of mutual learning, on equal footing, among researchers from different disciplines, multiple stakeholders, and community members

c) To create and integrate knowledge which is "solution-oriented, socially robust, and transferable to both the scientific and societal practice" (Segalàs and Tejedor 2013)

Despite (or perhaps thanks to) the lack of clear consensus among scholars on the concept of transdisciplinarity, a substantial body of studies discussing the concept and features of transdisciplinarity has been published over the past decade. Klein explains transdisciplinarity as "a holistic vision; a particular method, concept or theory; a general attitude of openness and a capacity for collaboration; as well as an essential strategy for solving complex problems" (2000c, 4) that is "transcultural, translational, and encompasses ethics, spirituality, and creativity" (2004, 516). Wickson, Carew, and Russell (2006) argue that the fundamental features of transdisciplinary research that distinguish it from other cross-disciplinary approaches to research include:

1. *Problem focus* (starting with a problem that is "'in the world and actual' as opposed to 'in my head and conceptual'" [1048])[3]
2. *Evolving methodology* (involving "the development of a shared and evolving methodology that has fused different disciplinary approaches" [1051])
3. *Collaboration* (including multiple stakeholders and community members who provide "a type of 'reality check' for research processes and outcomes" [1051])

This summary of the fundamental features of transdisciplinary research can be enhanced by the description suggested by Pohl and Hadorn (2007) who describe the key attributes of transdisciplinary research as follows: "Transdisciplinary research identifies, structures, analyses and deals with specific problems in such a way that it can: a) grasp the complexity of problems, b) take into account the diversity of life-world and scientific perceptions of problems, c) link abstract and case-specific knowledge, and d) develop knowledge and practices that promote what is perceived to be the common good" (30).

Montuori (2008, 2012) makes an important contribution to the discourse on transdisciplinarity by outlining the five dimensions that constitute the foundation of applied transdisciplinarity. These five dimensions of transdisciplinarity are:

1. "Inquiry-based rather than discipline-driven"
2. "Trans-paradigmatic rather than Intra-paradigmatic"
3. "Complex thinking rather than Reductive-Disjunctive thinking"
4. "Integration of the inquirer rather than 'objective' elimination of inquirer"
5. "Creative inquiry rather than reproductive inquiry" (Montuori 2012)

Although the discourse on transdisciplinarity is widely diffused and one shared conceptual framework that could guide transdisciplinary researchers in their pursuits is still evolving, some unifying themes have emerged from the contributions of various scholars. These unifying themes are:

- *Transcendence of disciplinary boundaries* (transgressing the narrow scope of traditional disciplinary worldviews through the merging of diverse disciplinary approaches, insights, and methodologies to generate new knowledge and insights that otherwise would not be possible)

- *Knowledge integration* (bringing together various bodies and types of knowledge and know-how from diverse sources to form a new understanding of the problem under investigation, create new conceptualizations and methodological approaches, and expand or transform knowledge within participating disciplines)

- *Focus on pressing real-world problems* (identifying and seeking workable solutions to specific societal problems)

- *Complexity* (addressing multidimensional "messy" or "wicked" problems that are too complex for disciplinary or even interdisciplinary research)

- *Contextualism* (maintaining that knowledge is not neutral or objective but is relevant to context and the prerequisites of the knower)

- *Joint problem solving* (involving researchers, practitioners, policy makers, stakeholders, social groups, and individual citizens in the design and implementation of research and leading to a solution that is greater than the sum of its parts)

- *Interconnectedness* (developing multiple nodes of connections between different bodies of knowledge and between different individuals or groups of individuals)

- *Diversity* (transcending and integrating different perspectives and perceptions through collaboration of researchers from different disciplines and through active participation of multiple stakeholders)

- *Social inclusion* (involving marginalized groups and ordinary citizens as valuable contributors to the research process)

- *Reflexivity* (emphasizing the value of collaborative deliberation and collective experimentation)

- *Recursiveness* (including theoretical refinement and continuous experimentation throughout the research process leading to a new knowledge)

- *Mutual learning* (aiming to achieve some kind of "symmetry of enlightenment" (Maasen and Lieven 2006, 404) between participating actors and appreciating each other's knowledge and contributions to the research process)

- *The promotion of the common good* (aiming at shaping a more equal society and the improvement of the human condition)

- *Universality* (having universal applicability)

- *Greater wisdom* (leading to wider public understanding and more enduring societal impact)

This summary of the characteristics of transdisciplinarity suggests that even though the interpretations of transdisciplinarity vary from one scholar to the other, transdisciplinarity is part of a social process and a form of the "democratic governance of knowledge" (Novy, Habersack, and Schaller 2013, 439). From this perspective, transdisciplinary research can be seen as "public-good research" initiated by urgent societal problems (Pohl and Hadorn 2007). In starting research with "life-world" problems and aiming to generate knowledge that is socially valuable, transdisciplinary research, as many believe, might be able to contribute to solving these problems that cannot be satisfactorily addressed from the disciplinary perspective.

Notes

1. Basarab Nicolescu is an author of numerous works on transdisciplinarity and a cofounder of the International Centre of Transdisciplinary Research and Studies (in French: Centre International de Recherches et Études Transdisciplinaires—CIRET), a worldwide organization, founded in 1987 and located in Paris, France, that aims to promote and advance transdisciplinarity around the world.

2. While Nicolescu respected and remained open to different interpretations of transdisciplinarity, he criticized the Zurich School's vision of transdisciplinarity for "the refusal to formulate any methodology and by its exclusive concentration on joint problem-solving of problems pertaining to the science-technology-society triad" (Nicolescu 2005).

3. Although the notion of transdisciplinarity as problem-oriented research is generally supported by scholars (Hadorn et al. 2008; Mobjörk 2010; Roux et al. 2006; Russell, Wickson, and Carew 2008), not all authors agree that the idea of problem solving is exclusive to transdisciplinary research. Hammer and Söderqvist (2001), for example, argue that multidisciplinary and interdisciplinary research can also be considered problem-oriented.

Suggested Readings

Futures 65 (January 2015). Special issue "Advances in transdisciplinarity 2004–2014," edited by Roderick J. Lawrence.

Maldonato, Mauro, and Ricardo Pietrobon (eds.). *Research on Scientific Research: A Transdisciplinary Study.* Brighton [England]; Portland, OR: Sussex Academic Press, 2010.

Morin, Edgar. *On Complexity.* Cresskill, NJ: Hampton Press, 2008a.

Nicolescu, Basarab. *Manifesto of Transdisciplinarity.* Albany, NY: SUNY Press, 2002.

CHAPTER FOUR

From Scientific Research to Societal Benefit: The Need for Transdisciplinarity

Facts are uncertain, values in dispute, stakes high and decisions urgent.

—Funtowicz and Ravetz (2008, 365)

In 2010, in a correspondence to the journal *Nature*, a group of 24 international scientists expressed an urgent need for funding of transdisciplinary scientific collaborations. Upon this funding, the scientists claimed, depends the future of Europe (Vasbinder et al. 2010). They argued that a modern science that still maintains and reinforces disciplinarity could not properly understand the effects of new technologies on our complex, interconnected systems (such as biodiversity and climate) and that a "sciences recast" was needed so that scientists would be better able to fulfill their promise to society, which is "to deliver a better understanding of systems that humanity needs for adequate food, energy, water and health without causing damage to the environment" (876). This message confirms the perceived need of the science community in addressing complex issues through transdisciplinary research. It also reminds us that, even after years of discourse on the topic, practices and cultures that support transdisciplinary research have not yet been properly established.

The need for transdisciplinarity is not new. It has been reflected in discussions and publications since 1970 when the First International Seminar on Interdisciplinarity was held at the University of Nice, France. At this seminar, a group of scientists, including an astrophysicist Erich Jantsch, a physicist and mathematician André Lichnerowicz, and a philosopher Joseph Kockelmans, raised concerns about the increasing specialization within academic disciplines (and resulting from it a fragmentation of knowledge) and expressed the need for an integrated approach to solving complex social, economic, environmental, and technological problems. Transdisciplinarity was envisioned as a vehicle for the much needed synthesis of the sciences and the humanities as well as a new mode of knowledge production that could create more visible links between science and society (Apostel et al. 1972).

A "transdisciplinary vision" introduced at that seminar was not widely recognized at that time and remained largely unexplored in the scholarly literature until the early 1990s (Bernstein 2015) when transdisciplinarity was "rediscovered, unveiled, and utilized rapidly to meet the unprecedented challenges of our troubled world" (Nicolescu 2002, 1). Since then—during the last decade in particular—the number of publications about transdisciplinarity has hugely increased, including a wide range of books, peer-reviewed journals, and conference proceedings. Transdisciplinarity has transformed from "a buzzword promoted by a relatively small number of academics and scientists with a western worldview" (Lawrence 2015, 1) to a practicing concept in many corners of the world. As Klein (2014) observes, there has been an "exponential growth in publications, a widening array of disciplinary and professional contexts, and increased interest in science-policy bodies, funding agencies, and public and private spheres" (68).

The renewed awareness of the need for transdisciplinarity that has occurred in the last few years arises in response to five major factors:

1. A heightened awareness of the inherent complexity of the reality and global interconnectedness brought about by social, political, and economical change; the need to understand these complex multidimensional global systems that are not referable to the conceptual framework of any single discipline or set of disciplines

2. A growing concern about a host of urgent complex problems (the so-called real-world problems or life-world problems) that have intensified in recent decades such as climate change, unsustainability, inequities between rich and poor, world poverty, violence, and risks to human health resulting from new technologies, among others

3. A demand for integrated solutions to these urgent complex problems, which, if not dealt with effectively, could lead to "potential self-destruction of our species" (Nicolescu 2002, 7)

4. A realization among scholars that contemporary science, which is still largely composed of compartmentalized academic disciplines, can neither properly understand nor cope with these urgent problems, which are too complex to be properly addressed by any single scientific discipline (or a set of disciplines)

5. The need for a more democratic governance of knowledge production focusing on joint problem solving and requiring the engagement of multiple actors in the research and decision-making process

Despite the perceived urgent need to bridge the gap between knowledge production and society, there has been substantial opposition (even in the most recent past) to the idea that it is necessary to transcend disciplinary boundaries in order to create integrated knowledge required to address the full complexity of real-life situations. This opposition persists as the result of a prevailing approach to knowledge production. Macdonald (2000b) describes this situation as follows:

> We have been taught (wrongly, of course) that it is possible to engage in disciplinary analysis without ultimately having to commit ourselves to contemplating our place in the universe. Unfortunately, the lesson has been so well learned in existing disciplines that it is unlikely to be transcended from within them. Transdisciplinarity, by contrast, is a discipline that demands its disciples to exact this commitment of contemplating their place in the universe as a precondition to discipleship. (70)

There has been, however, a growing recognition among scholars regarding the limitations of the existing disciplinary structures and disciplinary approaches to research that promote further specialization rather than cooperation and thus cannot address the full complexity of real-life situations. The specific concerns expressed by scholars include:

1. Hyper-specialization within individual scientific disciplines and proliferation of "sub-disciplines" that hinder the scientists' ability to achieve a larger-scale insight and more global perspective on problems and issues of the real world and to attain sufficient breadth of knowledge to recognize opportunities in related disciplines and to capitalize on cross-disciplinary collaborations. As Max Neef (2005) puts it, "If I were asked to define our times, in few words, I would say that we have reached a point in our evolution as human beings, in which we know very much, but understand very little" (14).

2. The limitations and distorted priorities of disciplinary methodologies that typically abstract an object from its context and focus on generalizable and typical conditions to be formalized in theories and laws that are rarely applicable to concrete problems caused and shaped by real-world situations and occurring in specific localities. Sarewitz (2010) describes this as follows: "Disciplinary views of the world distort as much as they reveal by artificially isolating and simplifying particular components of natural and social systems—components that happen to be amenable to precise measurement, mathematical description, or experimental replication—and then treating those edited versions as if they are discrete, puzzle- or clockwork-like pieces of a reconstructable whole" (65).

3. An implicit disciplinary hierarchy, in which a higher ranking is assigned to the "hard" and natural sciences relative to the social sciences and humanities.

4. The exclusion of valuable actors such as educators, stakeholders, practitioners, and citizens from the research process who can serve as useful sources for implementation of solutions to problems, found in the real world, with which scientists are not necessarily familiar and thus might have challenges with grasping contradictions, diverse perspectives, and opposing interests.

5. Institutional constraints for the implementation of cross-disciplinary[1] projects and impediments to obtaining funding for cross-disciplinary research projects, especially in new research areas (e.g., forensic anthropology, psychological economics, bioinformatics, geochemistry, and sociobiology), for which it is difficult to make the distinction of disciplinary matter.

6. Challenges associated with undertaking cross-disciplinary, cross-sectorial research projects that can hinder career advancement, have adverse effects on peer recognition and a sense of professional identity, and limit opportunities for funding and publication and the dissemination of research results.

These concerns have led to calls for a new research paradigm, namely transdisciplinarity, which, in contrast to the conventional structured model of disciplinary knowledge production, is rooted in "messy" real-life problems (versus theoretically simplified versions of problems). Furthermore, transdisciplinarity applies research strategies that include people from the "life-world" in the process of joint problem solving at a high level of integration and mutual learning. As Pohl and Hadorn (2007) observe, transdisciplinarity entails "participatory processes" meaning that transdisciplinarity "goes beyond doing research *on* actors [emphasis added] and implies that actors can help shape the research process" (427). In doing so, transdisciplinarity merges a wide range of insights and expertise resulting from the integration of diverse perspectives and experiences that is needed to address complex issues.

Note

1. The term "cross-disciplinarity" refers here to any kind of research that involves boundary crossing between two or more disciplines.

Suggested Reading

Nowotny, Helga, Peter Scott, and Michael Gibbons. *Re-thinking Science: Knowledge and the Public in an Age of Uncertainty.* Cambridge, UK: Polity, 2001.

CHAPTER FIVE

The Disciplinary Continuum: From Disciplinarity to Transdisciplinarity

> Before there can be transdisciplinarity, there must be disciplinarity.
> —Roderick Macdonald (2000b, 69)

Defining Disciplinarity

The *Oxford English Dictionary* (1989) provides multiple meanings of the term "discipline," ranging from training to authority to a system of rules to the self-control of behavior. According to other sources, the word "discipline" has Indo-European roots and originates from both the Greek term "didasko" (teach) and the Latin term "(di)disco" (learn) and thus conveys the double meaning of knowledge and power (Hoskin and Macve 1986). As a verb, the word "discipline" also means punishing and enforcing obedience.

Although these various interpretations of the term "discipline" place emphasis on training, control, and rigorous set of instructions, the contemporary meaning of the terms "discipline" and "disciplinarity" is not supposed to carry the tone of stringency and inflexibility or suggest that a knowledge-producer should be controlled and constrained (i.e., "disciplined") during the conduct of research inquiry. In the English language, the word "discipline" first appeared in the 16th century to refer to branches of knowledge, particularly to medicine, law, and theology

(Shumway and Messer-Davidow 1991). In this context, the modern use of the term "discipline" refers to a specific organized field of knowledge, the defining characteristics of which distinguish it from other fields of knowledge, and the term "disciplinarity" refers to a historical tradition of knowledge creation and knowledge organization.

Disciplinarity as Social Practice

Disciplinarity as a social practice is a relatively new development. Knowledge has assumed a disciplinary form only about two centuries ago, and a discipline-based knowledge has been produced in academia for just a little longer than a century (Klein 1996). The development of disciplinarity has been linked to several historic and social forces and events, including the industrial revolution, the general "scientification" of knowledge, technological advancements, evolution of the natural sciences, agrarian agitation, and formation of the first scientific societies such as the Royal Society in the United Kingdom and the Academie des Sciences in France. The trend toward a greater division of knowledge into specific disciplines was further propelled by the demand of industries for specialists and, as a consequence, by disciplines recruiting more and more students to their ranks. The development of more sophisticated and more expensive instrumentation within individual disciplinary fields has also contributed to further "professionalization" of knowledge in the 20th century (Flexner 1979; Klein 1996; Shumway and Messer-Davidow 1991).

Akin to the concept of faculties in academia, disciplines were originally divided into three basic categories: natural sciences, social sciences, and humanities. The first two "science" categories emerged in the 18th century as the result of the breakup of natural philosophy into independent natural sciences and of moral philosophy into the social sciences. The third category (the humanities) came into being in the 20th century in order to include the disciplines that did not hold or claim the designation of "sciences" (Shumway and Messer-Davidow 1991).[1] The defining characteristics that distinguish disciplines from one another include objects and subjects of research, concepts, epistemology, terminology, common theoretical assumptions, and established methodologies such as the principles of research discovery and verification of research results. In *Becoming Interdisciplinary*, Augsburg (2006) lists 16 elements that characterize "any given discipline":

1. Basic concepts
2. Leading theories

3. Modes of inquiry (or research methods)

4. What counts as a problem

5. Observational categories

6. Representational techniques

7. Types of explanation

8. Standards of proof

9. General ideals of what constitutes the discipline

10. Assumptions and world views

11. Disciplinary perspective

12. Seminal texts/books

13. Major thinkers

14. Major practitioners

15. Official professional/academic associations and leading academic journals (116–119)

Discipline-specific vocabulary as one of the defining characteristics of a discipline is missing from Augsburg's list, which is a serious oversight. Lisa Lattuca, a prominent researcher of interdisciplinarity, considers a disciplinary language as "one of the most distinctive and binding aspects of a disciplinary community" (2001, 29). Similarly, Ertas, Tanik, and Maxwell (2000) agree that a field of study can be described as a discipline given that it has "unified tools, techniques, and methods, and a well-developed jargon" (4).

Disciplines are also supposed to document and communicate knowledge in standard forms as well as to have some institutional manifestation such as established subjects taught at universities, respective academic faculties or departments, an undergraduate curriculum, typically embodied in the form of a major sequence of study, and respective academic faculties or departments. As an institutional form, a discipline is also supported by its recognition as a distinct discipline in a classification system (such as in library catalogs and databases), a professional association, which sponsors conferences, awards and prizes, the publication of scholarly journals, and the creation of a code of professional ethics, scholarly publishers that produce peer-reviewed journals, reference works, textbooks, and research monographs, and a system of social networks, including those sponsored or facilitated by professional associations and university departments (Becher 1989; D'Agostino 2012; During 2006).

The adherence to disciplinary norms and methods can be seen as a necessary and beneficial condition for the advancement of knowledge.

Kuhn (1962) argues that what holds the disciplinary communities together is their acceptance of a shared "paradigm" that provides guidance for their collective endeavors in a field of enquiry. Disciplinarity enables researchers to use a set of established practices and procedures, by which disciplinary knowledge is acquired, and then to communicate this newly acquired knowledge to other researchers in order to further its development without suppressing it. Therefore, it can be argued that disciplinarity makes a valuable contribution to society at large by facilitating "social mechanisms for distributing knowledge" (D'Agostino 2012). Furthermore, the evolution of knowledge is based (to a large extent) on disciplinary practice that helps create the range of relevant methodological approaches to a problem, provides a clearly defined structure for a project, and sets the boundaries on the parameters of research, dictating what should be included in research and what should be left out. It provides a researcher with a set of guidelines that determine the course of the researcher's inquiry as well as his identity. Disciplinarity also serves another useful function by helping researchers ensure the plausibility and testability of their hypotheses and enabling them to repeat the research done by others and to demonstrate the stability of their research findings. Geiger (1986) observes that "a discipline is, above all, a community based on inquiry and centered on competent investigators. It consists of individuals who are associated in order to facilitate intercommunication and to establish some degree of authority over the standards of that inquiry" (29). Knapp (2010) concludes that disciplines are "not a bad thing but they must be viewed for what they are: a *descriptive* means of categorizing our knowledge and paths of inquiry" (53).

Disciplinarity and the Compartmentalization of Knowledge

> "Nothing could be better than for each person concentrating on a legitimate specialization, laboriously cultivating his own backyard, nevertheless to force himself to follow his neighbors work. But the walls are so high that, very often, they hide the view."
> —Fernand Braudel, *A History of Civilizations*

Although the term "disciplinarity" has become synonymous with the organization and the systematic production of knowledge and the reputation of discipline-based scholarship have been, until recently, positive, the concept of disciplinarity is not so straightforward. Disciplinary specialization makes it more challenging for a researcher to address larger, more complex questions. For example, no single discipline can possibly explain the complex phenomenon of human thinking. Gaining insights into the workings of the human mind and the associated mysteries of consciousness calls for drawing on expertise from evolutionary biology, neuroscience, psychology, linguistics, philosophy, and semiotics, and then integrating these in such a manner as to generate a more comprehensive understanding of it. Repko, Szostak, and Buchberger (2013) cite the passage from *The Little Prince* by Antoine de Saint-Exupéry to illustrate how disciplinary specialization can blind researchers to the broader context of a situation within which the problem or idea exists:

> "Your planet is very beautiful," [said the little prince]. "Has it any oceans?"
> "I couldn't tell you," said the geographer . . .
> "But you are a geographer!"
> "Exactly," the geographer said. "But I am not an explorer. I haven't a single explorer on my planet. It is not the geographer who goes out to count the towns, the rivers, the mountains, the seas, the oceans, and the deserts. The geographer is much too important to go loafing about. He does not leave his desk." (2000, 45–46)

While using a strict disciplinary lens to examine a specific phenomenon enhances the particular body of knowledge for that discipline, complex problems are rarely susceptible to narrow specialized handling. Furthermore, extreme specialization can distort the perception and analysis of larger natural or social systems by artificially isolating and simplifying particular parts of these systems. The famous ancient parable about six blind men who examined an elephant by touching different parts of its body and who described the elephant in six different incommensurable ways illustrates this point of view.

Michel Foucault (1972, 1978, 1981) was among the first philosophers and historians of ideas who pointed out the limitations of disciplinarity as "a system of control in the production of discourse" (1972, 224) that had come to dominate much of modern life. Although Foucault used the term "discipline" in a more general sense, his observation included academic disciplines and their role of bringing about "discipline" in society. He argued that disciplines were simply "defined by a domain of objects, a set of methods, a corpus of propositions considered to be true, a play of rules and definitions, or techniques and instruments" (1981, 59).

It is generally believed that disciplinary research is not concerned with the peculiarities of specific cases or singular objects but with principles, scientific laws, and generalized explanations and aims to withdraw from the "real world" in order to better understand its complexities. A neo-Kantian philosopher Wilhelm Windelband introduced the terms "nomothetic knowledge" (the knowledge of general laws) and "idiographic knowledge" (the knowledge of singular or specific instances) to distinguish between the two components of knowledge production. He also believed that both nomothetic and idiographic components of knowledge deserve equal rights because any object of study (natural laws or specific human affairs) can become an object of a nomothetic as well as an idiographic analysis (Windelband 1980). Krohn (2010) thinks that the nomothetic component of knowledge can be exemplified by geometry and the idiographic component of knowledge can be exemplified in the science of surveying. He writes: "Since there is no real line, curve, or body that fits the demands of mathematical definition, they are ideally constructed. . . . Real things, those, which we can point at, are only approximations of ideal objects. . . . Surveying is oriented to the real world and therefore is in itself an interdiscipline. Geometry is a classical discipline (or subdiscipline if mathematics is the discipline)" (33). Other authors contributed to the academic debate by discussing the downsides of the dominant tendency to fragment knowledge by compartmentalizing it into "disciplines." Wilson (1998) observed that "the ongoing fragmentation of knowledge and the resulting chaos in philosophy are not reflections of the real world but artifacts of scholarship" (41). Sarewitz (2010) stipulated that even though disciplinarity is not synonymous with reductionism, it supports "an inductive, reductionist view of understanding, where larger-scale insight is supposed to arise from the accumulation of facts and insights acquired through inquiry focused at smaller scales" (65). Macdonald (2000b) defined disciplinarity is "the deployment of knowledge systems grounded in a relatively limited number of concepts which are held to have general explanatory power when applied to the world of experience" (69). Wilson (1996) concludes that "[s]taying within disciplinary boundaries means giving up trying to understand concrete phenomena" (195).

Nicolescu (2002) compared the trend toward greater specialization and fragmentation within disciplines to a modern Tower of Babel where "a theoretical particle physicist [cannot] truly hold a dialogue with a neurophysiologist, a mathematician with a poet, a biologist with an economist, a politician with a computer programmer, beyond mouthing more or less banal generalities" (41). This "process of Babelization," in Nicolescu's words, has resulted in large fragmented bodies of knowledge that show little overlap and thus are unable to address large-scale and large-scope contemporary problems of the real world. Figure 5.1 illustrates the concept of disciplinarity in which there is no evident cooperation or collaboration between disciplines.

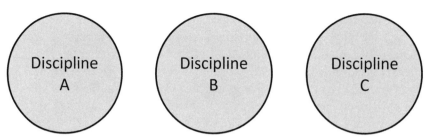

Figure 5.1 In disciplinarity, there is no overlap of the disciplines.

Disciplinarity and Boundary-Work

A common theme running through recent discussions of disciplinarity is the existence of arbitrary or artificial disciplinary boundaries, which hinder the exchange of ideas across disciplines, impede the progress of science, and make scientific research less relevant to society. Abbott (1995) describes disciplines as well-defined and differentiated epistemological and organizational units and institutional bodies that are separated by recognized boundaries. Klein (1996a) claims that "the underlying action of disciplining knowledge is control" (140). Ertas, Tanik, Maxwell (2000) argue that disciplines "inevitably develop into self-contained hard shells . . . and that [t]he longer a discipline evolves, the harder its shell becomes" (4). Roy (1977) describes this situation as "a balkanization of knowledge," with many "fiefdoms, each with its army (departmental faculty), local dialect (journals), and religious establishment (professional societies)" (162). Scholars generally agree that disciplinary boundaries are not natural but socially constructed (Fish 1989; Knapp 2012; Pahre 1996; Szostak, Gnoli, and López-Huertas 2016).

The concept of "boundary-work"[2] has been applied to describe the prevalent tendency of the disciplines to generate distinct boundaries. In the scholarly literature, boundary-work is described as comprising the set of strategies for creating boundaries around activities to distinguish them from others on the basis of differing values, methods, values, bodies of knowledge, and styles of organization (Gieryn, 1983; Jasanoff, 1987; Klein 1993). Thomas Gieryn, who coined the term "boundary-work" in his study on the demarcation of science from other intellectual activities, argued that boundary-work is likely to occur when "ideologists of a profession or occupation" pursue the following three goals:

1. "*Expansion* of professional authority or expertise into domains already claimed by other professions or occupations, thereby heightening the contrast between rivals

2. *Monopolization* of professional authority and resources, thereby excluding rivals from within by defining them as outsiders who are 'pseudo,' 'deviant,' or 'amateur'

3. *Protection of autonomy* over professional activities, thereby exempting members from responsibility for consequences of their work by putting the blame on scapegoats from outside." (Gieryn 1983, 791–92)

The development of the rigid organizational structure of higher education institutions, which typically groups specific disciplinary specialties together into faculties or departments that are cognitively and institutionally separated from each other, has led some to believe that "a discipline is at bottom nothing more than an administrative category" (Jencks and Riesman 1968, 523). Montuori (2005) points out to the existence of "clear parallels between the disciplinary organization of the university and the organization of thought" (151).

Although the majority of publications on disciplinarity focus on discussing disciplinary boundaries as barriers to research collaborations, less attention has been paid to the fact that crossing the boundaries is conceptually meaningful only in relation to the concept of the existence of disciplinary boundaries. Klein (1993) postulates that while boundary-work separates and differentiates through the construction and maintenance of boundaries, Gieryn's concept also suggests that boundary-work involves "the crossing, deconstructing and reconstructing of boundaries." This process of permeation of boundaries, Klein further explains, could occur across the borders that separate one discipline from another as well as across disciplinary groupings, taxonomic categories, and larger institutional constructs (186). She argues that "[i]f there is an undisputed truth about disciplinarity, it is that disciplines change [and they change] because they do not live in isolation" (Ibid.). She elaborates her argument by providing six "major and sometime overlapping" explanations for permeation of disciplinary boundaries:

1. "The epistemological structure of a particular discipline

2. Relations with neighboring disciplines

3. The pull of powerful or fashionable new tools, methods, concepts, and theories

4. The pull of problem solving over strictly disciplinary focus

5. The complexifying of disciplinary research

6. Redefinitions of what is considered intrinsic and extrinsic to discipline" (Ibid., 187)

More simply put, the boundaries between disciplines change due to either increasing differentiation within the disciplines or the integration of disciplines. The purpose of transcending disciplinary boundaries is always to advance the world of knowledge.

Hunt (1994) notes that in order to cross or change the boundaries, one needs to know where these boundaries are. She compares the history of disciplines to the history of human languages and argues that while the existence of disciplinary boundaries creates barriers between people, learning the language of a different discipline, similarly to learning a foreign language, opens up "previously unsuspected riches" and "creates a different relationship to one's own discipline" because we learn more from the otherness than from the sameness (2).

The Dialog between Disciplines

> Crossing boundaries is a defining characteristic of our age.
> —Julie Thompson Klein (1996, 1)

Although the question of knowledge production has historically been framed by disciplinarity, contemporary research is being increasingly characterized by an approach that rises above traditional disciplinarity and involves two or more disciplines working together. The three main forms of the "multiple disciplinary approach" (Choi and Pak 2006) include multidisciplinarity, interdisciplinarity, and transdisciplinarity,[3] all of which (as the prefix "multi-" suggests) refer to the involvement of several disciplines, although the degree of cooperation and integration among them varies.

It is still not uncommon to view "multidisciplinarity," "interdisciplinarity," and "transdisciplinarity" as interchangeable terms and to believe that all these terms refer to collaborations between disciplines or to team environments where the members of the team are from different disciplines. Indeed, upon first examination, the etymologies of these three terms connote the use of multiple disciplines (and their respective methodologies). However, while the distinction between multi-, inter-, and transdisciplinarity is not absolute (they all "overflow disciplinary boundaries," in Nicolescu's [2002] words [46]), their goals, approaches to research, and the degree of integration differ in significant ways.

Multidisciplinarity

Multidisciplinarity (also called by some scholars pluridisciplinarity or polydisciplinarity) is a research approach, in which researchers from two or more disciplines work collaboratively on the same theme *without* integrating the concepts, methodologies, or epistemologies from their respective disciplines. There is a broad agreement among scholars that multidisciplinarity is characterized by *juxtaposition* of disciplines rather than by their *integration*. The goal of the juxtaposition of disciplines is to add breadth of knowledge in an encyclopedic manner and attain a more comprehensive understanding of a theme being studied by presenting different perspectives without blending them. While each discipline contributes its unique methods and approaches to the theme at hand and thus broadens the base of knowledge and expertise, the existing disciplinary boundaries are not questioned and the participating disciplines retain their autonomy. For example, a literary work can be studied, with limited disciplinary interaction, within the history of literature, psychology, linguistics, and philosophy. While the study would draw on the knowledge from these different disciplines, it would remain within the boundaries of these disciplines. In Stokols et al.'s (2008) words, in multidisciplinary projects participating researchers "remain conceptually and methodologically anchored in their respective fields" (S97).

Multidisciplinarity is the first research approach on the disciplinary continuum where collaboration of disciplines is evident to some extent. However, it is important to keep in mind that multidisciplinary research is "essentially *additive*, not *integrative*" (Klein 1990, 56; italics original). Figure 5.2 illustrates the concept of multidisciplinarity in which multiple disciplines are connected but not integrated.

Bruce et al. (2004) reiterate this idea by observing that in multidisciplinary research, each discipline works in a self-contained manner; and thus, there is little cross-fertilization among participating disciplines. Research findings resulting from a multidisciplinary project are typically included in a collective final report, which is compiled in encyclopedic rather than synthesized manner.

Interdisciplinarity

Interdisciplinarity is a research approach in which researchers from two or more disciplines integrate the concepts, methodologies, tools, and epistemologies from their respective disciplines into the practice of other disciplines to generate a new conceptual framework for addressing a complex research problem or question. As the prefix "inter-" suggests, interdisciplinarity implies a dynamic interaction between disciplines and involves approaching a research problem from multiple disciplinary perspectives simultaneously. The classic examples of interdisciplinary

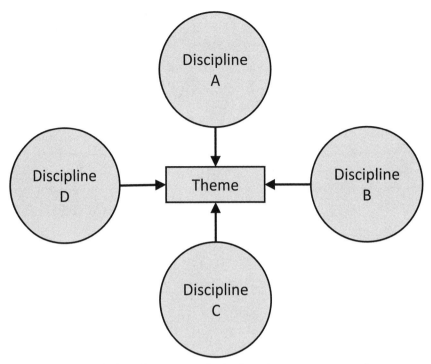

Figure 5.2 In multidisciplinarity, multiple disciplines are connected to present different perspectives on a theme but they are not integrated.

knowledge are molecular biology, which originated from cell biology and biochemistry, and paleontology, which was formed by the interaction of biology and geology. In the social sciences, area studies, women's studies, and qualitative research have been among the most influential interdisciplinary movements in the postwar period.[4]

The key characteristic of interdisciplinarity is integration of diverse disciplinary insights in order to create a more holistic perspective on a specific question, a particular issue, or an identifiable research problem. It involves the development of a shared methodological approach across multiple disciplinary frameworks. Furthermore, interdisciplinarity includes the transfer of methods from one discipline to another. For example, biomimicry, an interdisciplinary field, which aims to create nature-inspired technological innovations, transfers the methodology from biology to engineering sciences.

Similar to multidisciplinarity, interdisciplinarity remains within the framework of disciplinary research, in which disciplinary identities are preserved. It integrates disciplinary insights but not the disciplines that produced them. Unlike multidisciplinarity, in which disciplines remain separate and are "neither changed nor enriched" (Klein 1990, 56), interdisciplinarity synthesizes the knowledge and methodologies from two or more disciplines.[5] It creates a new body of knowledge, which stems from the combination of different points of view on a research problem and thus it can be seen as more than the simple sum of the parts.[6] Although this new body of knowledge has roots within the parent disciplines, it is itself unique and different from it. Newell (2000) points out that theoretical appeal of interdisciplinarity can be captured in the two terms—"balance" and "dynamism." In interdisciplinary research, Newell argues, "reductionism is spe-

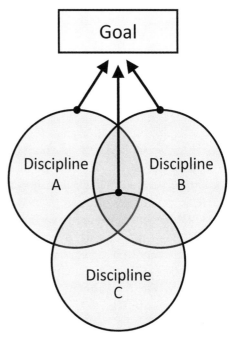

Figure 5.3 In interdisciplinarity, the "spheres of knowledge" intersect and are, to some extent, integrated.

cific; depth of knowledge is balanced by breadth; and disciplinary conflict is balanced through integrative tension. Interdisciplinarity thrives in a dynamic environment where disciplines evolve, new disciplines emerge, and questions, issues, and problems shift over time" (44–45). Figure 5.3 illustrates the concept of interdisciplinarity that employs a significant amount of integration between disciplines.

Transdisciplinarity

While transdisciplinarity has much in common with interdisciplinarity, it differs from it on a number of key issues. Those issues concern the goals of disciplines, the degree of their integration, and the structure of research teams.

The goal of transdisciplinarity is "the understanding of the present world, of which one of the imperatives is the unity of knowledge" (Nicolescu 2002, 44), whereas the goal of interdisciplinarity is the integration of multiple disciplines in order to gain a more complete perspective on a particular research inquiry. From this perspective, transdisciplinary approach to research is "far more comprehensive in scope and vision" (Klein 1990,

65) than interdisciplinary approach. In transdisciplinary research, the whole is not only greater than its disciplinary parts but also has qualitatively different characteristics. As Manderson (2000) puts it, "the aim of bringing together diverse disciplines in a transdisciplinary project is not to *transcend* that knowledge base but rather to *transform* it" (91). McMichael (2000b) makes a semantic analogy between the idea of transportation as "a process of moving something across an intervening space" and the idea of transdisciplinarity that "transports" research to new "emergent" experience "to new planes of insight and fulfillment" (203–4).

Transdisciplinarity not only transcends disciplinary boundaries through more comprehensive frameworks but "dissolves" the boundaries between disciplines in such a way that the participating disciplines become "deeply embedded in each other" (Somerville and Rapport 2000, xiv). What is more, transdisciplinary research transcends the divide between science and society by acknowledging the relevance and value of the experiential knowledge of diverse nonacademic stakeholders such as those from the government, industry, and civil society who all work together on addressing a complex social problem. Through exploring the diversity of academic and nonacademic perspectives, "[research] horizons become fused" (Makkreel 1997, 153) and this increases the chance of success in finding solutions to the problem at hand. Figure 5.4 illustrates the

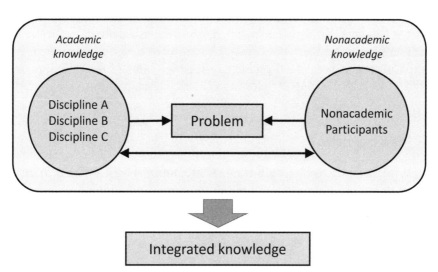

Figure 5.4 Transdisciplinarity synthesizes relevant academic and nonacademic knowledge with the goal of developing integrated knowledge to address a specific real-world problem.

transdisciplinary research model, in which both academic and nonaca-demic participants collaborate as equally valuable team members as they strive to synthesize their relevant skills and different perspectives in order to create a new integrated knowledge that can be applied to problem solving and issue resolution.

The Role of Transdisciplinarity in the Disciplinary Continuum

> Transdisciplinarity does not strive for mastery of several disciplines but aims to open all disciplines to that which they share and to that which lies beyond them.
>
> —Freitas, Nicolescu, and Morin,
> *Charter of Transdisciplinarity* (1994)

The participants of the seminal First International Seminar on Inter-disciplinarity held in 1970 at the University of Nice, France, envisioned transdisciplinarity as a set of axioms to be shared by different disciplines (Apostel et al. 1972). In his 1972 post-seminar chapter *Towards Interdisciplinarity and Transdisciplinarity in Education and Innovation*, Erich Jantsch who, along with Piaget, Lichnerowicz, and Kockelmans, is considered one of the pioneers of transdisciplinarity, described a multi-level cross-disciplinary hierarchy, which he called a knowledge pyramid. In this knowledge pyramid, Jantsch placed multidisciplinarity on the bottom, interdisciplinarity in the middle, and transdisciplinarity at the top. He argued that while in multidisciplinarity disciplines were simply connected, in interdisciplinarity disciplines were coordinated by higher level of understanding, which he called "axiomatics." In transdisciplinarity, an even higher level of understanding ("axiomatic of axiomatics") coordinated not only the disciplines but also interdisciplines. Jantsch conceived transdisciplinarity as superior to other cross-disciplinary approaches. Nicolescu criticized Jantsch for "[falling] in the trap of defining transdisciplinarity as a hyperdiscipline" (2007, 36) and argued that transdisciplinarity is not a discipline or a superdiscipline, even though it is "nourished by disciplinary research" (2002, 45).[7]

Although multi-, inter-, and transdisciplinarity can be seen as the disciplinary continuum, transdisciplinarity is not an expanded or a more advanced form of multi- and interdisciplinarity. Among the three forms of multiple disciplinary approaches, transdisciplinarity is the form that is most radically distinct from disciplinarity because it is "at once between the disciplines, across the different disciplines, and beyond all disciplines" (Nicolescu 2002, 44). Furthermore, transdisciplinarity transcends not only disciplinary boundaries but also the boundaries between science and society. Transcendence of boundaries and the emphasis on the construction of novel methodologies tailored to addressing specific complex problems are the key defining characteristics of transdisciplinarity. Desmond Manderson, one of the participants in the colloquium on transdisciplinarity at L'Abbaye de Royaumont, Ansieres sur Oise, held on May 25–29, 1998, suggested the term "new solutions" that he believed both captured the essence of transdisciplinarity as an endeavor to find workable solutions to societal problems and served as a metaphor for transdisciplinarity as an innovative research methodology that dissolves the boundaries between disciplines and creates a new solution in which the different disciplinary constituents can no longer be separated (Manderson 2000).

At the same time, Nicolescu argues, transdisciplinarity is neither antagonistic to disciplinary research nor strives to replace the methodology of disciplines. It complements and enriches disciplinary research by providing disciplines with new insights, which cannot be generated by disciplinary methods. Furthermore, transdisciplinarity is not being "disrespectful" of disciplinary boundaries. It rather "rebels" against and is not being constrained by these boundaries (Nicolescu 2002, 2008, 2010a, 2010b).[8]

The history of transdisciplinarity cannot be separated from the history of disciplinarity and its successors—multi- and interdisciplinarity. One way to understand transdisciplinarity versus multi- and interdisciplinarity is to see these concepts as a continuum that originates in disciplinarity and gradually defines different ways of multiple disciplines working together. From this perspective, disciplinarity is the precondition for transdisciplinarity and disciplines are "the essential structural underpinning of transdisciplinarity" (Somerville 2000, 97). Patell (2009) reiterates this point by observing that ". . . the success of the multi-inter-trans [continuum] has not eclipsed or weakened the traditional disciplinary structure; rather, its force has reinvigorated and thus strengthened the disciplines from within, intradisciplinarily" (104). In this respect, transdisciplinarity can be described as "intellectual outer space" where the "inner space" is constituted by disciplines (Somerville 2000, 98).

Another way to understand transdisciplinarity versus multi- and interdisciplinarity is to look at how these approaches would handle the same societal problem differently, such as, for example, the problem of school-related shootings in the United States.

Multidisciplinary approach. A variety of disciplines may partner to conduct research on school-related shootings. These disciplines may include psychology, psychiatry, sociology, criminology, and media studies. The goal of researchers engaged in such a multidisciplinary collaboration is to generate a multi-perspective view on this research problem but without blending their perspectives. For example, a psychologist may focus on the mental health trauma experienced by the communities in which school shootings occur. A psychiatrist may examine specific causes contributing to school shootings such as depression, suicidal tendencies, and personality disorders. A sociologist may focus on specific social factors of school shootings such as race, masculinity, and religion. A criminologist may study how school shootings compare to other types of victimization in schools such as bullying. A mass media researcher may focus on the Rashomon effect[9] to examine why observers of the same event may provide divergent accounts of what happened. While each of these disciplines contributes its own unique knowledge and methods to the research topic at hand, they offer limited perspectives on this complex societal phenomenon. The result of their collaboration may be a collective final report compiled in encyclopedic rather than synthesized manner, although this report can provide a rich area for future research on the topic.

Interdisciplinary approach. Researchers from the aforementioned disciplines may also form an interdisciplinary partnership to study school-related shootings. The goal of their partnership will be to integrate different disciplinary perspectives on this societal phenomenon into a more coherent body of knowledge. This can be accomplished by the creation of a shared methodological approach that may call into question the assumptions of the participating disciplines and result in the emergence of new assumptions. For example, the psychologist, sociologist, and criminologist may develop a shared methodological framework upon learning of the relevant theories and methods of the other disciplines. Such a shared framework may consider a variety of social, psychological, and cultural contexts that are conducive to school shootings such as peer relationships, social marginalization, or troubled home environment. This interdisciplinary collaboration may result in a mixed-methods multilevel analysis and interpretation of this societal problem and lead to a coauthored article or a series of coauthored articles.

Transdisciplinary approach. A transdisciplinary team conducting research on school-related shootings may also include (in addition to researchers from the aforementioned academic disciplines) school administrators, policy makers, and individuals targeted in shooting attacks such as students, faculty, and staff. It can also include other groups or individuals impacted by shooting attacks such as police, emergency personnel, fire departments, and ambulance crews. The goal of such a transdisciplinary team is to examine and synthesize the contributions from these academic and nonacademic participants in order to provide a useful roadmap for responding more effectively to school shootings or preventing them from occurring. Such transdisciplinary collaboration may result in policy recommendations regarding the availability of guns, the increased regulation of the gun industry and its implications for safer communities, or the development of school antiviolence policies.

Advocates of transdisciplinarity argue that real-world problems are transdisciplinary by nature and that no single academic discipline, or even a group of related academic disciplines, can possibly explain complex societal problems facing the humanity today, much less craft solutions to these problems. This is especially true when nonacademic stakeholders are not actually involved in the problem investigation and solution development effort.

Notes

1. Disciplines have also been categorized as "hard" (e.g., physical sciences) or "soft" (e.g., the humanities), "pure" (e.g., mathematics) or "applied" (e.g., engineering) and those that engage with "living systems" (e.g., biology) and those that engage with "non-living systems" (e.g., history). Becher (1981, 1994) also introduced the difference between "rural" and "urban" disciplines.

2. According to Wikipedia, the concept of boundary-work comes from the science studies. Boundary-work "comprises instances in which boundaries, demarcations, or other divisions between fields of knowledge are created, advocated, attacked, or reinforced" (https://en.wikipedia.org/wiki/Boundary-work).

3. The list of cross-disciplinary forms in this chapter is not exhaustive. It doesn't include such forms as pluri-disciplinarity, post-disciplinarity, proto-disciplinarity, and meta-disciplinarity (among others), the discussion of which is outside the scope of this book. López-Huertas (2013) groups the combinations of disciplines together in one category—"multidimensional knowledge."

4. While the origins of interdisciplinarity can be traced back to the mid-1920s when the formation of the United States Social Science Research Council was formed, it was not until late 1960s and early 1970s when the concept of interdisciplinarity became popular due to the recognition that 'big' societal questions such as poverty or peace are too complex to be adequately dealt with by separate disciplines (Klein 1990).

5. Romero Lankao et al. (2013) distinguish between academic-driven and issue-driven, or contextualized, interdisciplinarity. While the former is a "pure curiosity driven research" (30), the latter aims to bridge the divide between research and practice and is concerned with "issues that emerge from fundamental societal dilemmas" (ibid.) that cannot be addressed by any single discipline.

6. Klein (2010) refers to two metaphors proposed by the Nuffield Foundation—bridge building and restructuring—to illustrate the concept of interdisciplinarity. She writes: "Bridge building occurs between complete and firm disciplines. Restructuring detaches parts of several disciplines to form a new coherent whole. The Foundation also noted a third possibility that occurs when a new overarching concept or theory subsumes the theories and concepts of several existing disciplines, akin to the notion of transdisciplinarity" (21).

7. Despite his criticism, Nicolescu acknowledged Jantsch's "historical merit" which, he believed, was "to underline the necessity of inventing an axiomatic approach for transdisciplinarity and also of introducing values in this field of knowledge" (Nicolescu 2007, 36).

8. Nicolescu (2010b) defines a disciplinary boundary as "the limit of the totality of the results—past, present and future—obtained by a given set of laws, norms, rules and practices." He states that the above definition of a disciplinary boundary applies to multidisciplinarity and interdisciplinarity as well, which he considers to be "just continuous extensions of disciplinarity: there are multidisciplinary and interdisciplinary boundaries as there are disciplinary boundaries" (2014, 189). He argues that only transdisciplinarity has no boundaries and bases his argument on his theory of the multiple levels of reality and of the Hidden Third (discussed in Chapter 3 of this book).

9. The term "Rashomon effect" was suggested by Heider (1988) and was derived from the title of Akira Kurosawa's film in which four witnesses of a crime describe the event in different and incompatible ways.

Suggested Readings

Alvargonzález, David. "Multidisciplinarity, Interdisciplinarity, Transdisciplinarity, and the Sciences." *International Studies in the Philosophy of Science* 25, no. 4 (2011): 387–403.

Becher, Tony, and Paul Trowler. *Academic Tribes and Territories: Intellectual Enquiry and the Culture of Disciplines*, 2nd ed. Buckingham, UK: Society for Research into Higher Education & Open University Press, 2001.

Foucault, Michel. *Discipline and Punish: The Birth of the Prison*. New York: Pantheon, 1978.

Hunt, Lynn. "The Virtues of Disciplinarity." *Eighteenth-Century Studies* 28, no. 1 (1994): 1–7.

Klein, Julie Thompson. "Blurring, Cracking, and Crossing: Permeation and the Fracturing of Discipline." In *Knowledges: Historical and Critical Studies in*

Disciplinarity, edited by Ellen Messer-Davidow and David R. Shumway, 185–214. Charlottesville, London: University of Virginia Press, 1993.

Klein, Julie Thompson. *Interdisciplinarity: History, Theory, and Practice.* Detroit: Wayne State University Press, 1990.

Repko, Allen F., and Rick Szostak. *Interdisciplinary Research: Process and Theory*, 3rd edition. Los Angeles: Sage Publications Inc., 2016.

CHAPTER SIX

Transdisciplinary Research as a Collaborative Enterprise: Promises and Challenges of Transdisciplinary Initiatives

In science, novelty emerges only with difficulty, manifested by resistance, against a background provided by expectations.
—Thomas Kuhn (1962, 64)

An integrative collaborative approach to research is at the heart of transdisciplinary initiatives. This approach, also known as team science, aims to merge diverse knowledge, perspectives, and experiences of multiple research partners who work together on finding solutions to complex research problems that cannot be resolved within the framework of a single discipline or even the combination of disciplines.

Unlike multi- and interdisciplinary collaborations, transdisciplinary collaborations go beyond crossing disciplinary boundaries to also include the crossing of cultural and organizational boundaries and the boundaries between practice and research and between research and society (Klein 2004; Ramadier 2004). Many transdisciplinary projects involve hundreds of research participants with different disciplinary, demographic, cultural, and ethnic backgrounds and from a wide range of fields and sectors, including academia, government, industry, the public and private sectors, and the general public.

A significant body of publications[1] has examined contextual factors at different levels of analysis (interpersonal, organizational, environmental, sociopolitical, and technological) that influence the effectiveness of transdisciplinary teams. While specific suggestions for enhancing the productivity of transdisciplinary teams vary among different authors, four key factors contributing to success of transdisciplinary initiatives have been cited most frequently: (1) diversity of transdisciplinary teams as a creative force; (2) adherence to transdisciplinary ethics; (3) the importance of establishing and sustaining interpersonal trust within transdisciplinary teams; and (4) readiness for collaboration by teams and individuals.

Diversity of Transdisciplinary Teams as a Creative Force

Studies have shown that research teams composed of diverse members, who come from different disciplinary backgrounds or have been trained in different fields, are better able to generate innovative solutions to problems and perform better in creative tasks than teams that are more homogeneous in their approaches (Hong and Page 2004; Horwitz and Horwitz 2007; Jackson, May, and Whitney 1995; Milliken and Martins 1996). Hadorn et al. (2008) point out that diversity stimulates creativity and innovation in transdisciplinary teams because diverse problem-solvers can contribute to a research project not only their scientific or specialized knowledge but also their nonscientific knowledge. Such non-scientific knowledge, the authors argue, can take multiple forms, including "the interpretation in the life-world (systems knowledge); knowledge about the need for change, desired goals and better ways of acting (target knowledge); and knowledge about technical, social, legal, cultural and other means of redirecting the existing behavior (transformation knowledge)" (Ibid., 36). The convergence of scientific and nonscientific expertise and the interrelation of abstract and case-specific knowledge enable transdisciplinary teams to perceive contradictions and opposing interests as well as grasp multiple perspectives and views regarding the problem at hand. The convergence of expertise also helps the teams improve problem identification and problem analysis and customize research results to specific stakeholders and target groups.

The formulation of a specific societal problem, which is the starting point of any transdisciplinary research project, can also be articulated differently, not only by the different disciplines involved but also by individual and institutional partners engaged in the project (Rosenfield 1992; Bergmann et al. 2012). From this perspective, members of a transdisciplinary team can act as "filters for each other" (Klein 1990a, 21). Also, learning new skill sets and new problem-solving approaches can enrich the disciplinary identities of collaborating researchers themselves and stimulate new understanding of the fields outside their disciplines. As many disciplinarians acknowledge, rigorous disciplinary training does not prepare them for dealing with broad, systemic, or "wicked" problems because their training enables them to focus only on certain aspects of a problem and to frame and address it only from their own disciplinary perspective (Aslin and Blackstock 2010; Bardwell 1991; Bowonder 1987; Rittel and Webber 1973; Syme 2005). The input from other professionals with regard to research objectives, relevant steps in the research process, and the methods for collection and analysis of data, along with the resulting from this input synthesis of multiple perspectives, is essential for the achievement of a balanced and integrated solution to multifaceted research problems.

The formation of diverse research teams can also help customize research to specific targeted societal groups, including those groups that exist at the margins of society or have experience with sociocultural exclusion or oppression (such as migrant workers, homeless people, and people with mental disabilities, among others). The inclusion of these other participants, who have significant stakes in the solution to a complex societal research problem, fosters an open and inclusive research culture which can, in turn, help create strategies for reducing the damage and suffering caused by sociocultural exclusion and make knowledge more applicable to local contexts (Hollaender and Leroy 2001; Moulaert et al. 2005; Moulaert 2010).

At the same time, as scholars almost unanimously agree, transdisciplinary research cannot be successfully carried out simply by bringing together disparate team members. It requires the transformation of multiple disciplinary perspectives, experiences, and values represented among team members. This process of transformation could make an overall research outcome greater than the sum of its parts and enable the emergence of unique novel properties that could be further translated into innovative solutions to a difficult societal problem (Rosenfield 1992; Katz and Martin 1997).

Adherence to Transdisciplinary Ethics

The question of diversity is closely related to the question of transdisciplinary ethics, the main goal of which is to support a culture based on open communication, democracy, mutual learning, and respect among all team members. This ethics also presupposes a desire to contribute to the improvement and advancement of society.

The fundamentals of transdisciplinary ethics were formulated in 1994 at the First World Congress on Transdisciplinarity in Convento da Arrabida, Portugal, and further included in Article 13 of the *Charter of Transdisciplinarity*:

> The transdisciplinary ethics rejects any attitude, which refuses dialogue and discussion, no matter whether the origin of this attitude is ideological, scientific, religious, economic, political or philosophical. Shared knowledge should lead to a shared understanding based on an absolute respect for the collective and individual diversities united by our common life on one and the same Earth. (Freitas, Nicolescu, and Morin 1994)

A shared commitment to transdisciplinary ethical norms is one of the key factors influencing the effectiveness of transdisciplinary teams (Stokols et al. 2003). This shared commitment is also a necessary condition for navigating potential interpersonal conflicts and addressing communication barriers. Transdisciplinary ethics rests on the recognition that while different types of participants play different roles within the design and implementation of a research project, everyone on the team has something worthwhile to contribute and everyone has something new to learn from other team members (Balsamo and Mitcham 2010).

Other ethical norms impacting the effectiveness of transdisciplinary collaborations are associated with how power and control are distributed on a transdisciplinary team, how responsibility is shared among team members, and how rewards are administered. Questions about confidentiality, transmitting and sharing information, and the use of data often arise also because these questions can differ from field to field (Klein 1990). In addition, traditional standards of responsible scientific conduct such as maintaining data security, privacy, and integrity, settling claims to intellectual property ownership or licensing and protecting the rights of animal and human subjects all provide the ethical foundation for conducting successful transdisciplinary projects.

Establishing and Sustaining Interpersonal Trust

A number of studies highlighted the vital importance of establishing and sustaining interpersonal trust that enables a more positive collaborative approach within transdisciplinary teams. In the collaborative context, trust manifests itself in the sharing of risks and rewards, feeling comfortable in accepting and showing limits, being open to constructive criticism, and displaying mutual respect among team members. The importance of interpersonal trust is due to the fact that transdisciplinary team members are compelled to open themselves to greater vulnerability and risk than members of more homogeneous research teams because they have to cross professional and cultural boundaries, must often work outside their home organization, and will be dealing with less palpable products of the knowledge production process (Frescoln and Arbuckle Jr. 2015; Harris and Lyon 2013 Melin 2000).

Macdonald (2000b) considers a failure to trust those we work with as the greatest obstacle to transdisciplinarity and believes that the primary reason why we fail to trust others is that we fail to trust *ourselves*. He writes: "A failure to make ourselves vulnerable in the presence of the disciplinary other induces us to distrust the sincerity even of the disciplinary other who renders himself or herself vulnerable to us" (71). However, as Somerville (2000) points out, trust used in transdisciplinary collaborations must be "earned trust" and not "blind trust" (106).

Several factors have been suggested to promote the development of trust in collaborative teams. These factors include a demonstrated commitment to transdisciplinary ethical norms among all team members, the presence of shared values and experiences, the anticipation of future association, and the existence of effective policies related to funding and allocation of resources (Harris and Lyon 2013; Lewis and Weigert 1985; Mayer, Davis, and Schoorman 1995; Powell 2003).

Case studies of collaborative transdisciplinary research revealed that transdisciplinary teams were less productive during the first three years of a project but became more productive after a three-year period (Hall et al. 2012). One of the reasons for this situation is that the development of interpersonal trust takes time and this presents unique challenges faced by transdisciplinary collaborations. Many transdisciplinary collaborations are temporary and often dissolve after the project ends. A short-term project situation puts at risk the slow process of building trust and sustainable partnerships (Novy, Habersack, and Schaller 2013).

The process of establishing and sustaining trust presents even more challenges for virtual teams, which are commonly used in transdisciplinary research. Interpersonal trust is more transient and fragile in virtual teams because team members are geographically and culturally dispersed, work across different time zones, and communicate with each other primarily through the use of computer-mediated communication technologies (such as electronic mail, chat rooms, videoconferencing, and Skype). Because of that, members of virtual teams who "transcend time, space, and culture" (Jarvenpaa and Leidner 1999, 791) do not have opportunities to monitor each other's behavior through body language and this introduces a greater level of uncertainty than face-to-face communication. It lacks a "physical touch" and nonverbal cues, which are important for building and sustaining trust in teams (Jarvenpaa and Leidner 1999; Mayer, Davis, and Schoorman 1995; Olson and Olson 2000). A necessary condition for establishing and sustaining trust among team members is "regular and unconstrained" communication—both interpersonal and project-related (Stokols et al. 2008, S104).

Collaboration Readiness

Collaboration readiness is another factor that can enhance or impede a team's prospects for effective transdisciplinary collaboration (Hall et al. 2008; Morgan et al. 2003; Olson and Olson 2000; Stokols 2006; Stokols et al. 2003; Stokols et al. 2008). Multiple studies on research collaborations suggest that the more a team is "collaboration-ready" at the outset of a project, the better are the team's prospects for accomplishing the project's goals.

Hall et al. (2008) identified three major factors that increase the collaboration readiness of a research team:

1. Contextual–environmental conditions (such as broad-based administrative support; availability and quality of institutional resources; spatial proximity among researchers; and effective virtual connectivity of geographically dispersed researchers)
2. Intrapersonal characteristics (such as motivational factors and skills and qualities of a project leader)
3. Interpersonal factors (such as the narrower scope of disciplines represented among team members; small- or medium-sized teams; and researchers' positive experiences of collaboration on earlier projects)[2]

While these factors have a positive influence on the overall "collaboration readiness" of a research team (and, consequently, on the extent to which the team is likely to achieve its goals), other factors such as rigid administrative structures, large team size, the lack of collaboration history among team members and their geographic separation, inadequate remote collaboration tools, and the wide scope of disciplinary perspectives represented by team members can reduce their "collaboration readiness" and slow the progress of collaborative activities especially during the initial phase of a transdisciplinary project (Stokols et al. 2005).

Furthermore, team members who have not worked together on earlier projects tend to be less collaboration-ready (compared to those team members who have a history of working together) because it takes them more time to establish and maintain trust (Stokols et al. 2008). Other "collaboration readiness" factors include cooperative spirit, methodological flexibility, positive attitudes toward collaboration, willingness to devote significant amounts of time and effort to developing interpersonal relationships, effective interpersonal communication skills, and preparedness for inherent challenges of teamwork such as tensions, uncertainties, and complexities (Ibid.).

Other Beneficial Factors Impacting Transdisciplinary Collaborations

Other beneficial factors impacting the productivity of transdisciplinary teams that have been noted in the literature include:

- Shared acknowledgment of societal benefits from transdisciplinary research outcomes (Pohl 2011)
- Agreement on core aspects of the project at the outset such as research questions, desired outcomes, and methodological approaches (Sonnenwald 2007; Stokols 2006)
- The presence of a supportive empowering project leader capable of communicating a vision, generating and sustaining trust, willing to take personal and institutional risks, who is sensitive to socio-emotional needs of the team members, and skilled in conflict resolution (Morgan et al. 2003; Stokols 2006)
- Institutional structures and policies that support transdisciplinary research, including the provision of training and educational opportunities (Convergence 2014; Stokols et al. 2008)
- Negotiated and transparent distribution of resources (Novy, Habersack, and Schaller 2013)
- Career tracks and reward structures beyond the traditional academic disciplinary framework (Convergence 2014)
- A clear division of labor (Novy, Habersack and Schaller 2013)
- Agreement on a realistic timeline to achieve the team's goals (Sonnenwald 2007)
- Familiarity and social cohesiveness among team members (Harrison et al. 2003; Kerr and Tindale 2004)
- Availability of core facilities providing access to shared digital tools and resources (Cohen and Bailey 1997; Convergence 2014)

- Transparent and negotiated distribution of resources (Novy, Habersack, and Schaller 2013)
- Availability of effective tools for virtual communication for those projects in which team members are geographically dispersed (Olson and Olson 2000)
- Opportunities for informal communication that helps break down interpersonal barriers such as during workshops, retreats, and parties (Stokols et al. 2005)
- Availability of comfortable workspaces for team meetings (Inalhan 2003; Stokols et al. 2003; Stokols et al. 2005)
- A feeling of safety (Augsburg 2014)

Challenges of Transdisciplinary Collaborations

Numerous publications described specific challenges associated with achieving successful transdisciplinary collaborations.[3] These challenges can be grouped under three major categories: (1) inherent challenges, (2) institutional challenges, and (3) communication challenges.

Inherent Challenges

Some challenges faced by transdisciplinary teams stem from the characteristics inherent to transdisciplinary research such as the mega scope of research projects, heterogeneity of research teams, and goals that are large scale and far-reaching. As recent research suggests, it is more difficult to achieve successful collaborations in transdisciplinary teams than in disciplinary teams due to the size and complexity of transdisciplinary teams and their "loftier aspirations for achieving transcendent, supradisciplinary integrations" (Stokols et al. 2010, 474). While transdisciplinary teams have a great potential for tackling creatively real-world problems, they face significant challenges due to disciplinary, cultural, lingual, and geographical variables and thus the risk of collaboration failure can be high. Large and often geographically dispersed teams also require more time and more coordination to reach decisions. The lack of clearly defined methodologies for integrating knowledge from disparate disciplines has shown to further inhibit transdisciplinary collaborations (Harris and Lyon, 2013).

Institutional Challenges

Institutional challenges are due to what Fry (2001) called "the sociology of academia." These challenges stem from the inflexibility of departmental structures, research standards, performance evaluation procedures, and tenure and promotion policies in academic institutions that do not always support risk taking and where the split between the sciences and the humanities still exists. Disciplinary constraints on faculty appointment and promotion, inequitable allocation of research space, resources, and funding in favor of projects that correspond to academic departmental structures are all potential barriers to transdisciplinary collaborations (Eisenberg and Pellmar 2000). The lack of clarity with regard to sharing of resources and data also affect productivity (Ibid.). Concerns about tensions caused by uncertainties about research credit (especially for scientific publications, which is the main career currency in academia) and the lack of clear understanding about who has responsibility for the success or failure of a research project can also have adverse effect on transdisciplinary collaborations (Wray 2006).

Institutional missions, budgets, policies, and professional cultures differ between institutions and therefore create additional roadblocks to the formation of transdisciplinary partnerships. Concerns about the asymmetries of power and control, and sensitivity about actual or perceived differences in prestige and status between academic and nonacademic stakeholders, can also prevent collaborations from accomplishing their goals (Cohen 2000; Eisenberg and Pellmar 2000; Stokols 2006). While some changes within institutional structures, such as the establishment of interdisciplinary programs or research centers within universities, contribute to the recognition of cross-disciplinary endeavors, they do not create clear incentives to encourage faculty to engage in transdisciplinary research (Burggren et al. 2010).

Additional barriers are associated with multi-institutional collaborations versus single-institution collaborations. The high cost of coordination, different academic calendars, and negotiations over budgets, responsibilities, and intellectual property can slow down the progress of multi-institutional collaborations, especially large inter-institutional or international collaborations (Cummings and Kiesler 2007; Stokols et al. 2008).

Communication Challenges

While communication challenges faced by transdisciplinary teams stem from numerous factors, the challenges associated with communication across multiple disciplines have been cited most often in the literature on the topic. Transdisciplinary research takes place at the intersection of multiple disciplines, disparate sectors, and diverse cultures and requires a constant translation across disciplinary languages as well as ongoing negotiation between disciplines and life-worlds (Häberli et al. 2001; Macdonald 2000a). Learning a new disciplinary "language" and absorbing key concepts of other disciplines is time-consuming. It also takes time and effort to develop a common working language and establish a common ground from which participating disciplines can view the problem. Additional challenges arise from differences in concepts, methodologies, processes, attitudes, and experiences. These differences can be more prominent within established disciplines than within new or emergent research areas that have not yet been widely recognized as research fields (Convergence 2014).

Working in an environment with multiple disciplinary languages can be stressful. Although heterogeneity of transdisciplinary teams contributes to the generation of creative ideas and solutions, it can also lead to misunderstanding and confusion due to inevitable cognitive dissonance among team members resulting from a tendency to pigeonhole ideas according to disciplines and professional competences (Ibid.). Scientists often use scientific jargon as well as specialized language of their disciplines that other team members might not understand. Translating specialized language into a common vocabulary as well as disputes over terminology can hamper successful transdisciplinary communication. In order to work effectively together, all transdisciplinary team members must develop "multilingual fluency" and become "multilingual citizens" (Ibid.). This process takes a high toll on researchers' time and mental energy, and researchers need to be patient with respect to their own learning process and that of their peers.

Differences in "professional cultures" (Harris and Lyon 2013) and "cognitive cultural differences" (Klein 1996) further challenge effective communication within transdisciplinary teams. While diversity of disciplinary and cultural perspectives might stimulate creativity at some times, it might, at other times, increase tension between team members and become the object for a major dispute (Disis and Slattery 2010). Weaker social bonds due to having different networks of peers and belonging to different social and cultural communities can also increase the difficulty of developing coherence between team members (Cummings and Kiesler 2005).

Differing attitudes toward collaborative research can also impede effective team performance. For example, while the sciences are known as a "social, team-based enterprise" (Harley et al. 2010, 209), research in the humanities has been traditionally pursued by single scholars who place greater emphasis on individual research than researchers practicing in the life, physical, and engineering sciences (Martin 2014). Personal characteristics of team members and the diversity of cultural and ethical norms also influence the communication effectiveness of transdisciplinary collaborations.

For virtual transdisciplinary teams, reduced opportunities for socializing and information sharing such as during face-to-face interactions and regular meetings present additional communication challenges. Although virtual communication provides flexibility, lower costs, greater responsiveness, and improved utilization of resources, the use of computer-mediated communication technologies do not fully overcome communication barriers (Cummings and Kiesler 2005; Olson and Olson 2000). In order to collaborate successfully in the absence of face-to-face interaction, a sustained effective virtual communication is essential, which implies the encouragement of certain behaviors on the part of members of virtual teams such as establishing a regular pattern of communication, exchanging respectful and substantive responses, and conveying enthusiasm about the project (Jarvenpaa and Leidner 1999; Olson and Olson 2000). These behaviors has shown to foster a culture that is conducive to developing effective collaborations while irregular, inequitable, and unpredictable communication tend to hinder the progress of virtual teams (Ibid.).

Other Challenges of Transdisciplinary Collaborations

Other challenges of transdisciplinary collaborations cited in the literature include:

- Unfamiliarity with the concept of transdisciplinary research (Lawrence 2015)
- Conflicting goals among team members (Prokopy et al. 2015)
- Confusion about different types of cross-disciplinary projects ("cross-disciplinary illiteracy") (Jakobsen et al. 2004)
- Competition for funds (Roux et al. 2010)
- The lack of adequate training in integrated research (Massey et al. 2006)
- Unrealistic expectations about what transdisciplinary research can and cannot achieve (Stokols 2006)
- Difficulty in reproducing transdisciplinary research results (Brandt et al. 2013)
- The lack of effective publication culture for transdisciplinary research (Fry 2001)

- The lack of a "college of peers" (Kueffer et al. 2007)
- "The pull of disciplinary loyalties" (Klein 1990) and protection of intellectual turf (Eisenberg and Pellmar 2000)
- Extra time it takes to bear results from transdisciplinary projects (Burggren et al. 2010)
- "Personal chemistry" (Fry 2001)

To overcome these and other challenges, transdisciplinary team members must strike an appropriate balance between solidarity and diversity (Stokols et al. 2005) and develop a culture that is open, inclusive, and flexible in the way it approaches research problems (Burggren et al. 2010). They need to have high tolerance for ambiguity and keep critical distance with respect to their evaluative opinions concerning the initial research problem (Bergmann et al. 2012) so that they can more effectively integrate the depth and breadth of each other's expertise and take advantage of the diversity of disciplinary, cultural, and individual approaches to problem solving.

Despite the challenges of transdisciplinary collaborations, they are growing in popularity. There are powerful reasons why more and more researchers overstep the boundaries of established disciplines and engage in transdisciplinary research, including intellectual benefits and substantial rewards in terms of advancing the knowledge base and solving complex societal problems.

At the same time, transdisciplinary collaborations make tough demands on researchers' time, effort, and commitment and involve higher risks of failure than in other types of research collaborations. While there has been a proliferation of publications about barriers and facilitators of transdisciplinary collaborations during the last decade, gaps still remain for future research to address. One important topic in particular often goes unnoticed in literature, the topic on how researchers can become more "collaboration-ready" and more experienced in transdisciplinary approaches to research, which have been cited as the essential preconditions for success of transdisciplinary collaborations.

Notes

1. See, for example, Bergmann et al. 2012; Cummings and Kiesler 2005; Du Plessis, Sehume, and Martin 2014; Frescoln and Arbuckle Jr. 2015; Häberli et al. 2002; Katz and Martin 1997; Manderson 2000; McDonell 2000; Melin 2000; Novy, Habersack, and Schaller 2013; Rosenfield 1992; Stokols et al. 2005; Stokols et al. 2008; Stokols et al. 2010; Weingart 2000.

2. Hall et al. (2008) also point out that contextual–environmental collaboration-readiness conditions may be "more hard-wired into the physical and social environment" than interpersonal and intrapersonal factors which are "more-malleable human factors" and thus can "change over time as a result of collaborative processes" (S163).

3. See, for example, Convergence 2014; Cummings and Kiesler 2005; Eisenberg and Pellmar 2000; Häberli et al. 2001; Harris and Lyon 2013; Jeffrey 2003; Klein 2010; Klein et al. 2012; Macdonald 2000a and 2000b; Newell 2000; O'Donnell, DuRussel, and Derry 1997; Stock and Burton 2011; Stokols 2006; Stokols et al. 2008.

Suggested Readings

Cummings, Jonathon N., and Sara Kiesler. "Collaborative Research across Disciplinary and Organizational Boundaries." *Social Studies of Science* 35, no. 5 (2005): 703–722.

Maslow, Abraham H. *The Psychology of Science: A Reconnaissance*. New York, NY: Harper & Row, 1966.

Stokols, Daniel, Shalini Misra, Richard P. Moser, Kara L. Hall, and Brandie K. Taylor. "The Ecology of Team Science: Understanding Contextual Influences on Transdisciplinary Collaboration." *American Journal of Preventive Medicine* 35, no. 2 (2008): S96–S115.

CHAPTER SEVEN

Scholarly Communication in the Transdisciplinary Context: What Has Changed and What Has Remained the Same

New approaches to research, including transdisciplinarity, have not changed the core values and fundamental principles of scholarly communication—the generation and distribution of knowledge. Not only do researchers want to disseminate the results of their work to their peers and to the public, but they also need to ensure that their research findings are original. Martin (2014) writes: "The idea that a research lifecycle is incomplete until research results are disseminated is one of the fundamental principles of research. Scholars, thus, are responsible for accomplishing a dual task—of doing research and of communicating their research findings for the purpose of contributing to new knowledge" (53).

Throughout centuries, scholars used formal and informal methods of scholarly communication for disseminating their research results. The formal methods of scholarly communication include publication of peer-reviewed journal articles and scholarly monographs and submissions to conferences. These methods are still prominent in an academic environment and continue to affect the institutional criteria for hiring, tenure, and promotion (Harley et al. 2010; Weller 2011).

The informal methods of scholarly communication, sometimes referred to as "invisible colleges," consist of social networking activities among researchers. The concept of "invisible colleges" originated in the 17th century in the Royal Society of London whose members did not belong to any formal academic institution and therefore referred to themselves as "an invisible college" (Crane 1972). "Invisible colleges" served as an important channel for information exchange among scholars belonging to the same field of knowledge and allowed them to monitor research progress in their field, usually through manuscript reviews or regular personal meetings for the purpose of witnessing experiments and discussing research topics (Ibid.). Today, these channels primarily include web-enabled communication tools such as e-mail, blogs, wikis, discussion forums, social networking sites, and scholarly and professional hubs. A similar concept of "hidden universities" has also been used to describe a variety of informal methods of scholarly communication such as symposia, study groups, special panels and sessions at conferences, and subgroups within organizations and institutes. Although informal methods of scholarly communication are typically not considered as an important measurement of research impact or criteria for career advancement, they are highly regarded by researchers as a means for encouraging discussions, developing collaborations, publicizing their work, and determining who else is conducting related research (Martin 2014).

Even though the core values and fundamental principles of scholarly communication have remained constant throughout history, both formal and informal methods of scholarly communication have undergone profound transformations. These transformations can be attributed to several forces, which, collectively, accelerate the knowledge production and knowledge distribution. These forces include:

- Technological advancements
- A continuing move toward open scholarship
- A fundamental shift toward cross-disciplinarity in research
- Globalization of research collaborations
- New research funding policies
- Copyright law reforms
- Evolving roles of academic and research libraries

Technological Advancements

Technological advancements are, undoubtedly, one of the most powerful driving forces that have expedited and simplified the ways research is conducted, communicated, evaluated for quality, disseminated to the research community and to the public, and preserved for future use. Electronic publishing has helped to meet one of the most imperative needs of researchers—the need for exchanging research findings, keeping abreast of current trends and developments within and outside their area of expertise, and establishing research collaborations. Electronic communication has accelerated the peer reviewing process. The semantic web, cloud computing, text and data mining technologies, visualization tools, and Virtual Research Environments (VREs) have enhanced the ways researchers use scholarly literature, measure research impact, monitor emerging research trends, and communicate with their peers.

A Continuing Move toward Open Scholarship

A continuing move toward "openness" in research is one of the most momentous transformations in scholarly communication practice. The principle of openness has been introduced into nearly every stage of knowledge production and knowledge distribution—from data creation to the processes to the distribution of final research results. Although the move toward openness has found the most resonance in the open access publishing model, it has also been manifested by emergence of other approaches to performing research "in the open," such as providing open access to data, crowdsourcing, experimenting with open peer review, maintaining open presence through social networking sites, and participating in open online conferences.

A Fundamental Shift toward Cross-Disciplinarity in Research

A shift toward cross-disciplinarity in research has made overall scholarly communication practices more diverse and less rigid. As the research challenges are becoming more complex, often requiring researchers from different disciplines to work together, scholarly communication also moves beyond discipline-based collaboration patterns among researchers toward a greater cross-disciplinary integration. The publication of interdisciplinary journals, for example, promotes the integration of perspectives, theories, and philosophies from multiple disciplines and enables the dissemination of research discoveries across the boundaries of diverse scholarly communities.

Globalization of Research Collaborations

Research is increasingly becoming a global collaborative enterprise, which is manifested by the proliferation of international research collaborations that undertake increasingly ambitious large-scale projects. Global research activities are intensifying in all regions of the world, including emerging research markets, particularly in India, China, and Brazil (Sexton 2012). Consequently, the process of globalization of research has impacted the scholarly communication patterns to include a profusion of international coauthorships of research articles and patents, especially within the science, technology, engineering, and medical fields (National Science Foundation 2010; Ware and Mabe 2015).

Changes in Research Funding Policies

Research funding agencies' open access mandates initiated by the National Institute for Health in 2008 (and since then embraced by other funding agencies) have become crucial for transforming scholarly communication practices. These mandates necessitating public access to the results of federally funded research and requiring planning for data management have further promoted the open exchange of scholarly information, including published research and research data. The funders' growing emphasis on the societal impact of research increasingly requires scholars to prove the societal return on investment of publically funded research. This trend introduces a new merit evaluation criterion into the process of peer review and provides researchers with additional strategies for identifying effective scholarly communication venues.

Copyright Law Reforms

Copyright law reforms such as open access and Creative Commons licenses and author addenda to publication agreements are creating a more balanced approach to copyright management by preserving authors' rights for broader use and reuse of their work and thus increasing the impact and visibility of their research.

Evolving Roles of Academic and Research Libraries

The roles of academic and research libraries continue to evolve as their services and operations are being increasingly embedded in facilitating the new scholarly communication environment. These new roles include the establishment of institutional repositories, implementation of research data management services, creation of partnerships in the research process and scholarly publishing, assistance with intellectual property issues, and management of open access publishing funds.

Scholarly Communication in the Transdisciplinary Context

Like any new endeavor that reaches beyond conventional approaches, transdisciplinarity is challenging some of the traditional scholarly communication practices such as peer review. It is also reconsidering some long-held understandings about the knowledge production such as the belief in the autonomous and self-justifying nature of scientific research.

"Transdisciplinarization" of Peer Review

Peer review process has traditionally been used as a "valuation" tool to evaluate disciplinary excellence. In the transdisciplinary context, peer review is facing new challenges. Transdisciplinary research has by definition many attributes and that makes it particularly difficult to evaluate by using traditional evaluation approaches. Specific challenges of "transdisciplinarization" of peer review include:

- *Uncertainties and conflicting assumptions among reviewers*

  The process of evaluating transdisciplinary research creates uncertainty and conflicting assumptions among reviewers due to the lack of agreed-upon standards about the quality of research evaluation traditionally provided by academic disciplines such as the evaluation of research goals, focus, values, norms, and expectations. This is especially true among reviewers who belong to "conceptually distant disciplines" such as "hard sciences" (physics, astronomy, and mathematics) and "soft sciences" (the social sciences and humanities) (Huuotoniemi 2010).

- *Extending peer review beyond the boundaries of academic disciplines*

  Transdisciplinarity questions the concept of a "peer" by including nonacademic reviewers in the peer review process such as policy makers, practitioners, artists, and community members. The expertise and input of nonacademic "peers" is particularly valuable in evaluating the extent of the societal impact of a specific research project such as evaluating the project's environmental, educational, or aesthetic impact (Holbrook 2010a, 2010b).

- *Introducing new criteria for evaluating grant proposals*

  Recent developments in research funders' policies are further contributing to the "transdisciplinarization" of the peer review process by introducing the societal impact criterion in the evaluation of grant proposals. For example, all research proposals submitted to the National Science Foundation are now required to include a "broader impact" statement describing how the proposed research would benefit the society. The new societal impact criterion for evaluating grant proposals challenges the process of peer review. One of the key concerns of the advocates of peer review is whether the use of the societal impact criterion in grant proposal peer review is undermining one of the long-standing beliefs that "science is best pursued *without* regard to social relevance" (Miller 2010, 340) and thus questions disciplinary knowledge as autonomous and self-justifying. Furthermore, the demand for social accountability of research places another unique strain on the peer review system by asking specialists in a particular discipline to judge not only the intellectual merits of a grant proposal but also its societal implications in which they might lack expertise (Holbrook 2010b).

• *Expanding the definition of a "peer" in scholarly publishing*

  Publishers are also expanding the definition of a "peer" beyond the boundaries of specific academic disciplines by introducing new approaches to article review and ranking. For example, PubMed Commons, a pilot service launched by the National Institutes of Health, is now allowing any author in PubMed to comment on any article included in the PubMed database. The Public Library of Science (PLoS), an influential open access publisher, is testing the Open Evaluation system that allows users to rate PLoS articles on four dimensions: interest level, the article's significance, the quality of the research, and the clarity of the writing. Frontiers, another prominent open access publisher, has developed a new evaluation system that uses algorithmic methods for post-publication review of published research that allows readers to indirectly contribute to ranking of a published article.

Challenges of Transdisciplinary Scholarly Communication

While transdisciplinarity challenges some of the long-established scholarly communication practices such as peer review, it also faces its own challenges as it strives to foster scholarly communication that spans multiple disciplinary fields, organizations, and cultures. Some of these challenges stem from the need to converse across diverse disciplinary languages and different disciplinary cultures. As Klein (2004) observes, "there is no transdisciplinary *Esperanto*" (521).

While disciplinary diversity poses significant challenges for transdisciplinary scholarly communication, this diversity can also be seen as an invitation to creative interaction rather than as a handicap to be overcome (Loibl 2006). Hadorn, Pohl, and Bammer (2010) note that in order to exploit fruitfully such creative interaction, transdisciplinarians need to learn each other's disciplinary language including the understanding of data collection techniques, knowledge of analytical frameworks, and awareness of research results of previous work in the field. Hunt (1994) makes an acute observation about the value of learning the language of another discipline. She writes that learning the language of another discipline is similar to "learning a foreign language and experiencing a foreign culture [because it] creates a different relationship to one's own discipline and [because it helps] you gain a certain distance from your own discipline and a measure of imperviousness to the conventions that define it. . . . But you don't have to expatriate just because you learn a foreign language and enjoy visiting abroad" (6).

Another unique challenge faced by transdisciplinarians in the area of scholarly communication is their varied expectations with regard to how research outcomes should be disseminated. While it is expected that all transdisciplinary collaborators must benefit from the collectively produced new knowledge and have an opportunity to use and disseminate this new knowledge through their own channels, the choice of these channels vary. Researchers typically disseminate new knowledge through publishing papers in peer-reviewed journals, engineers—through the generation of patents, educators—through teaching, policy makers—through making recommendations at the government level. These differences can complicate scholarly communication among transdisciplinary researchers. Coauthorships that result from transdisciplinary collaborations require significant translation work, intense negotiations, and agreed-upon decisions on formats and terminologies for different fields. Although multiorganizational and multinational coauthorships are becoming a norm within many science fields, coauthorships across multiple sectors and social groups are still rare and require exploration and development. Furthermore, current publishing structures hinder transdisciplinary research because research papers that span multiple disciplines do not always have a distinct publishing avenue or assign value to researchers who are not listed as lead or senior authors (Carroll et al. 2014).

Scholarly communication challenges also arise from the fact that transdisciplinary researchers are often geographically and organizationally dispersed and thus rarely have an opportunity for a face-to-face interaction, which is important for networking and socializing. Innovative technologies for virtual communication offer transdisciplinarians a set of tools and services that enable them to communicate more effectively across "time, space, and culture" (Jarvenpaa and Leidner 1999, 791) and create a stronger sense of connectedness with their peers. This enables transdisciplinarians to pursue projects that would not have been feasible without the flexibility and the power of advanced technologies that include:

- *Computer-mediated communication (CMC) technologies*

  Videoconferencing, shared electronic whiteboards, synchronous video chats, and group support systems (GSS) enable transnational communication within large transdisciplinary virtual teams, bridge cultural and geographical distances, and allow a more effective handling of diversity issues that typically stem from language and time differences.

- *Virtual Research Environments (VRE)*

  VREs offer researchers a set of online tools and services such as shared videoconferencing, electronic whiteboards, instant messaging, project management tools, virtual networked computing, and shared access to research instruments, applications, and documents. These tools and services facilitate core research activities and provide space for a cost-effective and sustainable real-time interaction within transdisciplinary teams.

- *Peer-to-peer (P2P) grids*

  P2Ps are another popular trend in scholarly communication that enable a group of computers to form self-organized and self-configured peer groups that can collaborate without the need of a centralized management infrastructure.

- *Collaborative writing and sharing tools*

  The collaborative writing spaces such as Google Docs, Box, and Dropbox provide scholars with shared asynchronous spaces for collaboratively constructing, modifying, and rapidly disseminating documents without exchanging long e-mails.

- *Participatory media*

  Participatory media that includes blogs, wikis, mashups, podcasts, tagging, and social bookmarking, enhances participatory research by adding to research teams the participants from the group being studied and by building relationships between the researchers and the researched.

- *Social networking technologies*

  Social networking sites lower interpersonal barriers to collaboration for geographically and organizationally distant researchers and compensate them, at least to some degree, for reduced opportunities for socializing.

Expanding the Network of Transdisciplinary Scholarly Communication

The growing recognition of transdisciplinarity as an innovative approach to research and the successful pursuit of large-scale transdisciplinary projects have expanded the scope of transdisciplinary scholarly communication activities. Today, these activities are taking place in many parts of the world and include the publication of transdisciplinary journals, creation of transdisciplinary organizations and networks, and organization of conferences on transdisciplinarity.

Transdisciplinary journals in particular serve as an important forum for discussing complex issues across a wide variety of research fields.

These journals also play a critical role in consolidating discourse that is scattered across various publications. Some journals devote special issues on transdisciplinary topics.[1] There are also numerous individual papers devoted to transdisciplinarity that are published within disciplinary and general publications.

Examples of transdisciplinary journals include:

- *Epiphany: Journal of Transdisciplinary Studies*
  http://epiphany.ius.edu.ba/index.php/epiphany/index

  Dedicated to the creation of holistic approach to humanities and social sciences.

- *Futures*
  http://www.sciencedirect.com/science/journal/00163287

  Promotes diverse ideas, visions, and opinions about the futures of "cultures and societies, science and technology, economics and politics, environment and the planet and individuals and humanity."

- *International Journal of Transdisciplinary Research*
  http://www.ijtr.org/index.html

  Provides a platform for transdisciplinary research as it pertains to the integration of economics with the natural and social sciences and the humanities.

- *Transdisciplinary Journal of Engineering & Science* (TJES)
  http://www.theatlas.org/index.php?option=com_phocadownload&view=section&id=4&Itemid=167

  A peer-reviewed, open-access journal promoting transdisciplinarity and its applications in the natural and social sciences, humanities, and engineering. Basarab Nicolescu serves as editor-in-chief for this journal.

  Transdisciplinary scholarly communication is also sustained through the formation of transdisciplinary organizations that facilitate the dissemination and exchange of research among its members and with the public at large. The mission of these organizations is to promote transdisciplinary approach to research through publications, policy statements, committees, meetings, and conferences. Some of the most prominent transdisciplinary organizations are:

- *The International Center for Transdisciplinary Research* (in French: Centre International de Recherches et Études Transdisciplinaires—CIRET)
  http://ciret-transdisciplinarity.org/index_en.php

  Cofounded by Basarab Nicolescu in 1987, CIRET is a worldwide nonprofit organization located in Paris, France. CIRET serves as a virtual meeting space for transdisciplinary researchers from 26 countries, offers multilingual forums, reports on transdisciplinary projects from around the world, and publishes an online journal and the results of UNESCO-sponsored international colloquia. One of the major achievements of CIRET was the CIRET-UNESCO project "The Transdisciplinary Evolution of the University," which resulted in the organization of the International Congress "What University for Tomorrow? Towards a Transdisciplinary Evolution of the University" (1997), in a *Declaration* and a set of *Recommendations* later applied in a number of transdisciplinary programs around the world.

- *The Academy of Transdisciplinary Learning and Advanced Study (TheATLAS)*
  http://www.theatlas.org

  Founded in 2000, TheATLAS is a nonprofit organization committed to sustainable development through the integration of skills and knowledge from the disciplines in complex systems and engineering. TheATLAS funds and supports transdisciplinary research and educational activities around the world. It hosts biannual meetings on transdisciplinary and transcultural problems and provides a wide range of services to higher education institutions, including the provision of free educational materials and textbooks to students and faculty through its digital library. It publishes the *Transdisciplinary Journal of Engineering & Science (TJES)*.

- *td-net: Network for Transdisciplinary Research*
  http://transdisciplinarity.ch/en/td-net/Aktuell.html

  Emanated from a new research approach emphasized at a benchmark International Conference on Transdisciplinarity held in 2000 in Zurich, Switzerland, td-net is the Swiss-based network that serves as a communication and collaboration platform for researchers, educators, and stakeholders in society who are involved in inter- and transdisciplinary research and teaching. td-net also contributes to the further conceptualization of transdisciplinarity through the publication of books, organization of conferences, and the upkeep of "the toolbox for co-producing knowledge" that contains an overview of methods, practical experiences, and criteria for addressing the challenges of coproducing knowledge.

Transdisciplinary conferences have also become one of the primary means through which scholarly communication takes place. They provide a forum for discussion, exchange, and collaboration among the international community of transdisciplinary scholars and aim at collectively advancing the theory and practice of transdisciplinary research.

By developing these new approaches to scholarly production and communication, while capitalizing on the existing strengths of traditional practices, transdisciplinarity reaches new audiences and generates new forms of scholarly collaborations that are "not only 'multiple' with regard to disciplines, but also multiple with regard to cultures, scientific traditions and language" (Mittelmark et al. 2012, 3).

Note

1. See, for example, *Futures* 65 (January 2015), Special issue "Advances in Transdisciplinarity 2004–2014"; and *World Futures: The Journal of New Paradigm Research* 70: 3–4 (2014), Special issue "Transdisciplinarity."

Suggested Readings

Holbrook, J. Britt. *Peer Review*. In *The Oxford Handbook of Interdisciplinarity*, edited by R. Froderman, J. T. Klein, and C. Mitcham, 321–332. Oxford: Oxford University Press, 2010a.

Martin, Victoria. *Strength through Collaboration*. In *Demystifying eResearch: A Primer for Librarians*, 53–77. Santa Barbara, CA: ABC-CLIO, 2014.

Stokols, Daniel, Juliana Fuqua, Jennifer Gress, Richard Harvey, Kimari Phillips, Lourdes Baezconde-Garbanati, Jennifer Unger et al. "Evaluating Transdisciplinary Science." *Nicotine & Tobacco Research* 5, no. Suppl 1 (2003): S21–S39. doi: 10.1080/14622200310001625555.

Wickson, Fern, Anna L. Carew, and A. W. Russell. "Transdisciplinary Research: Characteristics, Quandaries and Quality." *Futures* 38, no. 9 (2006): 1046–1059. doi: 10.1016/j.futures.2006.02.011.

CHAPTER EIGHT

Transdisciplinarity in Practice: Projects, Funding, and Evaluation Criteria

> Transdisciplinarity is about the relationship between inquiry and action in the world.
>
> —Alfonso Montuori (2010, 10)

Characteristics of Transdisciplinary Projects

Transdisciplinary initiatives are not new. They have been implemented in a variety of ways throughout the last century. For example, the famous Bell telephone labs on new materials included scientists, engineers, economists, and industry and government workers. The design of satellite-based global positioning systems was the result of the integration of physical sciences and engineering. Agro-ecological research that was initiated in the early 20th century in Great Britain used transdisciplinary approaches through engagement with agricultural communities, social scientists, and nonscience knowledge systems such as local, experiential, and indigenous knowledge. The development of geothermal power that started in the 1950s in New Zealand was based on transdisciplinary knowledge exchange and collaboration of experts from multiple sectors.

Transdisciplinary projects vary in their nature, scope, and complexity. Research activities occur across physical sites, geographical locations, and social, cultural, and disciplinary relations and include participants from multiple fields, with diverse skill sets and various career trajectories. Based on the project goals, different transdisciplinary initiatives employ different organizational and management structures to support their activities. While the most visible transdisciplinary projects take place within universities, other research facilities such as laboratories, research centers, and experiment stations are also common for conducting transdisciplinary activities. Be it within a single university or across multi-organizational and multinational teams, the fundamental goal of transdisciplinary projects is the same—to address a concrete real-world problem through a transdisciplinary approach to research.

Although there is no single pattern of transdisciplinary research initiatives, transdisciplinary projects usually are:

- Problem-driven (starting with a specific societal problem or concern)
- Action-oriented (aiming to "translate" research findings into specific actions to address a specific societal problem)
- Large scale (requiring significant investment of time, budget, and resource allocation)
- Global in scope (attempting to address global societal problems that could not be addressed by a single discipline or a combination of disciplines)
- Systemic in approach (considering the wider system, in which a research problem is situated)
- Socially relevant (aiming at making significant and enduring societal impact)
- Highly collaborative (engaging multiple research participants and stakeholders)
- Heterogenic (involving research participants with different disciplinary, demographic, cultural, and ethnic backgrounds)
- Complex (including multiple tasks to be accomplished concurrently)
- Nonlinear (requiring extra flexibility because research could take unpredictable paths)

Funding of Transdisciplinary Projects

While transdisciplinary approach to research is becoming increasingly recognized as an innovative approach in knowledge production, transdisciplinarity is not yet considered mainstream in the area of publicly funded research (Convergence 2014). Even in the recent past, it was extremely difficult for researchers to obtain funding for transdisciplinary projects, especially at the early stages of transdisciplinary research.[1] This state of affairs was due to the fact that there used to be little recognition of the need for transdisciplinarity for tackling complex societal challenges (Somerville and Rapport 2000). Carroll et al. (2014) note that the unconventional research methods used by transdisciplinary teams do not "fit easily into grant proposals that require more detailed preliminary hypotheses or preparation" (22). Messerli and Messerli (2008) argue that the difficulty of obtaining research funding for transdisciplinary projects is due to the lack of well-defined research practices lending themselves to peer review.

The perceived lack of a shared conceptual framework for transdisciplinary research as well as the lack of guidance on how to establish effective transdisciplinary programs have also slowed the implementation of transdisciplinarity and, consequently, created obstacles for obtaining funding for transdisciplinary projects (Convergence 2014). In addition, a long-held perception of peer review as the basis of funding system put transdisciplinary research proposals at a disadvantage because "peer review of cross-disciplinary research [presented] the problem of the definition of a peer" (Morgan 1988).[2]

Over the past two decades, the growing recognition of transdisciplinarity as an innovative problem-oriented research approach has resulted in the expansion of funding for transdisciplinary projects. Furthermore, the success of several large-scale transdisciplinary collaborations, some of which are described later in this chapter, played an important role in catalyzing financial support of transdisciplinary projects. In the United States, major governmental funding agencies, such as the National Science Foundation (NSF), the National Institutes of Health (NIH), the Department of Energy (DOE), the Department of Defense (DOD), Food and Drug Administration (FDA), and the Defense Advanced Research Projects Agency (DARPA), have allocated significant financial resources for the development of complex large-scale transdisciplinary projects involving hundreds of researchers from a wide range of different fields and spanning multiple organizations. Some transdisciplinary initiatives such as the NIH-funded Transdisciplinary Research on Energetics and Cancer Centers and Transdisciplinary Tobacco Use Research Centers (TTURCs) have been operational for over 10 years.

A growing number of funding agencies are now requiring research grants to include cross-disciplinary teams, with the NSF still being a leader in funding cross-disciplinary research (Convergence 2014; Tachibana 2013). Transdisciplinary collaborations have also been promoted by prominent national research organizations such as the National Academies of Science, Engineering, and Medicine and the

Social Science Research Council. Funds from private research institutions and numerous foundations, although smaller in scope, also play an important role in supporting the development of transdisciplinary projects. For example, such organizations as the MacArthur Foundation, NIH Common Fund, and the Kavli Foundation invest funds to facilitate multi-disciplinary, multi-investigator initiatives aiming at advancing science for the public good.

Transdisciplinary research occurs across all fields and disciplines. However, the largest number of transdisciplinary projects has, by far, taken place at the intersection of the biological sciences and engineering where transdisciplinary collaborations are becoming a norm. This is mostly due to the substantial government funding of large-scale transdisciplinary research oriented toward the solution of problems related to the protection of the environment, sustainable food production, renewable energy, and improvement in human health. The examples of such large-scale projects include the NSF's biocomplexity[3] in the Environment Initiative (BE), which brings together science and engineering to gain a better understanding of the complex nature of environmental systems, and the National Nanotechnology Initiative (NNI), a U.S. Government Research and Development program, which integrates the expertise of multiple fields and agencies with the goal to advance nanoscience and nanotechnology, the fields that have wide-ranging applications across various sectors including energy, health, and manufacturing.

Other examples of transdisciplinary projects fostering the convergence of the biological sciences and engineering include:

- *The Brain Research through Advancing Innovative Neurotechnologies (BRAIN)*
  https://www.braininitiative.nih.gov

  Jointly sponsored by the NIH, DARPA, and NSF, with generous contributions from private foundations and research institutions, this initiative seeks to generate better understanding about how the brain works. It brings together expertise from neuroscience, synthetic biology genetics, nanoscience, optics, informatics, and computer science.

- *The Tissue Chip Projects*
  http://www.ncats.nih.gov/tissuechip/projects

  Supported by NIH, DARPA, and FDA, these projects integrate methods and insights from tissue engineering, analytical chemistry, cell biology, physiology, microfluidics, regulatory science, and drug development with the purpose of developing three-dimensional chips that mimic human physiology in order to predict drug efficacy and safety.

- *The Wyss Institute for Biologically Inspired Engineering at Harvard University*
  http://wyss.harvard.edu

  Supported by the philanthropic gift of $125 million from a Swiss entrepreneur and businessman Hansjörg Wyss, the institute aims to emulate biological design principles to develop innovative engineering technologies that could help address challenges in sustainability, energy, robotics, health care, and manufacturing.

More recently, transdisciplinary approaches to research have gained attention beyond the biological sciences and engineering. For social scientists, for example, transdisciplinarity presents a compelling opportunity to make a tangible impact on society by taking part in research projects that aim to advance understanding of concrete societal issues. Research funding agencies in the United States have made a promising shift toward the inclusion of the social science disciplines in transdisciplinary projects. For example, the social sciences have been integrated into the research conducted by the Long-Term Ecological Research (LTER) Network created by NSF in 2011 to provide insights into the human dimensions of long-term ecological change. Another example is the NIH-funded Transdisciplinary Research on Energetics and Cancer (TREC) project that brings in such social science disciplines as psychology and health behavior to identify the social determinants of cancer. In an effort to advance the contribution of the humanities within transdisciplinary projects, the Medical Humanities Initiative at the Institute of Humanities Research (IHR) funds programs that bring together educators, researchers, and practitioners from the fields of medical humanities, medical ethics, and spiritual care. The goal of such programs is to enhance the understanding of the human dimensions of healing, health, and human well-being.

Other examples of projects that embody a community of transdisciplinary researchers include the following:

- *The Research Institute for Humanity and Nature*
  http://www.chikyu.ac.jp/rihn_e/

  This institute, based in Kyoto, Japan, conducts solution-oriented transdisciplinary research that focuses on negative anthropogenic environmental impact. The institute's research is organized into programs and projects and involves close collaborations with multiples stakeholders from various academic and civilian communities. The goal of these programs and projects is to understand the underlying causes of environmental degradation that stems from problems in human culture and then attempt to find integrated approaches to these problems. The institute collaborates with Future Earth (http://www.futureearth.org), an open international research platform for scientists of all disciplines, which aims to address sustainability problems through integration of transdisciplinary environmental studies.

- *The Centers for Population Health and Health Disparities (CPHHD)*
  https://cancercontrol.cancer.gov/populationhealthcenters/cphhd/

  The research conducted by these centers was completed in 2016 after 10 years of funding provided by the National Cancer Institute (NCI), the National Heart, Lung, and Blood Institute (NHLBI), and the Office of Behavioral and Social Sciences Research (OBSSR). The centers combined approaches from biological, physical, social, and behavioral sciences to enhance understanding of how neighborhoods affect health outcomes and aimed to address inequities associated with the two major causes of death in the United States—heart disease and cancer—and to develop interventions and identify policy and practice approaches to reduce health disparities. Highlights from the research conducted by CPHHD were published in the journal *Health Affairs* 35, no. 8 (2016).

- *The Earth Institute at Columbia University*
  http://www.earthinstitute.columbia.edu.

  The Earth Institute forges research and educational collaborations among experts in physical and life sciences, law, economics, public health, and policy in order to learn how to best address socio-environmental problems such as environmental degradation, rapid urbanization, natural hazards, infectious diseases, and the sustainable use of resources, and then use that knowledge to develop policies and generate practical solutions to these problems. The institute educates the next generation of leaders in sustainable development and earth sciences by offering undergraduate, graduate, and doctoral programs. It also offers customized executive education for working professionals who wish to earn certificates in such programs as conservation and environmental sustainability and sustainability analytics.

Encouraging Transdisciplinarity as "Publicly Good Research"

To further strengthen the connection between the publicly funded research and its beneficial impact on society, policy makers are now placing special demands on the research funding system for proving social relevance and accountability of research that they fund. In response to these demands, NSF has implemented requirements for demonstrating the societal benefits of research funded through this foundation. Specifically, NSF has updated its merit review criteria for evaluating research proposals by introducing the Broader Impacts Criterion (BIC). All research proposals submitted to NSF are now required to include a "broader impact" statement describing how the proposed research would benefit the society. To assist researchers with formulating their broader impact statements, NSF has provided the following list of examples of broader impacts:

- Advancement of discovery and understanding while promoting teaching, training, and learning
- Broadening the participation of underrepresented groups
- Enhancing the infrastructure for education and research
- Broad dissemination of research results to enhance scientific and technological understanding
- Benefits of the proposed activity to society[4] (NSF 2002)

In 2005, to further strengthen the relationship between science and society, NSF funded a transdisciplinary research program—Science of Science and Innovation Policy (SciSIP). The goal of SciSIP-funded projects is to gain a better understanding of the connection between publicly funded research and its societal impacts and to evaluate how publicly funded science and technology benefit society and to what end.

Evaluating Transdisciplinary Projects

Given the complexity, high expectations, and significant risk of failure of transdisciplinary collaborations, evaluation of the research quality of transdisciplinary projects is a difficult task. Krott (2002) argues that transdisciplinary projects are subject to three types of appraisal: (1) evaluation by a scientific community, (2) metascientific evaluation, and (3) political evaluation.

1. In an evaluation by a scientific community, scientists compare the research activities with the standards for research and their values to society.
2. In metascientific evaluation, the progress of a transdisciplinary project is analyzed by scientific methods only without making value judgments.
3. In political evaluation, the analysis is driven by facts, interests, and values of the participants, including the project stakeholders.

At this time, there is no recognized set of criteria for evaluating transdisciplinary research. Academic evaluation systems are still dominated by either intra-academic quality criteria, such as citation count and research funding, or by market-geared external criteria, such as applicability of research results to industry (Carroll et al. 2014; Novy, Habersack, and Schaller 2013). Many still consider transdisciplinarity to be contradictory to the fundamental principles of traditional scientific knowledge production (Lawrence 2015). What is more, the presence of diverse perspectives on a research problem and on its possible solutions makes it challenging for transdisciplinary teams to achieve a balance between different views and develop criteria for gauging the success of a transdisciplinary initiative. This diversity of perspectives also raises a wide range of questions about standards of quality, the practice of evaluating transdisciplinary research, and about who should be included in the evaluation process.

Even though transdisciplinary initiatives are still met with greater skepticism than more traditional research collaborations, the perceived urgent need to address complex societal problems plays an important role in shifting of the attention of funding agencies away from monodisciplinary research toward inter- and transdisciplinary efforts that can provide insights into some of the most pressing issues—from protecting the environment to curing disease to ensuring national security.

Notes

1. van Kerkhoff (2010) observes that it is even more difficult to obtain research funding for transdisciplinary research in developing countries, even when the goal of the funds is to assist developing countries. She argues that there is significant bias in international research funding toward the industrialized countries, which receive the major portion of all research funds.

2. To address this concern, the Center for Scientific Review (CSR) at the National Institutes of Health (NIH) created a Panel on Scientific Boundaries for Review in 1998. The purpose of this panel was to conduct a comprehensive evaluation of the organization and function of the review process conducted by the CSR. The proposed changes modified the peer-review process at NIH for reviewing cross-disciplinary proposals by using peer-review groups that include researchers from multiple disciplines who are themselves actively involved in cross-disciplinary research.

3. The word "biocomplexity," which is often associated with the NSF's biocomplexity initiative, does not yet have a dictionary status and has been defined in various ways. One of the frequently cited definitions of this term was provided by Michener et al. (2001) who define biocomplexity as "properties emerging from the interplay of behavioral, biological, chemical, physical,

and social interactions that affect, sustain, or are modified by living organisms, including humans" (1018).

4. NSF complements this list of examples with short sections that provide background information and examples of activities for each component of the broader impacts statement.

Suggested Readings

Brown, Valerie A., John Alfred Harris, and Jacqueline Y. Russell (eds.). *Tackling Wicked Problems: Through the Transdisciplinary Imagination*. London, UK: Earthsca, 2010.

Stokols, Daniel, Juliana Fuqua, Jennifer Gress, Richard Harvey, Kimari Phillips, Lourdes Baezconde-Garbanati, Jennifer Unger et al. "Evaluating Transdisciplinary Science." *Nicotine & Tobacco Research* 5, no. Suppl 1 (2003): S21–S39. doi: 10.1080/14622200310001625555.

Walter, Alexander I., Sebastian Helgenberger, Arnim Wiek, and Roland W. Scholz. "Measuring Societal Effects of Transdisciplinary Research Projects: Design and Application of an Evaluation Method." *Evaluation and Program Planning* 30, no. 4 (2007): 325–338.

Wickson, Fern, Anna L. Carew, and Alice W. Russell. "Transdisciplinary Research: Characteristics, Quandaries and Quality." *Futures* 38, no. 9 (2006): 1046–1059.

CHAPTER NINE

The Vision of a Transdisciplinary University

"University" is derived from the Latin word "universitas," or "whole."
How far we have come from that universal view to our fragmented
silos of knowledge removed from the whole of society.
—Neuhauser and Pohl (2015, 115)

In response to widespread demands for making scientific research more
pertinent to the problems of the real world and therefore more socially
valuable, transdisciplinarity is gradually obtaining a prominent role in
colleges and universities around the world. The underlying theme of a
transdisciplinary approach to education is the promotion of cognitive
flexibility that encourages students to learn and think across disciplines,
understand the interrelationship between academic research and society,
and become engaged citizens who are truly concerned about real-world
problems. This approach enables students to work more effectively on
research problems that benefit from using disparate viewpoints and prepares them for generating more socially valuable knowledge after they
graduate.

The vision of a unified approach to education can be traced throughout
the history of human thought—from Plato's Academy to von Humboldt's
integrative theory of education to the Annales School of History. Cicero's
ideal of the *doctus orator* ("the learned orator") and the concept of a
"Renaissance man" are also examples of the vision of unified education
(Klein 1990, 1996). In the United States, educators have long valued the
vision of integrative learning. This vision can be linked to the general

education movement that emerged after World War I, the core curriculum movements in the 1930s and 1940s, which resulted in enhanced curriculum for students, and the new social studies movement in the 1950s, which stressed inquiry-based learning.

The vision of a transdisciplinary university emerged in the 1960s and 1970s as part of a larger movement toward interdisciplinarity, when the concerns about the highly linear structure of universities and their failure to approach complex societal problems from multiple perspectives, led to calls for reforms in higher education systems around the world. The advocates of such reforms argued that the ultimate goal of existing educational structures was to produce highly specialized professionals. To achieve this goal, these structures tended to "funnel" students down this or that ever-narrowing disciplinary track and thus limited the students' exposure to the larger context of complex societal problems and to the perspectives of other professionals working on the same problems (Carroll et al. 2014).

The concerns about "over-specialization" within the higher education system were underscored by the participants convened at the First International Seminar on Interdisciplinarity held in 1970 at the University of Nice, France, and which was jointly sponsored by the Organization of Economic Co-operation and Development (OECD) and the French Ministry of Higher Education. The seminar participants argued that traditional discipline-focused approaches had been inadequate for understanding the complexity and multidimensionality of real-world problems and called for the development of cross-disciplinary approaches to teaching, learning, and research that would provide integrated strategies in addressing these problems. In the resulting seminal publication *Interdisciplinarity: Problems in Teaching and Research in Universities*, the seminar participants envisioned a new university as a "goal-oriented" system that would better equip students with the skills for tackling global complex issues in both professional and scientific environments (Apostel et al. 1972). In this publication, Jantsch (1972) described his idea of a "transdisciplinary university" as follows:

> The new purpose implies that the university has to become a political institution in the broadest sense, interacting with government (at all jurisdictional levels) and industry in the planning and design of society's systems, and in particular in controlling the outcomes of introducing technology into these systems. The university must engage itself in this task as an institution, not just through the individual members of its community. (1972, 102)

The vision of a transdisciplinary university was further developed in 1982 when OECD published the work *University and the Community: The Problems of Changing Relationships*, in which they presented the results of a worldwide survey on the relationship between universities and their communities. In this work, the OECD announced that in order for universities to fulfill their social mission, the "exogenous" form of interdisciplinarity (i.e., originating in the community and addressing its needs) must take priority over the "endogenous" form of interdisciplinarity (i.e., referring to the internal production of knowledge) (OECD 1982). More recently, Carroll et al. (2014) envisioned transdisciplinary universities as "places that provide a safe space for risk-taking, facilitate collisions between people and ideas, and instill a sense of the limits of individual or isolated knowledge and perspectives. These universities would not necessarily do away with disciplines, but would create environments that allow for a variety of approaches to problem-solving, and for the healthy and respectful intermingling of disciplines" (18).

One of the catalysts for a continued discourse on transdisciplinary education evolved from the urgent need for change in the relationships between natural, economic, and social systems and processes, known as sustainability. Sustainability requires active participation of a wide range of academics and stakeholders and thus is critically dependent on education as one of the most effective means that society possesses for creating a more sustainable future. In 1990, the Association of University Leaders for a Sustainable Future (AULSF) created the Talloires Declaration, a 10-point action plan for "incorporating sustainability and environmental literacy in teaching, research, operations and outreach at colleges and universities" (AULSF 1990). This declaration, signed by more than 400 university leaders from over 50 countries, explicitly called for supporting inter- and transdisciplinary approaches in higher education.

In response to these trends in higher education, universities began increasingly offering interdisciplinary courses or programs, either alongside or as an alternative to disciplinary subjects. Many degree programs in professional fields such as medicine, management, social work, and law started to include courses or course segments focused on integration of disciplines (Klein 1996). The importance of cross-disciplinarity and collaborative work within the higher education system was also progressively highlighted by accreditation standards. The greatest scope of interdisciplinary programs created during the last two decades of the 20th century occurred within the natural sciences and engineering giving rise to the proliferation of such interdisciplinary fields as biochemistry, environmental engineering, and nanotechnology. This trend was largely due to the large-scale government support and funding of biological and engineering research oriented toward the solution of urgent societal problems and the fact that several major breakthroughs and discoveries were made at the convergence of these disciplines (e.g., genetically engineered crops and cancer split tests). Significant efforts have also been made to revise the science, technology, engineering, and mathematics (STEM) education to incorporate problem-based learning and training across disciplinary fields, and the number of interdisciplinary undergraduate majors has grown in recent years (Science 2013). These trends toward interdisciplinary curricula have represented important initial steps on the road to creating transdisciplinary university environments.

The transdisciplinary educational model presents a paradigm shift for academic institutions that are traditionally organized around discipline-based departments. It generates new needs that span such areas as instructional design and curriculum development and impacts many institutions' policies and research agendas. New concepts and methodologies transform the ways that research has been treated in traditional disciplines. Ertas, Tanik, and Maxwell (2000) describe an ideal transdisciplinary curriculum as the one that involves multiple mentors, includes project or laboratory exercise modules, and consists of "true transdisciplinary courses," the boundaries of which are "the boundaries of the problem being addressed, not the artificial boundaries of disciplines" (8). This type of an ideal curriculum could not only present the concepts and questions covered in the course from multiple perspectives but also integrate knowledge, jargon, and skills that would enable students to grapple more effectively with the complexity of real-world problems.

While transdisciplinarity signifies a shift away from a traditional disciplinary approach to education, it does not imply that traditional disciplines will disappear. As the *Charter of Transdisciplinarity* states, "Transdisciplinarity complements disciplinary approaches [and] aims to open all disciplines to that which they share and to that which lies beyond them" (Freitas, Nicolescu, and Morin 1994). Even though the breadth in students' learning experiences provides a diversity of perspectives on a problem being studied, by itself it is not sufficient. In transdisciplinary education, disciplines still remain the "essential building blocks" (Klein 2008, 406) for two reasons. First, acquiring at least some disciplinary depth is necessary for students if they are to integrate disciplines into a more comprehensive context of the problem being studied. Second, even though job prospects for students trained in transdisciplinarity can be strong in government agencies and nongovernmental organizations, disciplinary depth can help the graduates become recognized and valued by a more conventional job market. Hugill and Smith (2013) echo this thought when they write that "[t]ransdisciplinarity paradoxically requires strong disciplines if it is to be meaningful" (193). With this in mind, transdisciplinary education does not mean that it would "do away with disciplines" but rather that it would aim for "the healthy and respectful intermingling of disciplines" (Carroll et al. 2014, 18).

Transdisciplinary education requires innovative pedagogies that would inspire and enable students to think and work across disciplinary, cultural, and sectoral boundaries. The report of the National Academies of Science Committee *Facilitating Interdisciplinary Research* (2005) has made specific recommendations for promoting interdisciplinarity in research and education. Although the report had not specifically addressed *transdisciplinarity* in research and education [italics added], most of the recommended approaches are applicable to the interdisciplinary and transdisciplinary educational contexts. The recommended approaches include:

- Creating collaborations capable of understanding and addressing the inherent complexity of nature and society
- Allowing faculty and students the flexibility to explore basic research problems at the interfaces of different disciplines
- Extending research partnerships to the humanities and other fields and sectors required to address complex societal problems
- Providing access to and understanding of the "generative technologies" that have the capacity to find new ways of looking at existing disciplines and generate new fields (National Academies of Science 2005)

Some of the specific recommendations for students described in this report include taking a wide array of courses, while developing expertise in a specific discipline; seeking courses at the intersections of traditional disciplines as well as courses that study complex societal issues; gaining research experiences that span traditional disciplines; looking for opportunities to study with course instructors who already have cross-disciplinary research experiences; and connecting with mentors from multiple disciplines. Some of the specific recommendations for faculty include designing curricula that incorporate interdisciplinary concepts and topics; offering interdisciplinary studies; teaching integrative courses that relate research methodologies of one discipline to other disciplines and to society at large; participating in training activities on interdisciplinary research techniques and collaboration skills; and taking part in summer immersion programs designed for those faculty members who wish to learn new disciplinary languages and cultures (Ibid.).

New ways of teaching and learning also require new sets of skills needed for constructive work in transdisciplinary contexts. The development of creative problem-solving skills has been recognized as one of the primary objectives for student learning in higher education due to the growing demand for critical thinking and cognitive flexibility in the workforce. Problem-learning skills entail the cultivation of such abilities as synthesizing, differentiating, and reconciling and include the capacity to seek solutions to problems that are too complex to be addressed through the lens of a single discipline or even through the combination of disciplines. The learning outcomes include the abilities to take account of multiple dimensions of a problem and analyze it from multiple perspectives (including disciplinary perspectives) and empathize with multiple stakeholders, to place problems and their possible solutions within a broader context, to compare and contrast ideas and develop arguments, to critically evaluate resources, and to tolerate volatility and ambiguity (Haynes 2002; Mansilla 2005; Zhou 2016). Transdisciplinary research, which, by its very nature, focuses on concrete problems rather than disciplinary distinctions, has a great potential for developing problem-solving skills.

Considerable emphasis is also placed on integrative and analytical skills necessary for working on complex research questions as well as on communication, project management, and team development skills (Klein et al. 2012). In 2013, Gallup, in collaboration with Microsoft Partners in Learning and the Pearson Foundation, conducted a study to identify and measure skills across interpersonal, intrapersonal, and cognitive domains that are critical to the education of students for long-term career success in the "knowledge-based, technology-driven, globalized environment" (21st century skills and the workplace 2013, 8). The seven skills identified by this study strongly resonate with the concept of transdisciplinarity and, by extension, with the vision of a transdisciplinary university. These skills include:

1. Collaboration (the ability to work in diverse teams, interact with external stakeholders, and collaborate with and learn from those who possess expertise in different fields of study)
2. Knowledge construction (the ability to analyze ideas and information to draw conclusions about a specific topic or issue)

3. Skilled communication (the ability to communicate with both individuals and groups in a positive and effective manner)

4. Global awareness (the ability to understand key social/global issues, how they are interconnected and relate to each other, and to one's disciplinary specialty)

5. Self-regulation (the ability to develop goals and plans independently, manage one's work and time, and evaluate one's learning process)

6. Real-world problem solving (the ability to use one's knowledge to develop workable solutions to real-world problems either within one's community or in the world at large)[1]

7. Intelligent use of technologies in learning (the ability to use technologies to support knowledge construction and expand problem-solving capability)

Although these skills should be ideally nurtured at all educational levels, graduate studies are particularly well positioned to develop these skills. These skills represent "a transition from a world of learning by being taught (an unfortunate but appropriate characterization for most secondary and undergraduate curricula) to a complex socio-technological world in which there is a requirement to guide one's own learning and life's work" (Derry and Fischer 2005, 6).

While educators realize the importance of providing students with a solid understanding of how to put their knowledge into a broader context, identify and untangle complex real-world problems, communicate across disciplines, and cooperate with various stakeholders, universities still often lag behind in promoting and supporting faculty who have the willingness and background to teach these skills. Despite the broadening support for inter- and transdisciplinarity in higher education, universities continue to be primarily constructed around what Gibbons et al. (1994) called "scientific" disciplinary knowledge, or Mode 1, in which the boundaries between academic disciplines are being supported by institutional structures and criteria for career advancement and promotion (Becher 1989; Becher and Trowler 2001; Klein 2004). As McClam and Flores-Scott (2012) observe, "[w]hile it may be true that academic institutions are being called upon to promote transdisciplinarity, these same institutions have been described as places where traditional discipline boundaries are deeply delineated, practiced, and defended" (232).

The progress toward transdisciplinary teaching and learning has been hindered not only by disciplinary silos but also by other considerable challenges reported by scholarly literature on transdisciplinary approach to education (Balsiger 2015 Carroll et al. 2014; Derry and Fischer 2005;

Klein 2008; McClam and Flores-Scott 2012). While many of these challenges are identical to those faced by transdisciplinary research collaborations, such as conservative institutional structures, impact on career tracks and academic reward, publishing constraints, and challenges with funding (as discussed earlier in Chapter 6), other intellectual and practical challenges are more specific to transdisciplinary teaching and learning. They include:

- *The need for team-teaching*

  The teaching of transdisciplinary research skills requires the participation of multiple faculty and mentors as well as the participation of external stakeholders in order to present concepts, methodologies, and terminology from different perspectives and within different social contexts, and to fill skill gaps.

- *Conceptual distances*

  Faculty from different disciplines have different ways of approaching research topics that are inherent in faculty's prior knowledge and experience.

- *The gap between science and practice*

  The long-standing traditions of separating the scientific enterprise from practice make it challenging to properly balance research and practice in education.

- *Time and effort intensive logistics and coordination*

  Significant time and efforts in logistics are required to initiate relations with and establish schedules for multiple teaching faculty members and external stakeholders. Managing the teaching process also demands considerable efforts in coordination.

- *Peer generalizations and biases*

  Disciplinary conformity is still privileged in academia. Not fitting the "typical teammate mold" can be stressful for transdisciplinarians who are often regarded by their peers as unfocused "dabblers" (Carroll et al. 2014).

- *Issues with mentorship and co-mentorship*

  Faculty mentors who tend to associate with their own specific disciplines might encourage their mentees to stick to a single discipline as well. Those mentors who support the idea of crossing disciplinary boundaries may find it challenging to be a co-mentor with a person from another discipline or disciplines.

- *Difficulty with sustaining student-driven programs*

  Because students tend to leave every few years, it may be difficult to sustain student-driven programs that include transdisciplinary courses.

Carroll et al. (2014) suggest three specific areas that universities should foster in order to create transdisciplinary environments. These areas are:

1. *Mentality*

   Transdisciplinary environments require a more flexible mentality that espouses humility recognizing the limitations of any group or individual knowledge and open-mindedness appreciating different perspectives and new ways of problem solving.

2. *People*

   Transdisciplinary environments require the support of diverse types of individuals, including those people who:

   • specialize in one discipline

   • specialize in one discipline but are also aware of how their expertise fits into a larger context

   • specialize in multiple disciplines and are able to bridge these disciplines together

   • do not specialize in any specific discipline but who are skilled in context thinking and connecting

3. *Groups*

   Transdisciplinary environments should facilitate the development and sustainment of frequent communication between "learners and doers" as well as interactions between ideas across different disciplines.

Brundiers, Wiek, and Redman (2010) also provide specific implementation strategies for experiential learning that can help bridge the divide between academic and nonacademic knowledge. These strategies include: (1) "bringing the real-world into the classroom" (e.g., inviting external guest lectures from governments, industries, and nongovernmental organizations to discuss actual cases from their practice); (2) "visiting the real-world" (e.g., enabling students to meet and talk with stakeholders outside of the classroom); and (3) "engaging with the real world" (e.g., exposing students directly to real-world problems through transdisciplinary projects or internships). The Transdisciplinary Case Study (TCS) developed at the Swiss Federal Institute of Technology (ETH) in Zürich, Switzerland, serves as an example of such experiential learning that combines learning, research, and practice used to acquire skills and competencies necessary for research in sustainable development (Scholz et al. 2006).

Despite the fact that teaching transdisciplinary research skills is "a costly enterprise" (Balsiger 2015), a growing number of universities around the world are taking steps to becoming more transdisciplinary. In Europe, an example of a university that is incorporating transdisciplinary strategies into its education and training programs is the Institute of Creative Technologies (IOCT) at De Montfort University, Leicester, United Kingdom, that undertakes teaching and learning at the intersection of science, technology, the humanities, and the arts (Hugill and Smith 2013). In the United States, the Institute for Design and Advanced Technology (IDE-ATE) at Texas Tech University has developed (jointly with the industry stakeholders) a transdisciplinary Master of Engineering program (Ertas et al. 2003). The Brown School at Washington University in St. Louis developed a Master of Public Health program that is using transdisciplinary approaches to problem solving in public health (Lawlor et al. 2015). In Canada, the Schulich School of Medicine & Dentistry at the University of Western Ontario has initiated a transdisciplinary ecosystem health program that studies the risks of ecosystem degradation to human health (Ecosystem Health Program 2016). In Australia, the Queensland University of Technology is offering an undergraduate course titled "Creative Industries: Making Connections," which aims to develop students' skills as communicators and collaborators in creative industries[2] (Park and Son 2010). The International University Reforms Observatory (ORUS), an international network of European, South African, and Latin American academics promotes discussions of university reforms within a transdisciplinary context (http:// www.orus-int.org/).

Furthermore, a sizable body of information resources supporting transdisciplinary teaching has emerged during the last two decades, including a wealth of teaching resources that are freely available on the web under the auspices of such initiatives as td-net, the Academy of Transdisciplinary Learning & Advanced Studies (TheATLAS), the International University Reforms Observatory, and the Centre International de Recherches et Études Transdisciplinaires (CIRET). Fellowships (such as the Christine Mirzayan Science & Technology Policy Graduate Fellowship Program), joint projects (such as Yale University's the Art of Public Health project), and immersion programs (such as the one at the University of Oklahoma-Tulsa School of Community Medicine) have been established to provide students with an opportunity to work together across different disciplines and community contexts.

The aforementioned efforts share a common goal, which is about opening up wider and more societally relevant perspectives on education. They also affirm the increasing importance of incorporating transdisciplinarity in all stages of education. At the same time, a transdisciplinary approach to education is often seen as an idealized educational model of the future.

As Newell (2010) observes, universities are "notoriously slow to change" (368). Current academic structures and reward systems—for students and faculty alike—are still based primarily on disciplinary achievements. The success of the vision of a transdisciplinary university will continue to depend on concerted systematic efforts by educators, policy makers, and other stakeholders to integrate knowledge and promote transdisciplinarity within the higher education system.

Notes

1. It is worth mentioning that across the skills included in this report, the skill for real-world problem solving was identified as the most critical skill for higher work quality later in career. At the same time, while this skill most positively correlated with future career success, the majority of the study respondents reported that they did not have the opportunity to acquire this important skill at school and developed it in their current jobs outside of school.

2. Broadly speaking, the term "creative industries" (also called "creative economies") refers to activities that are concerned with the production and commercialization of individual creativity; for example, music, design, publishing, crafts, media, advertising, the performing arts, and computer games.

Suggested Readings

McGregor, Sue L. T., and Russ Volckmann (eds.). *Transversity: Transdisciplinary Approaches in Higher Education.* Tucson, AZ: Integral Publishers, 2011.
Science. Special Issue: Grand Challenges in Science Education, April 19, 2013.

PART 2

A Natural Fit: Transdisciplinarity and Librarianship

Librarianship is inherently a transdisciplinary vocation.

—Nathan Filbert (2016)

CHAPTER TEN

Why Do Librarians Need to Know about Transdisciplinarity?

Of the many concepts and areas of librarianship . . ., the one consistent thread is change.

—Jeffrey Knapp (2012, 209)

As Part I of this book has affirmed, there is the apparent spread of transdisciplinary thinking into higher education, which is increasingly forming new alliances that bridge academic, industrial, nonprofit, and governmental sectors. Academic research is becoming more "restless" as it is being "pushed and pulled" in various directions away from traditional academic departments and university settings (Clark 1995, 247). More and more scholars and educators recognize the limitations of the existing disciplinary structures that promote further specialization rather than integration and thus cannot satisfactorily address the full complexity of real-life situations. It is also generally undisputed that breakthrough discoveries tend to occur at the intersections of traditional disciplines, rather than within their strict boundaries.

In addition to growing recognition of the importance of transdisciplinary research, university programs and accreditation boards no longer expect students to master only disciplinary or technical competencies but also to become adept at "soft skills" such as communication, problem solving, collaboration and conflict management, and critical and creative thinking skills (ACRL 2015). The goal behind this trend is twofold: to produce graduates who have a stronger sense of social responsibility, and orientate them toward the world in which problems require both specialized skills and integrative knowledge to cope effectively with complexity. In Klein's (1996) words, "the challenges of the modern world require integrative problem solving and, at a more comprehensive level, holistic thought and transdisciplinary schema [to] promote the unity of knowledge" (134).

While knowledge integration holds great promise for scholars, there are also myriad challenges for conducting such scholarship. According to Smith et al. (2009), these challenges include:

- A need to be familiar with larger, more diffused body/bodies of literature
- A need to decipher different, fluctuating vocabularies
- A need to work across, through, and between provinces of research and practice in a world structured around well-defined disciplines with traditional limits and boundaries
- A need to work in a professional context suspicious of or hostile to [cross-disciplinarity] (230)

The "research drift" (Clark 1995) toward transdisciplinarity impacts the practice of researchers and educators and has yet to make a considerable impact on the librarians' already complex role. As Klein (1996) predicted two decades ago, new information needs created by the challenges of the modern world would "land squarely on the desk of the librarian, whose job is to organize knowledge and make it accessible" (135). The impact of transdisciplinarity on librarians will be rather significant for three major reasons:

1) Transdisciplinarity challenges the traditional organization of knowledge, which is the libraries' primary commodity. In view of this trend, librarians will need to find new strategies for knowledge management that will support these new developments in knowledge production and organization.

2) Transdisciplinarity generates new user needs that span such areas as research support, access to resources, information literacy, and the reconfiguration of library collections that are still largely organized on a discipline-based model. Libraries that traditionally place their primary emphasis on the user rather than the needs of the libraries will need to reshape some of their services to accommodate new needs of their users.

3) Transdisciplinarity creates new competency and mind-set expectations for librarians. Some retooling and reskilling will be necessary for librarians to ensure that they live up to these expectations.

While all library types will be challenged by transdisciplinarity, academic and research libraries, in particular, will be at the forefront of this challenge. In academia, where libraries serve as the core of intellectual life on campus, librarians play an indispensable role as "connectors" between diverse communities, resources, and disciplines. As the following chapters show, traditional strengths of librarians should enable them to successfully respond to the research needs of transdisciplinary scholars. Moreover, the nature of library and information science is itself transdisciplinary: it shares research methods with multiple disciplines (education, computer science, linguistics, systems analysis, and cognitive psychology to name just a few examples) and plays a critical role in cross-disciplinary and cross-community intellectual exchange.

Although academic librarians are accustomed to communicating across the entire landscape of disciplines and scholarly communities, the needs and expectations for library services and collections in the transdisciplinary environment are not yet well understood or properly supported in academia. While the implications of interdisciplinarity have been, to some degree, explored in the literature,[1] the question of transdisciplinarity as it pertains to libraries has been much more muted. Some speculations on the subject exist in library-related publications but these are rare and scattered across different sources. A clear understanding of the implications of transdisciplinarity for library services and collections is hampered by a lack of research in this area.

Mapping transdisciplinary services in libraries can, indeed, be mind-boggling. Or it can be "a matter of simply identifying the obstacles [transdisciplinary] scholars face, and applying the principles of librarianship in order to remove those obstacles" (Knapp 2012, 209). In either case, librarians will be challenged to find solutions to some difficult questions, which, nonetheless, are necessary to address if the libraries are to maintain one of their core values—that is advancing the education of library users toward the world in which they will live and work. As transdisciplinarity pushes librarians into unfamiliar territories, they must be prepared to take on the challenge of supporting "restless researchers" and, in the process, enhance an understanding of their own role as transdisciplinary collaborators. This process must begin with a clear understanding of the nature of research activities that generate transdisciplinary information needs. Even though, as Lattuca (2001) observed, librarians are used to "living without the comfort of expertise" (133) and routinely conduct research in unfamiliar scholarly fields and with unfamiliar terminology, it is essential that they move beyond a vague awareness of transdisciplinarity toward a better understanding of its key concepts, practices, and challenges in order to design new approaches to research services or rethink old ones.

The ideas and analogies presented in Part II of this book are clearly in the formative stage. Due to the paucity of previous research on transdisciplinarity and librarianship, this author relies on a larger segment of literature on interdisciplinary librarianship as a good place to begin the exploration of models that can be transferred to designing services and building collections for transdisciplinary scholars. As discussed in Part I of this book, both inter- and transdisciplinarity seek to integrate insights across disciplines, although the degree of such integration differs significantly between inter- and transdisciplinarians. Transdisciplinarity also differs from interdisciplinarity in the degree to which nonacademic participants are integrated into the research process. Despite these differences, some information-seeking practices and challenges associated with finding relevant information are common to both inter- and transdisciplinarians and, therefore, similar strategies can be used for assisting these scholars. This thesis is based on insights and conclusions drawn from literature on inter- and transdisciplinarity. For the sake of clarity, the following chapters use the term "cross-disciplinarity" as an umbrella concept that covers both interdisciplinarity and transdisciplinarity, unless a clear distinction between these two types of scholarship is critical.

The chapters that follow do not attempt to offer concrete answers to pivotal questions or provide practical guidance to librarians for creating new services to meet the demands for transdisciplinary research and education. Instead, these chapters highlight the key areas of library functions that are likely to be impacted by transdisciplinarity, while reflecting on how transdisciplinarity as a special type of challenge for libraries may be approached in terms of transferable skills and collaborations across library units. However, to assist transdisciplinary scholars in a meaningful way, librarians need more than conceptual generalities. Hopefully, these chapters provide the framework for further exploration and an opportunity for dialog and discussions that might lead to creative solutions in this dynamic field. Through this dialog and these discussions, new insights may be revealed that will enable librarians to develop services that foster transdisciplinary research and thus forge closer partnerships between the disparate academic schools and departments at their institutions. In turn, enhanced research support for transdisciplinary efforts will provide librarians with a rich assortment of opportunities for outreach and collaboration and enable them to embrace and enact change to help their library grow. As Miller (2015) states, "the role of change agent is one that librarians increasingly will play in the future" (337).

Note

1. For example, Bates 1996; Klein 1996; Mack and Gibson, 2012; Palmer 1996.

CHAPTER ELEVEN

Envisioning a Universal Classification: Transdisciplinarity and Knowledge Organization

You who read me—are you certain you understand my language?
—Jorge Luis Borges, *The Library of Babel*

If libraries have meaning at all, it lies in the very categories that librarians apply to select, organize, and dispense knowledge. These categories change, split, and merge over time, but the essential fact of categorization remains.

—Susan E. Searing (1996, 338)

Discipline-based knowledge organization structures have long been recognized as an obstacle to cross-disciplinary scholarship (Ackerson 2001; Copeland 2012; Gnoli 2010; Knapp 2012; Palmer 2010; Palmer and Cragin 2008; Searing 1992, 1996; Spanner 2001; Szostak 2008; Szostak, Gnoli, and López-Huertas 2016). The two most widely used classification systems—Dewey Decimal System (DDS) and the Library of Congress Classification (LCC) system—are not flexible enough to keep pace with the evolution of knowledge or to accommodate connections between overlapping research areas. Although some LLC schedules include cross-disciplinary aspects of a particular topic and some new terminology has been developed to classify cross-disciplinary interests, the overall LCC system is firmly grounded in disciplinary knowledge. Furthermore, DDS and LCC were developed over a century ago (in 1876 and 1897 respectively) when cross-disciplinarity was not yet foreseen and are, therefore, challenged when disciplinary boundaries shift or new research trends and topics emerge. As new research areas emerge, they are either being "squeezed" "into pre-existing outlines of knowledge" (Searing 1992, 9) or retain inadequate categories or are being neglected because they fall outside the mainstream of established ways for organizing and communicating knowledge (Moseley 1995; Schummer 2004). In particular, the current classification systems are poorly suited in facilitating transdisciplinary scholarship because works are classified according to traditional disciplinary lines rather than in terms of phenomena that transdisciplinarians study. Although the prevalence of current discipline-based classifications reflects historical circumstances, their late 19th-century origins "inevitably limit them" (Searing 1992, 8).

Similar to the LCC system, the Library of Congress Subject Headings (LCSH) system has evolved along the disciplinary-based structure of academia (Knapp 2012). The hierarchical, rigid, and linear LCSH structure is neither intuitive nor current enough to reflect the issues of the present day (Copeland 2012; Denda 2005) and the assignment of subject headings "often lags far behind the evolution of a new subject area" (Ackerson 2001, 50). This situation is further complicated by the fact that works are cataloged according to different terminology employed by different disciplines and are often treated according to the perspective of a given disciplinary knowledge domain. Denda (2005) and Palmer (2010) point out the need for the development of cross-disciplinary ontologies that would place the disparate terminology from different disciplines into a suitable context and thus help researchers locate materials at multiple levels of focus and depth.

Searing (1992, 1996) notes that the LCSH system partly compensates for the limitations of the "less hospitable" LCC system. Assigning multiple subject headings to a work in a library catalog enables a user to identify this work from several entry points while the classification system allows this work to carry only a single call number. At the same time, this situation results in inconsistent call numbers and that makes it difficult for scholars to locate works on topics spanning disciplinary boundaries. Robb (2010) and Knapp (2010) argue that allowing library users to "tag" items with their own descriptive terminology would encourage cross-disciplinary exploration and provide better "findability" to cross-disciplinary materials because subject headings assigned by a professional cataloger who assigns subject headings might not know the subject as well as a researcher.

In the same vein, several scholars examined the concept of "about-ness"[1] dominating library indexing practices and how this concept impacts cross-disciplinary information seekers. In the library and information science, the concept of "aboutness" and how it is determined is still a subject to ambiguity. Maron (1977) writes that "[t]he problem with *about* is that it is a very complex notion and we are unable to say precisely what it is we do when we make judgment of *aboutness*" (38). Milstead (1994) argues that more research in indexing is needed because "we have no idea of the mental processes involved when an indexer decides what a piece of information is 'about' " (578). The subjectivity of the indexing process ultimately leads to indexer inconsistency that puts an additional strain on the researcher who has to think about alternative indexing terms when conducting a bibliographic search. While the use of indexing rules and standards helps improve indexer consistency, indexing is still a subjective process that is open to an individual cataloger's interpretation of these rules and standards.

The relevance and precision of indexing terms can also be judged differently by an indexer mediating the meaning of a work on behalf of the reader and the reader who might have a different perception of what a work is about. Kleineberg (2013) writes that indexing within the library and information science is based on semantics (e.g., subject and topicality), while scholars need the indexing based on pragmatics (e.g., perspective, viewpoint, and injunction). Reynolds (1989) observes that "[r]eaders (or cataloguers) project their own perceptions, experiences, and level of comprehension onto the text. There is always a degree of tension between the new information and what the reader already knows or believes" (232). This situation leads to a "persistent and perhaps inherent conflict between what readers regards as the 'aboutness' of a document and what indexers define as its 'aboutness'" (Hutchins 1978, 34). Knapp (2010) makes a similar point when he writes:

> One of the problems with traditional cataloging methods is that they assume a sort of omniscience, or a sort of bird's eye view of how the totality of knowledge is organized in assigning subject headings and subject terms—in short, they are designed to help *librarians* locate items rather than the average scholar. And they assume that the scholar is aware of precisely what it is she/he is looking for, which is sometimes true—but not always. (58)

The current indexing practices present a challenge for all scholars but even a greater challenge for cross-disciplinary scholars who are primarily interested in finding works that investigate relationships and connections between phenomena and thus seek works that provide comments on particular aspects of a given phenomenon[2] (Szostak, Gnoli, and López-Huertas 2016). Weinberg (1988) argues that indexing fails the scholar because it focuses on "aboutness" while neglecting "comment." She quotes Lyons (1968) who defines comment as "that part of the utterance which adds something *new* (and thus communicates information)" (335). Hutchins (1978) makes a similar distinction between a "theme" (what the work is "about") and "rheme" (new information provided on the theme). He states that while novices and laymen may be interested in searching by theme, scholars are primarily interested in the rheme of a work.

The lack of consistent controlled vocabularies across online bibliographic databases is another barrier to cross-disciplinary scholarship (Gnoli 2010; Kutner 2000; Westbrook 1999). These databases follow the same discipline-based principle for classifying their content but tend to adopt their unique controlled vocabularies to describe the contents of a work. Although digital technologies have made a significant contribution toward guiding scholars to related or similar works, they are still not sufficiently responsive to more sophisticated cross-disciplinary queries (Palmer 2010). Furthermore, the increased likelihood of finding related or similar works across disciplines does so at the cost of increasing information overload (Wu et al. 2012). Having consistent interoperable vocabulary across diverse online bibliographic databases could not only help researchers to maintain a manageable grasp of information but also could facilitate construction of the Semantic Web, the goal of which is to enable computers to navigate across disparate online databases so that users can easily find and integrate information contained on the Web (Martin 2014; Szostak 2014).

In the absence of adequate library classification schemes and consistent controlled vocabulary, cross-disciplinary scholars have to rely on time-consuming and often ineffective strategies for finding resources they need such as tracing citations of key works in other disciplines, seeking the advice of colleagues, and consulting specialized bibliographies (Weinberg 1988). These scholars also rely heavily on serendipitous discoveries while browsing shelves in the library (Palmer 2010). Repko and Szostak (2016) point out that library catalogs are not set up to trace different disciplinary theories and methodologies that study a particular phenomenon, connect related phenomena (or parts of a particular phenomenon) studied by different disciplines, or identify the same phenomenon described differently by different disciplines. Therefore, works discussing the same phenomenon can be classified differently, either using different disciplinary terminology (Knapp 2012) or using identical terminology that describes different concepts (Spanner 2001). Also, works dealing with the same phenomenon can be scattered across multiple points of the classification schema according to the disciplines studying it. To complicate the matter further, a significant portion of cross-disciplinary research output (e.g., cutting-edge articles and symposium papers) is included in anthologies and other collective volumes and thus are not easily found through catalog records (Searing 1996). As a result, researchers may fail to identify important works because they do not know what terms to use for their search or they must know how to combine a variety of search terms and use different search strategies for identifying relevant resources in different disciplines.

To find relevant resources for their projects, cross-disciplinarians are forced to seek information in multiple areas and separate physical locations and this takes a high toll on their time and energy, which, in turn, impacts their productivity that often depends on quick and convenient discovery of relevant information resources. This situation also poses the risk of missing important documents that may result in the "reinventing of the wheel" due to the lack of awareness of previous research on their topic of study (Szostak 2008, 321). As Bush (2009) observes, "where the work resides very much influences how it gets found (or not) and used (or not)" (449).

The challenge of finding relevant information for their research projects is even more pronounced for transdisciplinarians who work on addressing real-world problems that "rarely arise within orderly disciplinary categories" (Palmer and Cragin 2008, 73) and "resist tidy slotting into existing classifications" (Searing 1992, 8). Transdisciplinarians rely heavily on finding "undiscovered public knowledge"[3] that can help them identify implicit connections within or across disciplines and discover promising links and hidden analogies they need for testing their hypothesis. As Beghtol (1995) observes, the risk of missing this valuable body of knowledge increases with cross-disciplinary interaction because the strategies for uncovering "undiscovered public knowledge" tend to be discipline-specific. Transdisciplinary researchers also depend on having easy access to the "hidden collections"—nonprocessed special collection materials such as nontextual items (art objects, photographs, audio and video recordings), thematic collections, and rare materials. Digitizing, cataloging, and making these materials easily accessible can save researchers' time and effort and thus facilitate and support cross-disciplinarity (Copeland 2012).

Transdisciplinarians also need to readily find works discussing transdisciplinarity and transdisciplinary methodologies to get a better understanding of these relatively new approaches to research with which they might be unfamiliar. In library catalogs, transdisciplinarity still does not have a designated subject heading. Individual works on transdisciplinarity can be found in library catalogs under the "Interdisciplinary Research" or "Interdisciplinary Approach to Knowledge" subject headings as well as under the subject headings for a relevant discipline or disciplines. Methods and theories employed in a work, as well as links and relationships between phenomena that transdisciplinarians are interested in, are rarely captured in subject headings.

Despite the limitations of discipline-based classification practices, libraries rarely develop alternative classification schemes. Searing (1992) writes:

> [F]ew libraries develop alternatives to the Library of Congress and Dewey classifications, because reclassifying a library is a complicated and extraordinarily expensive task. Moreover, as increasing distance in time from these systems' origins deepens sensitivity to the values embedded in them, it simultaneously nurtures skepticism that *any* system could be universal or value-free. . . . [M]ost librarians are resigned to the inadequacies of existing classification systems. Rather than embarking upon grand scale improvements, they focus on communicating the intricacies of the systems to library users, on promoting more sophisticated research methods than browsing, and on alerting users to implicit values in the systems. (9)

Nonetheless, a number of visionary librarians and information scientists across the world have called for a new approach to classification that would be capable of coping with the evolution of knowledge and thus better serve the needs of cross-disciplinary scholars. In the 1930s, S. R. Ranganathan introduced a novel (faceted) classification scheme that he called Colon Classification. Although still discipline-based, Colon Classification was capable of covering both the existing knowledge and newly discovered knowledge and assist users in locating works based on multiple facets. The Classification Research Group (CRG), formed in Great Britain in 1952, aspired to expand the postulational approach to facet analysis created by Ranganathan by developing the principles of faceted classification "unhampered by allegiance to any particular published scheme" (CRG 1955, 262) and rejecting all "existing classification schemes as unsatisfactory, in one way or another, for the demands of modern documentation" (Ibid., 263). The CRG developed these principles based on the theory of integrative levels as well as on the analysis of different dimensions of knowledge that are involved in the steps "between the world and classification" (Vickery 2008–2009). More recently, an international team of scientists has been working on the Integrative Levels Classification (ILC) experimental project (http://www.iskoi.org/ilc/index.php) that was inspired by the work of the Classification Research Group (CRG) and built upon the CRG's efforts. The ILC draws on an international team of collaborators to apply the theory of integrative levels (i.e., layers of complexity) to knowledge organization. Another, currently in progress, Basic Concepts Classification (BCC) project aims to break complex concepts that can be interpreted differently across disciplines and groups of people into "basic concepts" (such as entities, properties, and relationships) that can be readily understood across individuals and groups of people and are then subject to less ambiguity. Szostak (2011, 2014) argues that ambiguity could be significantly reduced by placing these basic concepts within logically organized hierarchies, allowing these basic concepts to be linked with each other, and then classifying scholarly works in terms of combinations of these basic concepts. Szostak (2014, 2016) also claims that BCC could also support development of the Sematic Web's controlled vocabulary structured around RDF triples that utilize the same kinds of basic concepts, namely entities, relationships, and properties.

Gutiérrez (2011, 2014) goes even further and calls for a new "complementary rather than substitutive" approach to knowledge organization, leading to the "declassification" of knowledge organization. He argues that the prevailing hierarchical classification of knowledge hinders communication in today's transversal knowledge environment because it can be perceived as "a weapon of domination" (2014, 394) that is "sending into exile every possible order but the one authorized by power" (2007, 35). He suggests replacing the tree-like representation of the hierarchical knowledge organization system based on Aristotle's logic with the postmodern concept of the rhizome.[4] He refers to Deleuze and Guattari (1987), who originally used this concept to describe the way in which meaning might be constructed of the world, and explains it as follows:

> Deleuze and Guattari . . . retrieved and rehabilitated the botanic metaphor by means of the rhizome, a set of anarchical, discontinuous, capricious and tangled roots, like those of the Southern mangroves, as a figure of epistemological dismantling. That is the nutrient from which sprouts the theory of declassification. (2011, 8)

Robinson and Maguire (2010) came to a similar conclusion when they examined the contrast between the tree-like model of the traditional hierarchical classification characterized by vertical fixed linkages and the nonhierarchical rhizome-like model of knowledge organization in which "non-hierarchical linkages, made pragmatically as they are needed, horizontally or across any number of levels, and linking elements of disparate nature when appropriate, crossing categories" (607).

A clear understanding of key information needs of cross-disciplinary scholars can provide a foundation for developing a more versatile approach to knowledge organization. Scholars who study cross-disciplinarity agree that cross-disciplinary research primarily involves the study of relationships between phenomena (or parts of a phenomenon) and the exploration of these relationships through the lens of different disciplines (Klein 1990; Salter and Hearn 1997; Szostak, Gnoli, and López-Huertas 2016; Weinberg 1988).[5] In particular, cross-disciplinarians need to know what previous research has been done in other disciplines or research fields about a particular phenomenon that confirms (or refutes) their theories. They need to know what theories and specific methods have been applied to these phenomena and these relationships, what evidence supports different theories, and what data have already been collected in investigating the phenomena and relationships they study. They also need their research publications to be found easily by other scholars researching the same topic. Szostak, Gnoli, and López-Huertas (2016) maintain that in order to achieve these goals, these scholars must be able to search by:

- The phenomena addressed in a work
- The relationships among phenomena addressed in a work
- The theory or theories applied in a work
- The method or methods applied in a work
- The disciplinary (or interdisciplinary) perspective of authors (61)

Advocates of this new approach to knowledge organization agree that the needs of cross-disciplinary scholars could be better served by an exhaustive phenomenon-based classification. In 2007, the participants of the conference of the Spanish chapter of the International Society for Knowledge Organization (ISKO), whose theme was "Interdisciplinarity and Transdisciplinarity in the Organization of Scientific Knowledge," called for an exhaustive and universal knowledge organization system (KOS), which was grounded in phenomena found in the real world, rather than in disciplines, and which did not employ different vocabulary in different disciplines. The conference participants argued that works should be classified in terms of phenomena, methods, and theories that themselves are defining characteristics of disciplines and thus the key areas that inter- and transdisciplinarians seek to transcend. The conference participants claimed that the new KOS (which could either complement or substitute for existing classification schemes) would simplify the classification of both scholarly and nonscholarly works and reduce conceptual ambiguity, thus facilitating scholarly communication across disciplinary boundaries. For this reason, the proposed classification would be especially beneficial to cross-disciplinary scholars while also aiding disciplinary researchers and general users. *The León Manifesto* (http://www.iskoi.org/ilc/leon.php) produced by the conference participants summarized these ideas from the conference participants as follows:

- "Instead of disciplines, the basic units of the new KOS should be phenomena of the real world as it is represented in human knowledge.
- The new KOS should allow users to shift from one perspective or viewpoint to another, thus reflecting the multidimensional nature of complex thought. In particular, it should allow them to search independently for particular phenomena, for particular theories about phenomena (and about relations between phenomena), and for particular methods of investigation.
- The connections between phenomena, those between phenomena and the theories studying them, and those between phenomena and the methods to investigate them, can be expressed and managed by analytico-synthetic techniques already developed in faceted classification." (2007)

Whether the vision of a "universal" classification can be achieved or not, transdisciplinary scholarship can be possible only if there is shared understanding across multiple scholarly communities. In *Manifesto of Transdisciplinarity*, Nicolescu writes:

> How can a theoretical particle physicist truly hold a dialogue with a neurophysiologist, a mathematician with a poet, a biologist with an economist, a politician with a computer programmer, beyond mouthing more or less banal generalities? Yet, a true decision maker must be able to have a dialogue with all of them at once. (2002, 41)

Libraries are in a good position to help in such a dialog by exploring and advocating a more versatile approach to knowledge organization. Even though research and knowledge grow more "restless," the libraries' core values continue to motivate their emphasis on the library user. As Umberto Eco (1997) comments on Borges's story *The Library of Babel*, "the real hero . . . is not the Library itself but its Reader, a new Don Quixote—restless, adventurous, tirelessly inventive, alchemically combinative—able to master the windmills that will keep on turning, indefinitely" (62).

Notes

1. Robert Fairthorne introduced the concept of "aboutness" in relation to information science. In his 1969 article "Content Analysis, Specification, and Control," he distinguished between the two kinds of aboutness—"extensional aboutness" and "intensional aboutness"—thus drawing a distinction between the "aboutness" intended by the author of a document and the aboutness actually expressed in that document. He argued that while "extensional aboutness" was fixed and unchanging because it was inherent to the document, "intensional aboutness" was inferred from the document and thus subject to interpretation by the reader engaged with its content.

2. The word "phenomenon" originally comes from a Greek verb *phainesthai* meaning "to seem" or "to appear." In general, the term "phenomenon" refers to an object or the aspect of an object that can be apprehended by the senses (such as through sights and sounds) as contrasted with the objects that can only be apprehended by the mind. In scholarship, the term "phenomenon" refers to an object of study.

3. The concept of "undiscovered public knowledge" developed by Don Swanson (1986) refers to sets of works or literatures that can reveal important, yet hidden connections and implicit links. These works and literatures are "mutually isolated and noninteractive" (Swanson and Smalheiser 1996, 295) because they do not cite each other and are not cited together with each other and thus they often remain undiscovered.

4. The concept of the rhizome has also been used to describe the rhizomatic nature of transdisciplinarity (see Chapter 1 of this book).

5. Some cross-disciplinary researchers focus on phenomena studied by a single discipline but apply methods or theories from multiple disciplines.

Suggested Readings

Repko, Allen F., and Rick Szostak. *Interdisciplinary Research: Process and Theory*, 3rd edition. Thousand Oaks, CA: Sage Publications Inc., 2016.

Rondeau, Sophie. "The Life and Times of Aboutness: A Review of the Library and Information Science Literature." *Evidence Based Library and Information Practice* 9, no. 1 (2014): 14–35.

Szostak, Rick, Claudio Gnoli, and María López-Huertas. *Interdisciplinary Knowledge Organization*. New York: Springer Science+Business Media, 2016.

CHAPTER TWELVE

Filling Collection Gaps: Areas of Concern and Possible Solutions

There are clear parallels between the disciplinary organization of the university and the organization of thought.
—Alfonso Montuori (2005, 151)

Developing a library collection that encourages and supports transdisciplinary research poses significant challenges for librarians who are faced with responsibilities to which the traditional collection development methods do not apply. In academia, libraries have been historically responsible for supporting the mission of their host institutions by developing focused collections intended to meet the needs of the faculty and students. Consequently, the organization of a typical academic library collection mirrors the institution's structure where boundaries are drawn along disciplinary lines represented by academic departments and programs. As Hickey and Arlen (2002) conclude, "the very organizational structure of libraries eschews the cross-disciplinary framework in favor of one based on the traditional 'pure' disciplines" (98).

Similarly, the funding structure and allocation of resources is reinforced by the disciplinary structures of universities. Reynolds, Holt, and Walsh (2012) describe the traditional collection development model in academic libraries as follows:

> Usually funding is by subject, with well-established disciplines histori-
> cally receiving more consistent support from academic libraries than
> newer subjects and interdisciplinary fields of study. This is traditionally
> accomplished either through allocation formulas or is based on historical
> allocations, the basis of which is often lost in the mists of time. . . . The
> subject funding structure can be rigid and often provides little flexibility
> for funding of new research areas as they arise. This can be especially true
> in economic downturns when library collection development budgets are
> static or decreasing. (98–99)

Although the growth of cross-disciplinary programs in academia tends
to make the boundaries of library collections more porous, the fund allocation matrix based on formula and overall dwindling support for library
resources over the last few decades are the major reasons why cross-
disciplinary materials are vulnerable to being overlooked by selectors. In
lean budget times, selectors may have a hard time justifying purchases of
resources that do not fit neatly into their discipline-based fund allocations. Furthermore, cross-disciplinarians rely heavily on journals in
emerging, cutting-edge fields and on conference proceedings, while
libraries are inclined to subscribe to mainstream disciplinary journals
rather than purchasing newer journals with less established reputations,
especially when funding is scarce (Searing 1996; Spanner 2001).

Another obstacle to developing an adequate collection for promoting
cross-disciplinary research is the division of responsibilities among
librarians whose selection assignments are based on disciplines that
match the academic program they support. Wilson and Edelman (1996)
observe that "nowhere is the traditional discipline-based university structure more clearly evidenced than in collection development where the
selection responsibilities of academic librarians are largely oriented
toward academic departments" (195). Metz and Foltin (1990) speculate
that the program-based division of labor makes subject selectors hesitant
to purchase materials that fall outside of their area of responsibility
because they want to avoid territorial disputes or because they assume
that another selector is already purchasing these materials. The scope of
the cross-disciplinary intellectual content is also much broader than that
of traditional disciplines so selectors must search more widely and more
creatively for relevant titles. This challenge is further complicated by
ambiguous or outdated classification categories and indexing terms
assigned to cross-disciplinary works that can discourage selectors from
acquiring the titles that fall outside the scope of academic disciplines
(Hickey and Arlen 2002; Metz and Foltin 1990). Moreover, new research
developments often entail the redefinition of research fields and involve

new terminology, or terminology can be used differently by different disciplines, which can lead to more confusion. Another challenge is that cross-disciplinary research is phenomenon-oriented whereas library collections are discipline-based. Szostak, Gnoli, and López-Huertas, who have written prolifically on cross-disciplinarity and knowledge organization, state: "An interdisciplinary work might be viewed as of tangential interest to all relevant acquisition librarians. If libraries were organized around phenomena rather than disciplines the value of interdisciplinary works would be more transparent" (2016, 40). In a similar vein, Robb (2010) argues that in order to encourage and support interdisciplinary research, a library collection should be focused on a topic, rather than individual disciplines. As an example, she cites the Oxford University Refugee Studies Library that has the world's largest collection of materials, including books, journals, and a large collection of gray literature, relating to the topic of forced displacement.

The traditional collection development methods, limited funding, and discipline-based division of responsibilities among selectors can lead to the situation where whole areas of cross-disciplinary knowledge are in danger of "falling through the cracks" during the collection-building process (Hickey and Arlen 2002). This situation contributes to a high level of insecurity for cross-disciplinary scholars and, as a result, adversely affects their productivity (Spanner 2001). The library's long-term failure to purchase works that are of importance to these scholars ultimately impacts the quality of the institution's teaching and research and undermines the academic library's mission.

Various approaches have been suggested by library literature for alleviating the problem of cross-disciplinary collection "cracks." Searing (1992) states that "[d]ividing the book budget by academic department is merely one model, albeit one frequently followed" (11). Canepi (2007) suggests that "[library budgets] are dynamic, not static, and the challenge for every library is to create an allocation formula that best incorporates the aspects most important to the specific institution" (14). Hickey and Arlen (2002) argue that allocating a portion of the budget for purchasing materials of interest to multiple academic fields will not only strengthen the presence of the library within the institution but also relieve subject selectors from "the perceived rigid compartmentalization" (104). They also suggest that librarians' selection assignments be made "according to degree of interrelatedness" (13) between intellectual domains in order to avoid gaps in the collection. Reynolds, Holt, and Walsh (2012) argue that a more holistic allocation structure is key to building library collections that are more reflective of cross-disciplinary campus communities. Specifically, they advocate for movement away from narrowly defined static spending allocations toward a more flexible budget structure that would have an option for purchasing cross-disciplinary materials through broad funds for science and technology, social sciences, and arts and humanities. They also note that patron-driven acquisitions (PDA) can be a useful means for addressing the needs of cross-disciplinarians. Ackerson (2001) highlights the importance of adding newly emerging areas to the approval profile in a timely manner. Knapp (2012) suggests designating a special budget line for purchasing journals in newer areas to ensure at least some level of funding for cutting-edge fields. Open-access journals may also help with budget issues for journals in these newer fields (Ibid.). Libraries can "collect" open-access journals into their collections by making them more visible through the venues that are familiar to scholars, for example, through electronic journal lists and research portals[1] (Martin 2014).

Various techniques have also been suggested to assist librarians in identifying cross-disciplinary titles, alert them to the need to coordinate with other selectors, and justify funding for important cross-disciplinary purchases. Bibliometric techniques, including citation, co-citation, and coauthorship analyses, have been a standard tool for measuring cross-disciplinary information transfer and use (Palmer and Cragin 2008). For example, Porter and Chubin (1985) have introduced an indicator known as "Citations Outside Category" (COC) that has been successfully used by numerous scholars as a tool for discovering cross-disciplinary research activities. COCs indicate those works in which a scholar in one field cites the work of a scholar in another field, thereby crossing a disciplinary divide. The authors postulate that COCs not only detect cross-disciplinary research but also "anticipate the convergence of particular skills to form new research specialties, and eventually disciplines" (174). Ortega and Antell (2006), Pierce (1999), Qiu (1992), and Schummer (2004) describe using author affiliation to assign disciplines for tracking cross-disciplinary information. White (1996) suggests using bibliographic "markers" such as keywords, phrases, descriptors, or subject headings to track down cross-disciplinary titles. He speculates that the occurrence of these "markers" in the literature by different authors can reveal hidden linkages between disciplines and that the reoccurrence of these "markers" can indicate the blurring of disciplinary boundaries. Lindholm-Romantschuk (1998), who conducted a study of the "intellectual territories" of disciplines, has observed that major scholarly journals that reflect the flow of ideas within and among academic disciplines can serve as excellent indicators of the intellectual direction of a discipline (62). More recently, clickstream data (i.e., a detailed web log data from aggregators, publishers, and institutional consortia) have been used to visualize and analyze the dynamics of scholarship (Bollen et al. 2009).

The value of proactive collaboration and regular communication among selectors responsible for interrelated disciplines has also been a common theme in the library literature (Hickey and Arlen 2002; Knapp 2010; Reynolds, Holt, and Walsh 2012; Spanner 2001). Collaboration activities could include the sharing of funds for purchasing materials in overlapping fields, cooperating on collecting for specific cross-disciplinary areas, and partnering when requesting additional needed funding for cross-disciplinary materials. Knapp (2010) states that "[t]he selection process should have a very social component to it to encourage selectors in fields that often cross over each other to work together for greater good of the collection" (57). Regular communication among library selectors such as the routing of review journals, publisher catalogs, notification slips, and other selection tools can help librarians see what knowledge areas, for which multiple selectors could be responsible, are being neglected and why. This can stimulate discussion among subject selectors and, as a result, help prevent inadvertent gaps in the collection (Metz and Foltin 1990).

Effective collection development for cross-disciplinary fields also depends on the degree of collaboration between librarians and faculty involved in cross-disciplinary research and teaching. Faculty-librarian collaboration can help librarians make better selection choices, evaluate current collections, guide future decision-making, and anticipate future collection needs of researchers engaged in cross-disciplinary scholarship. Searing (1992) observes that "collection development is the arena in which faculty and librarians most often come into conflict, and where values can collide rather nastily" (11). She advocates for a written collection policy that is jointly developed by librarians and faculty that would ensure a strong and relevant collection that has sufficient breadth and depth. Reynolds, Holt, and Walsh (2012) call attention to the need to extend the concept of "embedded librarianship" beyond the area of information literacy instruction and into the area of collegial collection development. As research and education become increasingly cross-disciplinary, librarians should not only make sure that their library collections are well stocked with the materials needed by cross-disciplinary scholars, but they should also increase their knowledge about the intellectual structure of cross-disciplinary fields. Embedding librarians into departments and research centers where cross-disciplinary research is taking place can increase librarians' awareness of new research initiatives on campus and alert them to the need for selecting relevant materials for these initiatives. Furthermore, it is crucial for librarians to anticipate the needs of researchers engaged in transdisciplinary research at their institutions. As Hurd (1992) ruefully remarks, "[i]t can be much too late if a library learns from a university press release that an interdisciplinary research center has been established. Such programs have been planned without librarian input on available library resources to support them or without opportunity for library staff to begin long-range planning for acquisition of materials or development of support services" (296). Conversely, better knowledge and understanding of the actual needs of cross-disciplinary researchers can help build the collection based on these needs rather than on "speculation" (Anderson 2011). In turn, greater connectivity with cross-disciplinary communities and anticipating the librarians' ability to serve these communities will strengthen the libraries' presence on campus and provide opportunities for further collaboration between researchers and librarians.

Note

1. For discussion of research portal initiatives in academic libraries, see Martin (2014), 135–139.

Suggested Reading

Pierce, Sydney J. "Boundary Crossing in Research Literatures as a Means of Interdisciplinary Information Transfer." *Journal of the Association for Information Science and Technology* 50, no. 3 (1999): 271–279.

CHAPTER THIRTEEN

Librarians as Boundary Intermediaries: Implications of Transdisciplinarity for Reference Services

We are no longer experts-masters and practitioners of a known body of knowledge. We are no longer experienced guides to a familiar terrain. We must be—can only be—explorers, scouts and pathfinders, navigating unbounded, evolving sources of information to map the way for users who are now fellow searchers.

—Fink and Loomis (1995, 3)

Assisting transdisciplinary scholars in locating information across multiple disciplines and various types of resources presents another challenge for librarians. While the purpose of a reference interaction between a librarian and a transdisciplinary scholar is the same as that of a traditional reference encounter, which is "to find the documents answering [the reader's] interest at the moment, pin-pointedly, exhaustively, and expeditiously" (Ranganathan 1961, 53), the unique challenge lies in the nature and scope of research questions posed by transdisciplinarians. They focus on finding solutions to real-world problems that "fall between the cracks of [established] disciplines" (Chubin 1976, 466) and "metaphorically encompass the several parts of the material field which are handled separately by the individual specialized disciplines" (Miller

1982, 11). This complicates the information-seeking process of transdisciplinarians as they strive to examine multilayered real-world problems from a variety of disciplinary perspectives and apply the techniques developed in one discipline to research conducted in another. This also complicates the work of reference librarians who attempt to answer questions that do not fit into traditional classification schemes, subject headings, and the databases' controlled vocabulary. Reference librarians must think broadly, creatively, and flexibly to discover alternative paths to finding materials needed by researchers working within a transdisciplinary paradigm.

Fundamental to meeting the wide-ranging information needs of transdisciplinary scholars is a clear understanding of their information-seeking processes and the challenges they face when looking for information across multiple disciplinary fields and knowledge domains. Due to the lack of research in this area, librarians often have little understanding of how transdisciplinarians gather and use information. Until such research is conducted and reported, a copious (and still growing) literature on the information-seeking behavior of interdisciplinary researchers is a good place to begin the exploration of information-seeking activities of transdisciplinary scholars. It is reasonable to suppose that the information-seeking behaviors of interdisciplinary and transdisciplinary scholars do not differ in dramatic ways. This assumption is based on the premise that both interdisciplinary and transdisciplinary scholars work on the boundaries of knowledge rather than within their core knowledge domains and thus struggle with gathering and translating information that is "intellectually distant or from unknown sources" (Palmer 2005, 1144). Moreover, it can be assumed that both transdisciplinary and interdisciplinary scholars (henceforth described as cross-disciplinary scholars in this chapter) face similar practical and intellectual challenges in targeting relevant material for their projects.

Information-Seeking Behavior of Cross-Disciplinary Scholars

One bit of knowledge may raise questions, lead to another fact or to a new conclusion, and so forth, which changes one's knowledge state and hence what one finds relevant and worth seeking.
—Case and Given (2016, 91)

The information-seeking practices of cross-disciplinary scholars differ significantly from those working within single disciplines (Bates 1996; Hurd 1992; McCain 1986; Palmer 1999). A significant segment of library literature examines the distinctive patterns of information-seeking processes of interdisciplinary scholars.[1] In 1996, the journal *Library Trends* devoted an entire special issue (vol. 44, no. 2) to studies on the interdisciplinary nature of knowledge and its implications for academic libraries. Representative of this research on the topic is the seminal nonlinear model of information behavior proposed by Allen Foster (2004) based on the findings of his study on information-seeking behavior of interdisciplinary researchers.[2] Foster's model includes three core processes—*opening*, *orientation*, and *consolidation*.

- *Opening* involves such activities as initial keyword searching, footnote chasing, probing, and browsing as well as more complex activities such as Breadth Exploration ("a conscious expansion of searching to allow exploration of every possibility" [233]) and Eclecticism ("accepting, gathering and storing information from a diverse range of both passive and active sources . . . for later incorporation and satisfaction of information needs" (Ibid.).

- *Orientation* includes "picture building" (i.e., defining the information problem and problem focus), reviewing (i.e., evaluating the already collected information to determine "where I am now"), and identification of relevant disciplines, concepts, key works and authors, and existing research).

- *Consolidation* is a reiterative process of refining, sifting, and verifying in order to determine whether enough material has been obtained to meet the present information need.

While the terms assigned to opening, orientation, and consolidation suggest sequential activities, Foster argues that these processes are neither fixed nor proceed in a straightforward, linear fashion. Instead, they "are analogous to an information seeker holding an artist's palette of information seeking opportunities, in which the whole palette remains available at any given moment throughout the course of information-seeking" (235). Furthermore, the core processes of opening, orientation, and consolidation take into account the interaction between their external context (social and organizational, time, the project, navigation issues and access to sources) and internal context (feelings and thoughts, coherence, and knowledge and understanding) and the information seeker's cognitive approach (flexible, adaptable, open, nomadic thought, and holistic). Although Foster does not write from the perspective of a reference librarian, his model, which he describes as "nonlinear, dynamic, holistic, and flowing" (235), provides a useful framework for librarians to keep in mind when serving cross-disciplinary scholars.

Multiple studies identified two typical information-seeking practices of cross-disciplinary scholars: probing and translating. Probing, a form of deliberate browsing for identifying scattered information outside of a researcher's domain, involves web-surfing, browsing journal issues, library and personal collections, publishers' catalogs, and bibliographic indexes. Translating involves assessing, interpreting, and grounding "intellectually distant" information with the background knowledge of the researcher's primary disciplinary domain (Palmer 2010).

Cross-disciplinary researchers also rely heavily on serendipity. Although not being used as a conscious information-seeking strategy, scholars in all disciplines recognize serendipity as a valuable tool for discovering new knowledge and generating new ideas (Cobbledick 1996; Delgadillo and Lynch 1999; Foster and Ford 2003; Palmer, Teffeau, and Pirmann 2009). The value of serendipitous discoveries is even more appreciated by cross-disciplinary researchers who have to search widely scattered information for their projects (Palmer, Teffeau, and Pirmann 2009).

Information-Seeking Challenges of Cross-Disciplinary Scholars

Another crucial factor for the provision of effective reference service to cross-disciplinary scholars is an understating of their unique information-seeking challenges. Although cross-disciplinary research practices vary, there are key challenges that all cross-disciplinary scholars face, including high-information scatter, acculturation to an unfamiliar discipline or disciplines, learning new disciplinary languages, information overload, and the need to keep up with new research findings across multiple disciplinary areas pertinent to the research under investigation.

High Information Scatter

The concept of information scatter introduced by L.J.B Mote (1962)[3] refers to the degree to which information on a specific topic is distributed ("scattered") across numerous resources. Information scatter is usually low within traditional academic disciplines where "the underlying principles are well developed, the literature is well organized, and the width of the subject area is fairly well defined" (Mote 1962, 170). Within cross-disciplinary fields, on the other hand, where the number of different subjects is immense while the organization of resources is nearly nonexistent, information scatter is very high. Relevant information may be found in different places, both within the classification system and in the physical library. This presents a serious challenge for cross-disciplinary scholars who must identify highly scattered authoritative materials outside their primary field and thus have a greater learning curve than that of disciplinary scholars (Westbrook 2003).[4] Klein (1994) describes this challenge as follows:

> The problem of interdisciplinary information is the problem of information scattering. Appropriate materials do not appear in a single location, nor are they readily identified by cataloguing, indexing, and online services, which tend to mirror existing disciplinary categories. Searchers must develop some expertise in moving across the varied assumptions, structures, and forms of disciplinary literatures as well as the invisible colleges, networks, and hybrid communities in which interdisciplinary knowledge often develops. (15–16)

Disciplinary Acculturation

Another challenge faced by cross-disciplinary scholars is the need to achieve a certain "disciplinary adequacy" (Jones 2012), or "disciplinary acculturation" (Spanner 2001), in two or more unfamiliar disciplines that are pertinent to their research. Smith et al. (2009) describe this process as becoming "intellectually bi- or multicultural" (217). This process involves a significant effort to "acculturate" to unfamiliar and sometimes conflicting disciplinary cultures and norms and requires researchers, at the very least, to become familiar with the basic elements of new disciplines.[5] White (1987) asserts that any meaningful crossing of disciplinary boundaries "must take place through a process of translation that is based upon rather full knowledge of the practices that define each community" (11). Bartolo and Smith (1993) observe that "the duality of the interdisciplinary search task—the need to find information and the lack of knowledge of another discipline—potentially heightens the level of uncertainty and anxiety for the researcher" (347). These tasks are particularly challenging for cross-disciplinary students who need to consult resources from multiple disciplines that are not linked through traditional coursework.

Learning New Disciplinary Languages

The knowledge of terminology of the "other" discipline, or disciplines, needed for understanding research literature and communicating with researchers outside their primary discipline, is another competency that cross-disciplinary scholars must master. The need for a constant "translation" between disciplines comprises one of the most laborious and difficult components of the cross-disciplinary research process (Palmer 2010). Jones (2012) describes the process of learning the language of another discipline as "becoming bilingual." Palmer (1996) notes that even "[E]xperienced researchers feel like novices as they look for information in unfamiliar contexts and attempt to become oriented and knowledgeable" (170). Galison (1997) observes that cross-disciplinarians often develop a "pidgin language," that is, a limited "interlanguage" that facilitates communication across disciplinary fields. The challenge of learning a new disciplinary language is magnified by the fact that similar concepts may be assigned different terms in different disciplines or the same concept may have multiple origins (Bates 1996; Westbrook 2003). To confront this challenge, cross-disciplinarians try to follow key names in the field, chase citations,[6] seek out scholars doing similar work, and rely on other time-consuming search strategies.

Information Overload

While information overload is a real problem for anyone involved in serious research, the burden of information overload is heavier for cross-disciplinary scholars. Large quantities of relevant information that they find across multiple disciplinary resources can be beyond the capacity of anyone to absorb and utilize effectively. As disciplinary literature becomes increasingly "fractured," (i.e., diffused into other disciplines, forming new intersections within a single discipline, or residing on the periphery), it also becomes more difficult for a researcher to know whether all relevant information has been discovered (Ackerson 2001). Wilson (1996) observes that "[s]pecialization in research is partly a response to, and defense against, [information] overload—i.e., one adjusts the size of the field over which one hopes to maintain expertise so that the burden of keeping up is manageable" (193). Wilson further stipulates that information overload is especially threatening to "solo" interdisciplinarians, such as humanities scholars, who typically conduct research individually, rather than in formal research teams. Wilson suggests that these "solo" researchers should actively seek collaboration and co- or multi-authorship in order to combat the threat of information overload.

The Difficulty of Keeping Current

Closely related to the problems of high scatter and information overload is the difficulty of keeping current both within and outside the areas of a cross-disciplinary researcher's expertise. Reading broadly across streams of literature in multiple specialties is a challenging task that takes a high toll on the researcher's time and energy. Because of that, cross-disciplinary researchers tend to "probe broadly" rather than "read broadly" (Palmer 1996). Information probing involves skimming through the tables of contents and abstracts of a wide range of research journals and general science magazines in order to discover segments of information and new ideas relevant to their research. While skimming helps researchers keep current, it also complicates their information-seeking work because it can result in the expansion or shift of research interests (Ibid.). To combat the challenge, cross-disciplinary researchers rely heavily on interpersonal networks as a way for gathering pertinent information not easily revealed through skipping scholarly literature (Crane 1972; Cronin 1982; Palmer 1996). Newby (2001) observes that cross-disciplinary researchers tend to have larger interpersonal networks than disciplinary researchers because they struggle with identifying authoritative information outside their native disciplines.

Sources of Information

The sources of information for cross-disciplinary research are highly heterogeneous. No single source, however comprehensive, can satisfy all the information needs of cross-disciplinary researchers. Furthermore, different disciplines rely on different modes of communicating research. For example, in most scientific fields, where the currency and expediency of access to latest research findings is crucial, research is almost exclusively communicated through articles published in peer-reviewed journals, while in the humanities, where individual scholarship still predominates, research is principally communicated through solo-authored monographs. Spanner (2001) also notes that newer cross-disciplinary fields communicate new knowledge differently from traditional disciplines as they rely more heavily on conference proceedings rather than scholarly journals.

Considering diverse sources of information is especially important when a topic involves research done on the intersection of fields whose disciplinary norms and culture differ significantly and thus affect how and through which channels research is being communicated. Knapp (2010) advocates the value of full-text searching (versus subject heading searching) for cross-disciplinary scholars for whom defining the disciplinary "ingredients" of research and becoming aware of resource types is more important than identifying specific books or articles. Knapp's idea is aligned with Sandstrom's (1994) vivid description of how cross-disciplinary scholars "forage" for resources in "patchy information environments" (432) and with what Bates (1989) called "berrypicking of information," the process in which researchers gather information "in bits and pieces" and where each bit and piece of new information can change the direction and the essence of the original query.

While a systematic and productive information search is key to research in any discipline, transdisciplinary scholars have to engage in significantly more laborious information-seeking process—and of a different kind—than researchers in traditional disciplines. Transdisciplinary scholars make significant use of information scattered across a wide spectrum of books, journal articles, data sets, gray literature, "invisible college" resources, and ephemera. Finding relevant information in libraries where knowledge organization systems are still imperfect for their purposes is one of the key challenges for transdisciplinary researchers.

Much of the success of cross-disciplinary information search relies on the reference librarian's ability to accomplish four overarching goals: (1) identify which disciplines are likely to be relevant to the research under investigation, (2) select a wide range of potentially useful information sources specific to these disciplines, (3) determine the span of time over which these resources are still useful to current research,[7] and (4) construct a search strategy that is narrow enough for targeting the most pertinent material among large quantities of information.[8] This approach echoes Newell's (2007) advice to interdisciplinary scholars who "need to start broadly and narrow the focus towards more specialized sources as the topic takes shape" (85).

General sources of information are the same for both cross-disciplinary and discipline-based scholars, even though their information needs differ. Peer-reviewed journal literature still constitutes the most important information base for most scholars who need to gain insights into current research and technological developments. Large multidisciplinary databases such as JSTOR, Web of Science, and Proquest Research Library provide a useful "one-stop searching" capability, which is a good starting point for conducting cross-disciplinary literature research. However, multidisciplinary databases are insufficient for conducting research on more advanced or obscure topics (Jones 2012; Scimeca and Labaree 2015). To delve deeper into a more advanced or obscure topic, a preliminary search in a multidisciplinary database should be supplemented with further searches in pertinent subject-specific databases (Ibid.) as well as in topical databases that cut across disciplines (Repko and Szostak 2016). Identifying subsequent work that cites a particular article is another useful tool for cross-disciplinarians to "connect the scholarship of different disciplines by building on the connections discovered by previous scholars" (Newell 2007, 87).

At the same time, relying solely on research articles and overlooking other resources when assisting cross-disciplinary scholars poses a serious risk of missing highly relevant materials. The following resources should also be consulted:

- *Subject encyclopedias and handbooks*

  Subject encyclopedias and handbooks can play a key role for cross-disciplinary scholars who need to familiarize themselves with the fundamental concepts of a particular discipline, its history, terminology, methodologies, key authors, and primary fields involved in its formation.[9]

- *Disciplinary dictionaries*

  Disciplinary dictionaries are useful for developing familiarity with the terminology of a particular discipline.

- *Books*

  Books provide pertinent background information for researchers who need to learn about basic research methodologies outside their main field of study and interpret how these methodologies from new intellectual domain may be applied to their own research.[10] Browsing print books in the physical library can also result in serendipitous discovery of materials that otherwise would have been missed through direct searching (Palmer, Teffeau, and Pirmann 2009).

- *Review articles*

  Review articles are an effective entry point into scholarly literature in any discipline. They can provide cross-disciplinary scholars with a succinct introduction into an unfamiliar topic and direct them to key references in the field. Cross-disciplinary review articles, in particular, are a valuable source of information about research across multiple disciplines.

- *Government documents*

  Government documents reporting on research results from government-funded projects are an excellent primary source of information in many research areas. In addition to reporting research findings, government documents are also useful for finding data, policies, judicial acts, and information on patents.

- *Conference proceedings*

  Conference proceedings reflect the latest innovations in many fields. They provide access to original, cutting-edge research at an unvarnished level prior to its appearance in peer-reviewed journals and thus can offer a unique perspective on that research compared to that in a corresponding article.

- *Dissertations*

  Recent dissertations can be a valuable source for understanding the state of the art in a particular research field. Another value of dissertations resides with the list of key references on a topic.

- *Technical reports*

  Technical reports are particularly useful in the information-gathering stage of a research project because they often provide progress updates on a new line of research, as required by funding agencies.

- *Subject-based bibliographies*

  Subject-based bibliographies can help identify scattered information and aid the process of probing into the peripheral areas outside of the research-er's primary discipline "to increase breadth of perspective, to generate new ideas, or to explore a wide range of types and sources of information" (Palmer 2010, 183).

- *Primary data*

  Primary data from multiple data sources are essential to all research endeavors.

- *"Invisible college" resources*[11]

  "Invisible college" resources can satisfy a number of information needs of cross-disciplinary scholars such as connecting to other researchers, getting up-to-date on current developments in the field, and discovering new ideas and relevant research findings. Furthermore, "invisible college" resources "facilitate boundary spanning [by helping] transmit ideas across disciplines" (Cronin 1982, 224).

- *Web-based materials*

  Web browsing that Rowlands et al. (2008) describe as "bouncing" and "flicking" can lead researchers to more traditional literature resources that otherwise might not have been discovered.

- *Nonacademic sources of information*

  While multi- and interdisciplinary scholarship places little emphasis on seeking research input from nonacademic domains, transdisciplinary schol-arship requires researchers to identify relevant nonacademic information resources, such as newspaper articles, artifacts, eyewitness testimonies, tele-vision broadcasts, works of art, and oral histories. Such items can be relevant to a research inquiry and help transdisciplinary researchers think more com-prehensively about the context of a topic under investigation. Consulting these sources is especially important for transdisciplinary researchers who actively seek to engage nonacademic stakeholders in the research process.

Synoptic Reference

The polymathic approach to reference services, or "synoptic reference," proposed by Scimeca and Labaree (2015) brings reference librarians closest to the understanding of how to effectively frame transdisciplinary research questions and search for information on a wide-range of subjects that do not fit into traditional subject headings and the controlled vocabulary of disciplinary databases. Even though Scimeca and Labaree apply the concept of synoptics[12] to the provision of reference services for interdisciplinary scholars, this concept can also be effective in assisting other cross-disciplinary scholars, including those pursuing transdisciplinary investigations.

Scimeca and Labaree base their concept of synoptic reference on methodology for dealing with the history of philosophy suggested by a German philosopher Wilhelm Windelband in his *Introduction to a History of Philosophy* (1901). Windelband argued that three factors were necessary in order to understand the formation and development of a discipline's concepts and problems: (1) the pragmatic factor defining the concept or problem that is being discussed, (2) the historical factor determining the historical context of that concept or problem, and (3) the individual factor taking into account the unique position of an individual thinker or school of thought in analyzing the concept or addressing the problem under investigation. Drawing on Windelband's methodology, Scimeca and Labaree propose the following stepwise strategy for providing synoptic reference:

Step 1: Reaching a clear understanding, both by the scholar and the librarian, of the concept under investigation (the pragmatic factor). This step can be accomplished through a careful reference interview.

Step 2: Investigating the historical background (the historical factor). This step involves consulting the resources that provide a historical overview of the chosen concept.

Step 3: Examining the subject-specific perspective (the individual factor). This step includes utilizing discipline-based resources that are pertinent to the concept being researched.

While most reference librarians are already well-versed in performing these individual steps during their reference interactions with library users, the uniqueness of synoptic reference lies in its holistic approach to a research inquiry; thus, it can help librarians more effectively meet the information needs of those scholars who are not confined by the boundaries of a single well-established discipline. Furthermore, synoptic reference "forges an intellectual partnership between the librarian and the patron [who are] actively participating in the collaborative learning process that results in an integrated acquisition of knowledge" (482).

Notes

1. See, for example, Bates 1996; Foster 2004; Jones 2012; Klein 1996a; Knapp 2012; Palmer 1996, 2001; Palmer and Neumann 2002; Scimeca and Labaree 2015; Searing 1992, 1996; Spanner 2001; Westbrook 1999, 2003. In 1996, Library Trends devoted an entire special issue (vol. 44, no. 2) to studies on the interdisciplinary nature of knowledge and its implications for academic libraries.

2. Foster's nonlinear model has undergone at least two updates. See Foster, Urquhart, and Turner (2008) and Foster and Urquhart (2012).

3. Also see Bradford's law of scattering (Bradford 1948).

4. While information scatter presents a significant challenge for cross-disciplinary researchers, it also serves important functions. Information scatter promotes connections between disciplines and cultivates integration between disparate knowledge fields. Chubin (1976) observes that information scatter keeps knowledge from becoming "sect-like" and that without information scatter researchers would be divided into small groups, only communicating, reading, and citing each other. Information scatter also promotes innovation and discovery that often occur not inside the core of an established academic discipline but on the margins between disciplines (Chubin 1976; Crane 1972).

5. For a description of the basic elements of a discipline, see Augsburg (2006, 116–119). Also, see Chapter 5 of this book.

6. Bates (1996) and Palmer (1996) recommend this strategy for an initial information search—to discover conceptual connections to a cross-disciplinary topic not through subject terms but through citations that can lead to similar research being conducted in different disciplines.

7. For example, it is important to keep in mind that information in the humanities fields maintains its usefulness for a long time, while information in the biomedical fields ages rapidly.

8. Jones (2012) makes a good point when she writes that the challenge for interdisciplinary researchers is "one of selection of the most relevant sources, rather than discovery [and that helping them] formulate sufficiently narrow searches is essential to their success and their time management" (178). Part of this challenge is that there are rarely corresponding subject headings or controlled vocabulary terms for cross-disciplinary topics; and therefore, keyword searches are often necessary.

9. Repko and Szostak (2016) advise to consult encyclopedias with "great care" because the authoritativeness of an encyclopedia article largely depends on the scholarly credentials of the article's author (131).

10. Fortunately for cross-disciplinarians, book catalog records often reflect some of the topical diversity of a book by listing more than one subject heading that can be used to perform relevant searches and thus yield additional references on the topic (Searing 1992).

11. "Invisible colleges" are informal methods of communication within the scholarly community. In the past, these methods included marginal note-taking on the manuscripts of fellow researchers as well as personal meetings of scholars to witness experiments and discuss research topics (Price 1961, 1963; Crane 1972). Nowadays, "invisible college" activities include web-enabled communication tools such as blogs, discussion forums, social networking sites, e-mail, virtual collaboratories, and scholarly hubs.

12. When explaining the concept of synoptic reference, Scimeca and Labaree refer to the less predominant usage of the term "synopsis," which is defined by the *Oxford English Dictionary* (1989) as "a mental act, faculty, or conduct pertaining to, involving, or taking a combined or comprehensive mental view of something."

Suggested Readings

Foster, Allen. "A Nonlinear Model of Information-Seeking Behavior." *Journal of the American Society for Information Science and Technology* 55, no. 3 (2004): 228–237.

Knapp, Jeffrey A. "Plugging the 'Whole': Librarians as Interdisciplinary Facilitators." *Library Review* 61, no. 3 (2012): 199–214.

Palmer, Carole L. *Work at the Boundaries of Science: Information and the Interdisciplinary Research Process*. Dordrecht, The Netherlands: Springer Science & Business Media, 2001.

Scimeca, Ross, and Robert V. Labaree. "Synoptic Reference: Introducing a Polymathic Approach to Reference Services." *Library Trends* 63, no. 3 (2015): 464–486.

CHAPTER FOURTEEN

The Process of Becoming: Reflections on Transdisciplinary Learning and Information Literacy Instruction

Is it not a pleasure after all to practice in due time what one has learnt?

—Confucius

The vision of transdisciplinary learning can be tracked back to Confucius and his ideas on education, the focus of which (as the aforementioned quote implies) was on the interrelationship between knowledge and practice. This classic idea resonates strongly through the modern discourse on transdisciplinarity as "the relationship between inquiry and action in the world" (Montuori 2010, 10).

Although the vision of transdisciplinary learning stems from deep historical roots, research on transdisciplinary pedagogies is still at an early stage. There is no comprehensive conceptual framework for transdisciplinary teaching and learning. Consequently, there are no clearly defined learning objectives and learning outcomes and no agreed-upon inventory of skills and competencies expected of students who are taking transdisciplinary courses.[1] This state of affairs is partly due to the fact that there is still no single coherent strand that runs through the wide range of definitions for transdisciplinarity that has been offered. However, valuable guidance and insights can be found across multiple sources and forums discussing innovative pedagogical approaches to higher education and these approaches can be applied to developing effective transdisciplinary teaching environments.

The idea of the four pillars of learning articulated at UNESCO's International Commission on Education (Delors et al. 1996) is still relevant today and may provide an excellent conceptual framework supporting curriculum enhancement for transdisciplinary courses. The four pillars of learning have been envisioned as necessary conditions for a more encompassing lifelong education in the 21st century. This concept was further expanded by Nicolescu (1997) who believed that these four pillars form the foundation of transdisciplinary knowledge and interpreted them in such a manner that they reflected his vision of transdisciplinarity. The four pillars of learning—in their original form (Delors et al. 1996) and as interpreted by Nicolescu (1997)—are as follows:

- *Learning to know*: combining a broad general knowledge with an in-depth knowledge of a small number of subjects (Delors et al. 1996); distinguishing "what is real from what is illusory" and "being capable of establishing bridges—between the different disciplines, and between these disciplines and meanings and our interior capacities" (Nicolescu 1997).

- *Learning to do*: developing occupational skills and the competence to deal with real-life situations and work in teams (Delors et al. 1996); the acquisition of professional or occupational competencies as well as "an apprenticeship in creativity" (Nicolescu 1997). The latter refers to developing "a flexible, interior core that could quickly provide access to another occupation should it become necessary or desirable [and] discovering novelty, creating, bringing to light our creative potentialities" (Ibid.).

- *Learning to live together*: appreciating interdependence "in a spirit of respect for the values of pluralism, mutual understanding and peace" (Delors et al. 1996); fostering a "transcultural, transreligious, transpolitical and transnational attitude" that makes space both for open unity and complex plurality that are not antagonistic but rather enable us "to better understand our own culture, to better defend our national interests, to better respect our own religious or political convictions" (Nicolescu 1997).

- *Learning to be*: developing one's personal attributes without disregarding "any aspect of a person's potential (such as memory, reasoning, aesthetic sense, physical capacities and communication skills) and an ability to act with greater autonomy, judgment and personal responsibility" (Delors et al. 1996); developing an understanding that "being" is not synonymous with "existing" but is a "a permanent apprenticeship," in which we are "discovering our conditioning, discovering the harmony or disharmony between our individual and social life, testing the foundations of our convictions in order to discover that which is found underneath" (Nicolescu 1997).

A Project 2061 published in 1989 by the American Association for the Advancement of Science (AAAS) may also provide direction in the formulating of learning outcomes for transdisciplinary learners. The learning outcomes that were suggested by *A Project 2061* included "being familiar with the natural world and respecting its unity; being aware of some of the important ways in which mathematics, technology, and the sciences depend upon one another; understanding some of the key concepts and principles of science; having a capacity for scientific ways of thinking; knowing that science, mathematics, and technology are human enterprises, and knowing what that implies about their strengths and limitations; and being able to use scientific knowledge and ways of thinking for personal and social purposes" (AAAS, 1989, xvii-xviii).

These competencies cannot be taught with just one approach. The assumption that authoritative knowledge comes only from an established disciplinary expert is negated in a transdisciplinary world. New ways of working with knowledge must be employed that will support transdisciplinary education requiring all learners to "confront differences in perspective not just from disciplines but also from people who think, learn, and perceive differently from them in order to complete a group task or interact productively in a community" (Newell 2010, 365–366). Because transdisciplinary learning is inquiry driven rather than driven by the purview of a single discipline or a set of disciplines, various pedagogies—both time-tested and emergent—must be considered.

Exploring Relevant Pedagogies

The following list, while far from being exhaustive, pulls together the strands of relevant pedagogies that may inspire further exploration of transdisciplinary teaching and learning and, consequently, contribute to developing new approaches to information literacy instruction for transdisciplinary students.

- *Integrative learning*
  The pedagogical practices that use integrative approaches to teaching and learning align most closely with the concept of transdisciplinary learning.

While not synonymous with integrative learning, transdisciplinary learning requires some of the same "habits of mind" identified in the 2004 *Statement on Integrative Learning* developed jointly by the Association of American Colleges & Universities (AAC&U) and the Carnegie Foundation for the Advancement of Teaching (CFAT):

> Integrative learning comes in many varieties: connecting skills and knowledge from multiple sources and experiences; applying theory to practice in various settings; utilizing diverse and even contradictory points of view; and, understanding issues and positions contextually. Significant knowledge within individual disciplines serves as the foundation, but integrative learning goes beyond academic boundaries. Indeed, integrative experiences often occur as learners address real-world problems, unscripted and sufficiently broad to require multiple areas of knowledge and multiple modes of inquiry, offering multiple solutions and benefiting from multiple perspectives (13).

- *Interdisciplinary learning*

Interdisciplinary learning focuses on interaction and collaboration between two or more disciplines. It has been primarily used in academic programs within the social sciences and the humanities such as women's studies, area studies, religious studies, and American studies as well as in more "traditional" disciplines such as philosophy, anthropology, and literature. Interdisciplinary teaching applies methods and insights from a variety of relevant disciplines to examine an issue, topic, or question from multiple perspectives and then integrates these perspectives into a more complete and coherent analytical framework. Although a similar meaning is sometimes applied to both "interdisciplinary" and "transdisciplinary" teaching, the misinterpretation of these two terms may result in confusion and a failure of properly defining student needs and creating effective instructional designs. Rosenfield (1992) points out an important difference between interdisciplinary and transdisciplinary research with regard to different levels of interactivity and her explanation can help clarify the difference between interdisciplinary and transdisciplinary teaching. According to Rosenfield, interdisciplinarity involves researchers who "work *in parallel or sequentially* from disciplinary-specific bases to address common problems" (1351), while transdisciplinarity involves researchers who work "*jointly* using [a] shared conceptual framework that draws together concepts, theories, and approaches from the parent disciplines' (Ibid.; emphasis added). Thus, transdisciplinary learning takes interdisciplinary learning a step further by "[facilitating] collaborative learning through a shared conceptual framework" (Park and Son 2010, 83–84).

- *Experiential and service learning*

Experiential pedagogies, promoting students' interpersonal and intrapersonal learning and engaging students in situations rooted in the complexities of the real world, encourage peer interaction and require students to be "active agents in the learning process rather than passive recipients of information" (DeZure 2010, 375). These pedagogies also support the development of skills that are essential for transdisciplinary problem solving such as the ability to pose and scope a research problem, tailor-relevant methodologies to solving the problem, and draw on strengths of, and contributions from, different disciplines and research methodologies for accomplishing a common task. Experiential learning has become a mainstream pedagogical approach in vocational or professional programs. It combines academic study with fieldwork as a way to develop students' practitioner skills and their capacity for applying classroom knowledge to complex or ambiguous real-life situations. Service learning is part of experiential learning that includes service in the community and an ongoing, structured reflection that helps students develop a sense of social responsibility. Both pedagogical approaches blur the lines between theoretical and practical knowledge and foster students' personal, intellectual, and social capacities that are in accordance with the vision of transdisciplinary education.

- *Rhizomatic learning*

  The idea of rhizomatic learning was proposed by Dave Cormier (2008) who was inspired by the concept of the rhizome, first posited by Deleuze and Guattari in *A Thousand Plateaus* (1987) as a symbol of nonhierarchical connectivity.[2] Cormier has extended Deleuze's and Guattari's concept of the rhizome to education by introducing the idea of rhizomatic learning, in which community becomes central to curriculum. The rhizomatic educational model (also known as the "community as curriculum" model) requires the creation of a specific context, within which the curriculum is constructed by all members of the learning community. In this model of learning, "the curriculum is not driven by predefined inputs from experts; it is constructed and negotiated in real time by the contributions of those engaged in the learning process. This community acts as the curriculum, spontaneously shaping, constructing, and reconstructing itself and the subject of its learning in the same way that the rhizome responds to changing environmental conditions" (Cormier 2008, Article 2).

- *Phronetic social science*

  Phronetic social science is a case-by-case approach to teaching advocated by Flyvbjerg (1998). This approach embraces mixed methodology unbound by disciplinary practices and uses "thick" analysis of the details of a studied phenomenon, from which more general insights can be gained. According to Flyvbjerg, "[t]he task of phronetic social science is to clarify and deliberate about the problems and risks we face and to outline how things may be done differently, in full knowledge that we cannot find ultimate answers to these questions or even a single version of what these questions are" (140).

- *Participatory action research as a pedagogical strategy*

  Participatory action research that has been used for curriculum design in higher education settings can be defined as a collaborative strategy to obtain empirically based insights with the primary goal of inspiring social transformations. Participatory action research as a pedagogical strategy uses a variety of educational activities tailored to a specific project in order to enhance students' participation and to generate practical knowledge within a particular field.

- *Applied research in education*

  Although educators teaching applied research might not describe their practices as transdisciplinary, many of them integrate knowledge and methodologies from multiple disciplines and involve stakeholders in their teaching process. Applied research in education aims to link research with action in order to generate new actionable knowledge that can help solve practical problems.

- *Translational studies*

  The field of translational research, which has progressed significantly in the last few decades in the health sciences, involves some of the same approaches as transdisciplinary research. It requires "translating" knowledge from theory to practice, implies the interaction of multiple disciplines and interweavement of different sectors and domains, and expects active community engagement. In the educational setting, the "bidirectional" manner, in which translational research moves—from basic research to practice-oriented research to population-based research and back—makes it particularly challenging for designing effective teaching programs in translational studies and might require developing customized curricula for students given the diversity of their educational backgrounds and research interests (Rubio et al. 2010).

- *Project-based and problem-based learning*

  Project-based learning is an action-oriented teaching method that places a strong emphasis on problem solving and critical thinking skills. It engages students into carefully designed projects and tasks that address authentic real-world questions. The idea of "learning by doing" can be traced back to the philosophical works of John Locke and Jean-Jacques Rousseau. It was further promoted by the Progressivists and revitalized in the 1950s in the works by Jean Piaget. Problem-based learning is a subset of project-based learning that is framed around a specific open-ended problem.

- *ICT-based learning*

  Information Communication Technology (ICT) is well suited to support and complement transdisciplinary learning because it promotes students' participatory and collaborative learning experience (Park and Son 2010). Ally (2004), who makes a connection between constructivist theory emphasizing critical thinking skills versus the mastery of facts and ICT-based learning, describes seven implications for online learning that can be used to design transdisciplinary courses:

1. "Learning should be an active process [in which] learners [should be able] to apply information in a practical situation.

2. Learners should construct their own knowledge rather than accepting knowledge given by the instructor.

3. Collaborative and cooperative learning should be encouraged to facilitate constructivist learning.

4. Learners should be given control of the learning process.

5. Learners should be given time and opportunity to reflect.

6. Learning should be made meaningful [and] include examples that relate to the learners so that they can make sense of information.

7. Learning should be interactive to promote high level learning and social presence, and help develop personal meaning." (18–20)

- *Situated learning*

  The theory of situated learning proposed by Lave and Wenger (1991) suggests that people learn best from each other through social activities in communities of practice and within specific "situated" contexts. Unlike students who are acquiring knowledge that is decontextualized from the "lived-in world" learning situations, such as working toward a degree in a classroom, students in the situated learning context learn in real-world settings through engagement in a community of practice formed by peers who are learning together, for example, during their internship in a hospital or a school.

The Uniqueness of Transdisciplinary Learning

> Learning is by its very nature transdisciplinary.
> —Moss, Osborn, and Kaufman (2003, 7)

What is actually unique about transdisciplinary learning? The answer to this question is not so clear-cut. A high level of integration and interactivity are the two characteristics that are regarded by the majority of scholars as the most distinguishing traits of transdisciplinary learning. Transdisciplinary learning starts from identifying a specific issue or problem, exploring it from multiple disciplinary angles in order to arrive at an integrative perspective on feasible solutions or improvement. In transdisciplinary learning, "integration becomes the purpose of education, not simply a tool" (Klein 2006, 14). Transdisciplinary education is also characterized by the highest level of learning interactivity that can be accomplished through the design of students' participatory framework, in which "teachers become interactive learning designers while students become knowledge producers" (Park and Son 2010, 84–85).

Various scholars have highlighted other characteristics of transdisciplinary learning that differentiates it from other types of learning. Nicolescu (1997) stipulates that transdisciplinary education "addresses the open totality of the human being and not just one of its components" and aims at achieving "equilibrium between analytic intelligence, feeling, and the body [to] reconcile effectiveness and affectivity." Along the same vein, Ertas et al. (2003) argue that in "the transdisciplinary educational model, students' characteristics, needs, interests, and personal learning processes are central to the learning experience [and that] these objectives are as important as the teaching of specific knowledge and skills" (Ertas et al. 2003, 6). These enact the notion of the four pillars of learning articulated by Jacques Delors et al. (1996)—learning to know, learning to do, learning to live together with, and learning to be—that determine the balance between thought and action and between self and others and validate and celebrate diverse ways of knowing, doing, experiencing, and being.

Davies (2009) believes that "the shift towards transdisciplinary learning is a shift in how we view the curriculum." He argues that a curriculum should enable students to "creatively move into, through, and across disciplines areas, in order to open meaning rather than be pinned down by [disciplinary] facts." From a transdisciplinary perspective, students should not be expected to simply do "Maths or English [but to see] how Maths and English connect to a topic, how the thinking in each area can be applied, and what sorts of questions these types of thinking ask." This stance is consistent with one of Nicolescu's main principles of transdisciplinarity, namely that it is "at once between the disciplines, across the different disciplines, and beyond all disciplines" (Nicolescu 2002, 44).

Tress, Tress, and Fry (2005) state that transdisciplinary learning "combines interdisciplinarity with a participatory approach" with the goal of generating "new knowledge and theory" (17). Park and Son (2010) echo this statement by saying that the key characteristic of transdisciplinary learning is the production of new knowledge through participatory collaboration "in which various levels of participation can control the overall quality of a conceptual framework and learning outcomes" (84).

Another unique characteristic of transdisciplinary learning is that it encompasses *all types of knowledge* about an issue or a question, including both academic and nonacademic knowledge. It draws together theories, methods, and concepts not only from parent disciplines but also from stakeholders' knowledge and lived experiences in order to explore deeply a topic or an issue and then transforms these into new knowledge. The uniqueness of transdisciplinary learning also lies in its striving for what Nicolescu (1997) describes as "the equilibrium between the exterior person and the interior person." He states that "[k]nowledge is neither exterior nor interior; it is simultaneously exterior and interior [and that] [t]he studies of the universe and the studies of the human being sustain one another" (2008, 9).

Links can also be made between transdisciplinary research as a collaborative enterprise and transdisciplinary learning as a synergetic experience. Both approaches presuppose an ethic of respect for the norms of a collectivity as well as for personal attributes and subjective experiences. This ethic is needed for establishing a common orientation toward a problem being solved and for a convergence of disparate views and perspectives necessary for finding solutions to the problem at hand. In the educational context, this approach implements the concept of the four pillars of learning articulated by Jacques Delors (1996) that determines the balance between thought and action and between self and others. Müller et al. (2005) compare transdisciplinary learning to a spiral, the cycle with no defined beginning or end, in which learning takes place through ongoing iterative interactions between internal interpretations and external actions. These views are also indicative of Schmitt's (2007) vision of transdisciplinary learning wherein students are "able to effectively communicate across disciplines, value other's expertise and knowledge, establish necessary relationships, ask important questions, integrate shared learning, and grow in self-confidence while successfully working with others."

Transdisciplinary learning also involves the application of mind habits that transcend disciplines and can be put to use across *any* subject matter. The distinguished educators Costa and Kallick (2009) have identified 16 "Habits of Mind" that can help students deal successfully with challenges, both in school and in the larger world. These Habits of Mind are "Persisting; Managing impulsivity; Listening with understanding and empathy; Thinking flexibly; Thinking about thinking (metacognition); Striving for accuracy; Questioning and posing problems; Applying past knowledge to new situations; Thinking and communicating with clarity and precision; Gathering data through all senses; Creating, imagining, and innovating; responding with wonderment and awe; Taking responsible risks; and finding humor" (Costa and Kallick 2009, X). The authors argue that these Habits of Mind are *transdisciplinary* in nature and by that they meant that "there is no 'subject matter' to the Habits of Mind; rather, they are applicable in *every* subject matter" (3).

McGregor (2015c) further asserts that transdisciplinary learning requires such "transformative mind habits" as "seeing patterns, using one's imagination, being able to explain abstractions, creating multidimensional models, playing with intellectual ideas, and pulling results together to generate solutions" (106). She believes that these mind habits become even more powerful when used in conjunction with the knowledge of boundary objects[3] that enable learners to "create links, bridges or modes of transcending borders so people can connect in reflective, knowledge generating communities, operating at the borders between disparate worlds" (Ibid.).

Other "habits of mind," mentioned in the literature on transdisciplinarity, that are required for effective transdisciplinary learning, include the abilities to manage complexity, adapt to change by modifying one's attitude and thinking, find a proper balance between breadth and depth of training, and collaborate with diverse groups of people. It is also imperative for students to develop competencies and attitudes needed to thrive in a collaborative environment, such as an aptitude for openness toward all plausible solutions and unintended side effects, a sense of social responsibility, negotiation and conflict resolution skills, and humanitarian and ethical attitudes.

Although fostering transdisciplinary habits of mind is an important goal for all learners in all fields, these habits of mind must be developed *in addition to* and *along with* specific in-depth disciplinary knowledge. As Nicolescu (2002) has stated, "The transdisciplinary method does not replace the methodology of each discipline, which remains as it is. Instead, the transdisciplinary method enriches each of these disciplines, by bringing them new and indispensable insights, which cannot be produced by disciplinary methods" (122).

The uniqueness of transdisciplinary learning has been well summarized by Davies (2009) who postulates that transdisciplinary learning helps people see problems in even more than three-dimensional depth because it "models much of the way we learn in the real world—facing real problems, seeking solutions, and crossing boundaries to find answers." Derry and Fischer (2005) proffer a similar argument, writing that "if the world of working and living relies on collaboration, creativity, definition and framing of complex problems—and if it requires dealing with uncertainty, change, and intelligence that is distributed across cultures, disciplines, and tools—then [higher education] programs should foster transdisciplinary competencies that prepare students for having meaningful and productive lives in such a world." The authors also argue that a transdisciplinary educational model is more suitable for graduate students because students must first acquire sufficient depth in their primary discipline in order to place disciplinary knowledge within a larger context and analyze and synthesize knowledge across disciplines. Rosenfield (1992) provides a similar reason for placing transdisciplinary education at the graduate level because a solid grounding in one's primary discipline is necessary for appreciating the contributions that other disciplines make to the problem being addressed.

The Correlation between Transdisciplinary Learning and Information Literacy

> *In-formation* carries time-honored considerations and content regarding the process of becoming. *Literacy* refers to our skillful and competent participation in it.
>   —Nathan Filbert (2016, 199)

Although teaching information literacy to transdisciplinary students can appear, at first glance, as an unfamiliar task of considerable challenge, information literacy is a concept that is already deeply rooted in transdisciplinarity.[4] Even though transdisciplinarity originated outside the library domain, both transdisciplinary learning and information literacy transcend disciplinary boundaries by seeking a similar goal through participatory collaboration. According to Nicolescu (2002), the primary goal of transdisciplinarity is "the understanding of the present world, of which one of the imperatives is the unity of knowledge" (44). While not identical, this goal mirrors closely that of information literacy that was described as an "overarching literacy essential for twenty-first century living" (Bruce 2004, 8) and as "a way of knowing through learning to engage with the landscapes which constitute our working, educational and everyday lives" (Lloyd 2006, 580). From this perspective, transdisciplinary learning depends upon and draws significantly from the core concepts of information literacy, which has been inextricably associated with the acquisition of critical thinking and critical reflection skills, preparing students to handle complex and unpredictable challenges, both in everyday life and workplace situations (Lloyd and Somerville 2006).

Much of transdisciplinary learning overlaps the areas that are at the heart of information literacy. The correlation between transdisciplinary learning and information literacy is especially evident in three areas that concern (1) location and use of information across different disciplines and subject fields, (2) acquisition of skills for lifelong learning, and (3) collaboration in the process of knowledge creation and sharing.

Shenton and Hay-Gibson (2011) assert that information literacy is "especially suited to transdisciplinary thought" (166) because "the information literate individual will have acquired the knowledge, skills and understanding necessary to find and use information on a wide range of subjects" (168). Similarly, Lloyd (2006) defines information literate people as those who are "engaged, enabled, enriched and embodied by social, procedural and physical information that constitutes an information universe. Information literacy is a way of knowing that universe" (195). She further postulates that information literacy should focus on broad informational "landscapes" that involve "complex contextualized practices" (570) rather than on teaching specific information-seeking skills. These statements clearly echo Nicolescu's definition of transdisciplinary learning as "the study of the universal" (Nicolescu 1998).

Given that transdisciplinarity is a phenomenon that is of relevance to any subject matter (as discussed earlier in this chapter), then librarians, who are information experts and have traditionally worked in and across disciplines, are already well equipped for supporting transdisciplinary learning because information is "ubiquitous in that it pertains to everything" (Levitan 1980, 244). While recognizing the importance of disciplinary knowledge, which is in accordance with the principles of transdisciplinarity, librarians are also used to crossing disciplinary borders and acting as "translators" by providing cross-disciplinary vocabulary and concept translations for students, thus offering them opportunities to see connections as well as differences among disciplines.

Finally, the recently introduced concepts of transliteracy (or metaliteracy) signify a move toward a holistic and participatory approach to the acquisition and communication of knowledge. Similar to transdisciplinarity, these concepts emphasize the transcendence of existing concepts and approaches. Transliteracy transcends the barriers between the academia and the wider community through social media networks and aims to "map *meaning* across different media" (Ipri 2010, 532; emphasis added). Metaliteracy informs and unifies multiple literacies (such as digital, visual, data, and media literacies) under a common framework.

A comparable pattern between transdisciplinary learning and information literacy can also be detected with regard to the acquisition of skills for lifelong learning. Furthermore, developing information literacy and transdisciplinary literacy requires similar cognitive abilities such as those for critical thinking and critical reflection. Just as transdisciplinary habits of mind are "essentially acontextual" because they can be put to use across different subjects and different situations (Shenton and Hay-Gibson 2011), so are information literacy skills that are not limited to the academic environment. Lifelong learning is at the heart of the transdisciplinary education and information literacy has been increasingly recognized as the foundation for lifelong learning that is "common to all disciplines, to all learning environments, and to all levels of education (Association of College and Research Libraries 2000). In *Alexandria Proclamation on Information Literacy and Lifelong Learning*, UNESCO (2005) asserted that "[i]nformation literacy lies at the core of lifelong learning [because it] empowers people in all walks of life to seek, evaluate, use and create information effectively to achieve their personal, social, occupational and educational goals."

More recent perspectives present an even more discernible shift to the holistic view of information literacy as an overarching skill set that can rightly claim its place as an essential component of transdisciplinary learning. In the *Framework for Information Literacy for Higher Education*, the Association of College & Research Libraries (ACRL 2015) continues this evolving vision in its attempt to reformulate its previous *Information Literacy Competency Standards for Higher Education* developed in 2000. The change of terminology used in the *Framework* is significant. Instead of defining information literacy as "the ability to locate, evaluate, and use effectively the needed information" (ACRL 2000), it is defined as "the set of integrated abilities encompassing the reflective discovery of information, the understanding of how information is produced and valued, and the use of information in creating new knowledge and participating ethically in communities of learning" (ACRL 2015). The *Framework* offers information literacy instruction a more advanced conceptual approach for leading information literacy efforts. At the same time, as argued by Filbert (2016), the *Framework* is still not strong enough to support transdisciplinary learning. Evidently, more research is needed in this area in order to "validate librarianship's transdisciplinary potential" (Ryan 2016, 199).

The inextricable link between transdisciplinary learning and information literacy is also revealed in their emphasis on collaboration and teamwork. Transdisciplinary learning is often discussed in terms of collaboration among multiple disciplinary experts, stakeholders, and other relevant participants. Similarly, information literacy is best accomplished through collaboration among library peers, faculty, and other professional experts. While the idea of information literacy as collaborative endeavor is not new, it has been primarily understood in terms of the partnership between librarians and disciplinary faculty who work together on accomplishing mutually desired learning outcomes for their students. To support transdisciplinary learning, information literacy should not be predicated solely on the involvement of disciplinary faculty but also involve the development of new partnerships. The unique place of academic librarians in the university who are themselves part of the multidisciplinary network of fellow librarians and have access to research resources within and across disciplines make them especially valuable transdisciplinary players and put them in an ideal position for supporting transdisciplinary learning.

Transdisciplining Information Literacy Instruction

Transdisciplining information literacy instruction presents unique challenges (and opportunities) for librarians. While librarians are in a good position to support students' learning across multiple contexts and perspectives, little research has been reported on how students develop transdisciplinary competencies in the library setting. Despite the conceptual appeal of transdisciplinarity, scholars have focused more heavily on interdisciplinary teaching and learning. However, publications offering ideas for teaching interdisciplinary information research processes is a good place to begin the exploration of models that can be transferred to designing transdisciplinary information literacy instruction. For example, Newby (2011) observes that a valuable framework for designing graduate courses in interdisciplinary programs can be provided by the categories of information-seeking behavior of academic scholars. Utilizing an understanding of information-seeking behaviors reported by library science literature (e.g., Ellis 1993; Foster 2004; Palmer 2001), Newby proposes the following elements for designing a course for graduate students in interdisciplinary programs:

Orientation. Becoming familiar with the culture and terminology of an unfamiliar discipline and understanding the organization of knowledge for this discipline as well as the organization of information in academic libraries and specific disciplinary databases.

Chaining/citation linking. Following references found in bibliographies as well as conducting citation searches in such databases as the Web of Science and some search engines, such as Google Scholar.

Browsing/probing. Exploring a semi-defined area of interest and determining networking mechanisms.

Monitoring. Keeping up with current research and knowledge of research fronts.

Consolidation and integration. Refining and sifting through information resources and knowing when enough information has been found (226).

Even though Newby writes about developing an information literacy course for interdisciplinary students, her proposed model can be successfully adopted for developing an introductory transdisciplinary information literacy instruction.

Newell's (2000) description of two "predictable mistakes" that result in a failed interdisciplinary course can also help librarians avoid these mistakes when teaching information literacy skills to transdisciplinary students:

- *Choosing a topic that is too broad*

  Newell argues that in order to present multiple disciplinary perspectives, a topic must be "delimited" to make sure that "the disciplines confront one another instead of talking past each other" (47).

- *Leaving disciplines implicit*

  Newell highlights the importance of the students' understanding of disciplines that contribute an appreciation of their "contrasting contributions" in order to integrate these contributions "into a more comprehensive understanding of the topic" (Ibid.).

Ertas et al. (2003) present a transdisciplinary model for engineering education in which instructors play the role of "mentors or guides [who] assist students in discovering, applying and understanding information, technical knowledge, and skills" (6). The authors provide concrete recommendations for student learning activities that can supply ideas for the delivery of transdisciplinary information literacy instruction. These activities include both independent projects and team projects that focus on accomplishing the project goal rather than on acquiring technical knowledge. Dold (2014) describes a hypothetical example of the situation, in which students in three behavioral health fields benefit from applying critical information literacy's transdisciplinary approach to problem solving. She suggests that the primary value of librarians in terms of teaching critical information literacy to transdisciplinary students lies in the librarians' ability "to understand the vocabulary of each field [and to] show the student where the disciplines overlap and where they diverge" (181).

Integrating transdisciplinarity in information literacy instruction is challenging but of critical importance if the library is to strengthen its status at a time when some are predicting that librarianship might fade away. Furthermore, it is a worthy area for librarians to break into new roles and responsibilities by targeting this area with their existing skills and simultaneously maintaining the library's core value as an evolving entity. Two of the greatest challenges facing librarians in providing support for transdisciplinary learners stems from the need to develop appropriate pedagogies and cultivate specific mind habits that will enable librarians to think and work across disciplinary, cultural, and sectorial boundaries. Students engaged in transdisciplinary learning require access to a large and complex mass of resources, including resource types that have not been traditionally introduced during information literacy sessions. Transdisciplinary students also require new information-seeking skills and strategies in identifying resources, key authors, and research trends outside their disciplines in order to work effectively on a research problem that can benefit from disparate viewpoints and methodologies of multiple disciplines. Likewise, becoming familiar with an unknown disciplinary culture and its language is one of the most formidable challenges for librarians who, too, will have to leave the relative safety of their subject expertise for what Donald Schön (1995) called the "swampy lowlands" of real-world problem solving.

If we accept that information literacy has a deep connection with transdisciplinarity, then we can envision transdisciplinary information literacy as a concept that offers a solid theoretical footing for transdisciplinary learning. Ideally, there should be little to separate the two. By understanding both the concept of transdisciplinarity as a whole and the differences between various approaches to transdisciplinary learning, librarians will be better equipped to choose the type of instruction best suited for their students.

In practice, designing information literacy instruction from a transdisciplinary perspective can take many forms, most of which will likely demand high levels of interaction, flexible delivery, and various types of synchronous and asynchronous communication. The emerging transdisciplinary pedagogies discussed earlier do not provide a clear path for development of information literacy instruction for transdisciplinary learning. Ideally, a transdisciplinary course should be co-taught with a librarian and an instructor who is already involved with, or has an interest in, transdisciplinary research.

The framework for transdisciplinary information literacy and effective pedagogical strategies for its implementation are yet to be developed. Not only will this concept and these strategies lead to the enhancement of student learning, but they will also provide librarians with a rich assortment of opportunities for working collaboratively with faculty on curriculum development and long-term assessments, thus making librarians valuable partners in transdisciplinary teaching and learning processes.

Notes

1. Although there is no systematic documentation supporting the following argument, the author suggests formulating the primary learning objective of transdisciplinary education as the development of students' ability to take a

specific problem as a starting point, then explore it from different disciplinary perspectives, and arrive at an integrative viewpoint on possible solutions. In this context, one of the primary learning outcomes includes the ability to integrate information harvested from different sources for the purpose of creating new knowledge through dialogs among disciplines and in collaboration with multiple experts, peers, and stakeholders.

2. The botanical term "rhizome" as a metaphor for transdisciplinarity has also been used to describe the rhizomatic nature of transdisciplinarity. The concept of the rhizome and how it applies to transdisciplinarity is discussed in more detail in Chapter 2 of this book.

3. Derry and Fischer (2005) define boundary objects as features that serve as communication interfaces among members of different disciplinary communities. Examples of boundary objects include products, ideas, standards, or designs that "cluster" at the edges of community borders and have a potential to connect people across the borders.

4. Not surprisingly, both concepts—transdisciplinarity and information literacy—have emerged at about the same time, in the early 1970s.

Suggested Readings

Filbert, Nathan W. "Framing the Framework: The Rigorous Responsibilities of Library and Information Science." *Reference & User Services Quarterly* 55, no. 3 (2016): 199–202. https://journals.ala.org/rusq/article/view/5929/7517.

Klein, Julie Thompson. *Finding Interdisciplinary Knowledge and Information.* In *Interdisciplinary Studies Today* (*New Directions for Teaching and Learning*, vol. 58), edited by Julie Thompson Klein and William G. Doty, 7–33. San Francisco, CA: Jossey-Bass, 1994.

Knapp, Jeffrey A. "Plugging the "Whole": Librarians as Interdisciplinary Facilitators." *Library Review* 61, no. 3 (2012): 199–214.

McGregor, Sue L. T. *Enriching Responsible Living Curricula with Transdisciplinarity.* In *Responsible Living*, edited by Robert Didham, Declan Doyle, Jørgen Klein, and Victoria W. Thoresen, 97–111. New York: Springer International Publishing, 2015c.

Newby, Jill. "Entering Unfamiliar Territory: Building an Information Literacy Course for Graduate Students in Interdisciplinary Areas." *Reference & User Services Quarterly* 50, no. 3 (2011): 224–229.

Nicolescu, Basarab. *The Transdisciplinary Evolution of Learning: Condition for Sustainable Development.* Bulletin Interactif du Centre International de Recherches et Études transdisciplinaires. CIRET, 1998. http://ciret-transdisciplinarity.org/bulletin/b12c8.php.

Searing, Susan E. "Meeting the Information Needs of Interdisciplinary Scholars: Issues for Administrators of Large University Libraries." *Library Trends* 45, no. 2 (1996): 315–342.

CHAPTER FIFTEEN

Becoming a Transdisciplinary Librarian: From Catching Up to Leading the Way

We are drowning in information, while starving for wisdom. The world henceforth will be run by synthesizers, people able to put together the right information at the right time, think critically about it, and make important choices wisely.

—E. O. Wilson (1998b, 294)

Currently, no study has identified the areas of knowledge and skill sets that librarians need or will need in the future to better support transdisciplinary research. It is, however, reasonable to assume that a traditional mix of core skills and competencies expected of any academic librarian (e.g., proficiency in the use of information discovery tools, expertise in knowledge organization, and skills in information literacy) already make librarians uniquely qualified for providing research assistance to transdisciplinary scholars, as long as these skills and competencies are continuously honed and kept up to date. An array of "top skills for tomorrow's librarians" (Schwartz 2016), which represent both a continuation and transformation of librarians' traditional practice, coupled with the newer skills required for supporting eResearch (Martin 2014), will further equip librarians with the intellectual confidence equal to that of their faculty peers and enable them to cope with the challenges occurring within their profession. A discussion of these necessary skills and competencies is outside the scope of this chapter. Instead, this chapter focuses on a broader picture by attempting to identify attitudes and mind-sets which are more directly, although not exclusively, related to supporting transdisciplinary research and which a transdisciplinary librarian needs to cultivate in addition to his or her regular professional competencies. True transformation must, in Miller's (2015) words, "take into account the whole person and individuals' social structures." This view is consistent with the concept of the "transdisciplinary attitude," which encompasses "the open totality of the human being" (Nicolescu 1998) and which is "always oriented towards the actualization of [one's] interior potentialities" (Nicolescu 2002, 133).

The Transdisciplinary Attitude

> Transdisciplinarity is simultaneously an attitude and a form of action.
>
> —Julie Thomson Klein (2004, 521)

The notion of a "transdisciplinary attitude" was introduced by philosopher Joseph Kockelmans in his essay "Why Interdisciplinarity?" (1979), which was included in the seminal collection of essays by participants in a postdoctoral seminar on interdisciplinarity held at Pennsylvania State University (1975–1976).[1] In his essay, Kockelmans describes transdisciplinarity not as a conceptual construct but as a particular attitude which is "oriented toward comprehending the contributions of each discipline from the perspective of man's search for meaning, which itself is suprascientific because inherently human" (153–154).

The notion of the transdisciplinary attitude was formalized by Freitas, Nicolescu, and Morin (1994) in *The Charter of Transdisciplinarity*, which described the three fundamental characteristics of the transdisciplinary attitude as follows:

> *Rigor, opening* and *tolerance* are the fundamental characteristics of the transdisciplinary attitude and vision. *Rigor* in argument, taking into account of all existing data, is the best defense against possible distortions. *Opening* involves an acceptance of the unknown, the unexpected and the unpredictable. *Tolerance* implies acknowledging the right to ideas and truths opposed to our own. [italics in original]

Nicolescu (1997) has further developed the idea of the transdisciplinary attitude, which he based on the idea of "the equilibrium between the exterior person and the interior person" and is characterized by "a new tolerance" that requires "putting into practice the transcultural, transreligious, transpolitic, and transnational vision." Klein echoed this idea by describing transdisciplinary attitude as "a general attitude of openness and a capacity for collaboration" (2000, 4) that is "transcultural, translational, and encompasses ethics, spirituality, and creativity" (2004, 516). In *Manifesto of Transdisciplinarity* (2002), Nicolescu describes the transdisciplinary attitude as "the individual or social capacity to preserve a constant, unchanging direction, no matter what the complexity of the situation or the hazards of life. On the social level, this direction is that of the flow of information crossing the different levels of Reality, whereas on the individual level, it is that of the flow of consciousness crossing the different levels of perception" (83).

Other scholars have offered their own interpretation of the transdisciplinary attitude. Becker et al. (1997) argue that the transdisciplinary attitude requires "theoretical, conceptual and methodological reorientations with respect to core concepts of the various . . . disciplines" (42) with the goal of achieving a transdisciplinary culture of cooperation. Benatar (2000) describes the transdisciplinary attitude as the state of being "sensitized" to a broader view of education and practice. Similarly, Klein (2009) writes that the transdisciplinary attitude is the one that is "capable of sensitizing all social actors to more comprehensive, inclusive modes of knowing and acting in the world" (40).

These varied views share the overarching idea of an "equilibrium" between the individual being and the social being, which are "two facets of one and the same world" (Nicolescu 2002, 89). In librarianship, as in other professions, this equilibrium refers to a balanced interaction between the dynamics of the interior life and external life, which enables a transdisciplinary dialog between the diversity of people and domains that is necessary for the advancement of knowledge. To achieve this equilibrium, one must discover the "bridges" that link "beings and things at the deepest level" (Nicolescu 2002, 89), upon which a true transdisciplinary dialog is founded. Only by having the transdisciplinary attitude, we can discover "our own place in this world" that is "one of the aspects of what is called happiness" (Ibid, 88–89).

Scholars of transdisciplinarity agree that the transdisciplinary attitude must be cultivated. Nicolescu (1997, 2002) envisions the transdisciplinary attitude as a conscious stand, a potential, which can be learned but which demands a high degree of personal commitment, or it "can forever remain non-actualized, absent in life and in act" (1997). Klein (2009) states that the transdisciplinary attitude must be continuously "brought about."

Claverie (2009) believes that the transdisciplinary attitude relies on the ongoing cognitive effort on the part of a researcher and requires constant motivation so that the researcher does not "fall back on reassuring habits of disciplines" (6). Augsburg (2014) argues that "one is not born a transdisiciplinarian" but "becomes transdisciplinary" through the cultivation of certain habits of mind and transdisciplinary "virtues."

The idea of the transdisciplinary attitude is closely related to the notion of a "transdisciplinary individual." Bruce et al. (2004) argue that the "ideal" personality traits of a transdisciplinary individual include flexibility, open-mindedness, creativity, adaptability, communication and collaboration skills, along with a curiosity about other disciplines and the willingness to learn from them. Godemann (2008) describes the traits of a transdisciplinary individual related to the capacity for knowledge integration, including the capacity for self-reflexivity, seeing beyond the boundaries of a familiar discipline, and openness to new ideas and processes.

In *Becoming Transdisciplinary*, Augsburg (2014) provides a good summary of skills and "virtues" of a "transdisciplinary individual" based on several studies that have emerged during the last two decades, focusing specifically of the insights from Giri (2002), Jacobs and Nienaber (2011), and Wall and Shankar (2008). The following list, based on Augsburg's summary, highlights the skills and traits that are more or less unique to those individuals working effectively in transdisciplinary teams:

- Ability to build networks within "unfamiliar" realms
- "Capacity to engage in meaningful dialogue, while suspending one's own point of view" (Augsburg 2014, 240)
- Having "a powerful societal conscience and awareness, [being] able to think in complex, interlinked manner, and be able to relate to the logic of complexity" (Ibid., 241)
- Inwardly felt need for points of views from others
- Being a coproducer of hybrid knowledge
- Ability to acknowledge the pain inherent in abandoning one's intellectual comfort zone
- Interperspectivity[2]
- Having a modest "positionality"[3]

Giri (2002) has expressed a more philosophical viewpoint on what it takes to become transdisciplinary. Drawing upon the insights from Sunder Rajan, Heidegger, the Hinduism, and Buddhism, she has created a list of transdisciplinary "virtues" (or "arts"), among which are the art of dialog, the art of authentic embeddedness, the art of acknowledged dependence, and the art of abandonment. The art of dialog enables one to engage in a meaningful conversation, while letting go or suspending one's own point of view as the only valid point of view. It helps overcome disciplinary divides in approaching problem solving, encourages the interaction of disciplines, and prepares the ground for the holistic analysis of a problem in order to solve it. The art of authentic embeddedness presupposes a firm grounding in one's "home" discipline. For Giri, being embedded in one's discipline leads to the widening of one's horizons such as the realization that there are "diversities and differences" in one's "disciplinary homes"—"homes whose doors and windows are ever open to the world"[4] (108). The art of acknowledged dependence is based on Giri's view of transdisciplinarity as "a field of relationship," in which disciplines and actors depend on each other, and this dependence enables each actor to acknowledge "what the self owes to the other" (113). The art of abandonment (or the art of "distantiation," in Giri's words) draws inspiration from Martin Heidegger, who believed that human beings must abandon their homes and move in strange lands in order to discover the meaning of life, and from the Indian perspective of *vanaprastha*, according to which one should abandon one's accumulated power and wealth in search for truth. The art of abandonment, as it applies to transdisciplinarity, requires one to have the courage to abandon the familiar grounds of one's home discipline in order "to discover the unexpected truths of reality on the borderland and wilderness" (9).

Transdisciplinarity as a Mind-Set

The most important task today is, perhaps, to learn to think in the new way.

—Gregory Bateson (1972, 462)

Transdisciplinarity has also been envisioned as a certain mind-set that includes the capacity for transdisciplinary thinking, combinatorial creativity, the balance between disciplinary depth and transdisciplinary breadth, and commitment to lifelong learning.

Transdisciplinary Thinking

Nobody is from just one place. Our borders are not primarily physical: they are, above all, symbolic.

—Ricardo Vieira (2014, 9)

Transdisciplinary thinking assumes that "everything is dependent on everything else, everything is connected, and nothing is separate" (Ouspensky 2001, 22). It is manifested in a capacity to establish conceptual bridges between disciplines, identify links and commonalities between seemingly disparate approaches used by different disciplines, and move creatively across knowledge domains. This type of thinking emerges from the researcher's area of subject expertise and then transcends it by eschewing traditional distinctions between science and art, theory and practice, academic and nonacademic knowledge. As Nicolescu (2002) puts it, "Transdisciplinarity can be understood as being both the science and the art of discovering . . . bridges . . . between different areas of knowledge and between different beings" (89) and "between the different disciplines, and between these disciplines and meanings and our interior capacities" (133). This capacity for discovering and establishing bridges enables one to see that knowledge domains are not separate or disconnected but related to each other and interdependent. The idea of transdisciplinary thinking can be linked to Deleuze's and Guattari's (1987) concept of the rhizome (discussed in Chapters 1 and 15 of this book) and Amselle's (1998) concept of "connections" that emphasizes the open, dynamic, and interdependent nature of human cultures. Vieira (2014) describes the process of cross-fertilization of ideas as cultural "metissage"—the continuous hybridization of knowledge and ideas across boundaries—and argues that this process must be actively sought and cultivated so that one can discover and create new knowledge (Vieira 2014).

Mishra, Koehler, and Henriksen (2010), drawing upon Root-Bernstein (1996) and Root-Bernstein and Root-Bernstein (1999), who studied key cross-disciplinary cognitive skills, propose the following seven key cognitive tools that enable people to think effectively across domains: perceiving, patterning, abstracting, embodied thinking, modeling, play, and synthesizing. The authors argue that while these cognitive tools "emerge out of disciplinary practices," they are "universal in their application" (27). Balsamo and Mitcham (2010) identified five mind habits for interdisciplinary practice that can be applied to transdisciplinary practice:

- *"Intellectual generosity.* A genuine acknowledgement of the work of others. This should be explicitly expressed to collaborators as well as mentioned via citation practices. Showing appreciation for other ideas in face-to-face dialogue and throughout a collaborative process stimulates intellectual risk-taking and creativity.

- *Intellectual confidence.* A belief that one has something important to contribute. Confidence avoids boastfulness and includes a commitment to accountability for the quality of a collaboration. Everyone's contribution to a collaboration needs to be reliable, rejecting short cuts and guarding against intellectual laziness.

- *Intellectual humility.* A recognition that one's knowledge is partial, incomplete, and can always be extended and revised. This is a quality that allows people to admit they do not know something without suffering loss of confidence or self-esteem.

- *Intellectual flexibility.* The ability to change one's perspective, especially based on new insights from others. This can include a capacity for play, for suspending judgment and imagining other ways of being in the world and other worlds to be within.

- *Intellectual integrity.* The exercise of responsible participation. Such a habit serves as a basis for the development of trust, and is a quality that compels colleagues to bring their best work and thinking to collaborative efforts." (269)

Combinatorial Creativity

The scientist needs an artistically creative imagination.

—Max Planck

The person's capacity to think effectively across domains has been connected to one's ability to generate creative ideas (Caper 1996; Feinstein 2006; Root-Bernstein 1996; Root-Bernstein and Root-Bernstein, 1999; Simonton 1999, 2000, 2003). Henriksen, Mishra, and Fisser (2016) define creativity as "a process of developing something that is novel, effective and whole (NEW)" (35). The importance of creative abilities has become especially apparent in recent years. Pink (2006) writes:

> Today, the defining skills of the previous era—the "left brain" capabilities that powered the Information Age—are necessary but no longer sufficient. And the capabilities we once disdained or thought frivolous—the "right brain" qualities of inventiveness, empathy, joyfulness, and meaning—increasingly will determine who flourishes and who flounders. (3)

Creativity has been unanimously considered in literature as an essential ability for transdisciplinarians who are involved in complex, multidimensional problem-solving processes. Montuori (2008a) speaks of the joy of transdisciplinary inquiry, a process that is mysterious, creative, and exciting but requiring hard work and psychological risk. He describes it as "a way of travelling along the web of connections, to explore the myriad relationship that connect us to the world and ultimately make up who we are" (18).

In recent decades, creativity has been seen as having a "combinatorial" nature (Eagleman 2011; Henriksen and Mishra 2015; Henriksen, Mishra, and the Deep-Play Research Group 2014; Popova 2012; Root-Bernstein and Root-Bernstein 1999; Simonton (2000, 2003, 2004). Henriksen and Mishra (2015) define combinatorial creativity as "a mindset that thinks across different disciplines and experiences, in order to connect ideas for new inspiration and construction" (7). Combinatorial creativity arises from a "rich personal micro-culture" (Popova 2012), which consists of a person's life experiences, avocations, and cultural, intellectual, and aesthetic interests. In turn, this "mental pool of resources" (Henriksen and Mishra 2015) encourages and inspires new combinations of ideas and provides content for making comparisons and drawing analogies. As Steve Jobs famously summed it up in an interview (Wolf 1995), "Creativity is just connecting things." Combinatorial creativity is similar to transdisciplinary thinking, which aims at discovering interconnections between disciplines and building "bridges" between scholarly discourses in order to enhance an understanding of a particular problem or issue.

Root-Bernstein (1996) and Henriksen and Mishra (2015) have demonstrated a strong connection between professional and personal creativity of highly accomplished people and how their personal creative endeavors (such as hobbies and artistic pursuits) contribute to their creativity in their professional lives by adding variety and dynamism to their work. Miller (1998) considers personal creative outlets as an essential part of a balanced psychology.

Multipotentiality (i.e., avoiding excessive task specialization and over-commitment to a single professional function) can also increase one's creative potential. Plucker and Zabelina (2009) write that "someone who focuses too tightly for long periods of time on a particular task is likely to experience functional fixedness" (9). Plucker and Beghetto (2004) believe that a flexible position between specificity and generality in which a person moves between positions "as the task or problem of the moment dictates" is optimal for creative production. Nicolescu (1998) makes a similar point when he writes that "every profession should be an authentically woven occupation, an occupation which would bind together in the interior of human beings threads linking them to other occupations. Of course, it is not simply a question of acquiring several competencies at the same time but of creating a flexible, interior core that could quickly provide access to another occupation should it become necessary or desirable."

Transdisciplinary Literacy

We must, in other words, become adept at learning.
                                                    —Donald Schön (1973, 28)

Just as a transdisciplinary researcher must maintain a balance between disciplinary depth and transdisciplinary breadth to address multidimensional research problems, a transdisciplinary librarian must maintain a balance between specialization and wider knowledge. Specialization refers, first and foremost, to having a comprehensive expertise in the library and information science as a discipline in its own right that enables a librarian to handle competently a wide range of research queries. Wider knowledge refers to developing complementary knowledge in other disciplines that enables a librarian to add greater depth of understanding when working with transdisciplinary researchers. This idea of a transdisciplinary librarian as both a polymath and a specialist is consistent with the view of transdisciplinarians as "pluri-disciplinary experts" (Nowotny, Scott, and Gibbons 2001). Ziman (1999) reiterated this idea by introducing the term "transdisciplinary ethos" that places emphasis on general scientific scholarship that can help researchers familiarize themselves with each other's practices and perspectives.

While formal educational opportunities can, to some degree, cultivate in librarians a wide breadth of knowledge, a continuous self-directed education is essential for becoming "transdisciplinary literate." Transdisciplinary literacy encompasses, at the very least, basic awareness of the developments in the life, physical and social sciences, and the humanities, coupled with the knowledge of key transdisciplinary concepts, trends, and practices. This knowledge will ensure that the transdisciplinary librarian remains relevant and competent even without a formal educational background in other disciplines.

Transdisciplinary librarians can self-educate themselves in a number of ways. Hickey and Arlen (2002) recommend that librarians regularly review materials in a broader call number range than the one normally associated with the librarian's area of responsibility. Browsing current issues of major scholarly journals can also alert librarians about emergent areas in cross-disciplinary research. Westbrook (2003) urges librarians to learn about the research agendas of interdisciplinary faculty members at one's institution and become aware of the wide range of theories and methodologies they use. Campus-wide or departmental publications can serve as a valuable source for information about pertinent transdisciplinary research projects, teaching, activities, and initiatives.

RSS feeds and social bookmarking have been suggested as tools for following blogs, book reviews, news, and tables of contents from relevant journals (Farkas 2007; Knapp 2010). Knapp (2010) recommends librarians to read—rigorously and regularly—periodicals written for educated audience such as *The New Yorker* and *Wired*. He cautions librarians against reading scholarly periodicals in disciplines, in which they are not experts. He states that "few, if any, librarians, have [sufficient] subject specialist expertise in all the disciplines that frequently come in contact with others" in cross-disciplinary studies (59).

Miller (2011) believes that the task of "keeping up" should be perceived as a "collective endeavor" rather than "an independent obligation" (3). She argues that the idea of communities of practice introduced by Lave and Wenger (1991) and further developed by Wenger, McDermott, and Snyder (2002)[5] offers information professionals a conceptual framework for developing and sustaining both general and subject-specific expertise, shifting more easily between their "generalist and specialist identities" (3), and "[supporting] the growth and development of each other's general, disciplinary, or interdisciplinary knowledge" (4) as well as for fostering the creation of tools and infrastructure for continuing professional development. In a similar vein, Knapp (2010) maintains that librarians should "cultivate a social dimension in their work" (60) to engage in discussion and information exchange with their peers with regard to developments in cross-disciplinary knowledge.

Notes

1. Nicolescu (2002), on the other hand, traces the idea of the transdisciplinary attitude to an Argentinian poet Roberto Juarroz who, Nicolescu believes, introduced the term in 1991.

2. For Giri (2002), the idea of "interperspectivity" stems from the views of an Indian philosopher Sunder Rajan: "[f]or Sunder Rajan, 'each perspective or point of view is such only as a member of a community of points of view; this is a community and not a collection, for each perspective, from within its own resources, refers to the possibility of others'" (105).

3. For Jacobs and Nienaber (2011), having "modest positionality" means adopting a humble attitude toward "the immensity of knowledge" and being able to admit that "it is impossible to ever perfectly solve or understand an issue completely. The pursuit of knowledge is always imperfect. Similarly there is never a perfect solution to a problem" (674).

4. A similar idea is expressed by Margaret Somerville (2000) who writes: ". . . just as international travel is not a permanent departure from our own home base and can give us new perspectives, insights, and solutions to difficulties we

face in our home countries, transdisciplinary activity is not an abandonment of our disciplines and should enrich our disciplinary activities rather than weaken, vulgarize, or detract from these, as it is often feared and sometimes simply assumed it will do" (98).

5. Wenger, McDermott, and Snyder (2002) define a community of practice as "a unique combination of three fundamental elements: a domain of knowledge, which defines a set of issues; a community of people who care about this domain; and the shared practice that they are developing to be effective in their domain" (27).

Suggested Readings

Augsburg, Tanya. "Becoming Transdisciplinary: The Emergence of the Transdis-
      ciplinary Individual." *World Futures* 70, no. 3–4 (2014): 233–247.
Giri, Ananta Kumar. "The Calling of a Creative Transdisciplinarity." *Futures* 34,
      no. 1 (2002): 103–115.
Montuori, Alfonso. "The Joy of Inquiry." *Journal of Transformative Education* 6,
      no. 1 (2008): 8–26.
Wenger, Etienne. *Communities of Practice: Learning, Meaning, and Identity.* New York,
      NY: Cambridge University Press, 2000.

Conclusion: Looking Ahead

Transdisciplinarity can no longer be avoided.
—Masini Eleonora Barbieri (2000, 124)

This book has provided a synoptic overview of the emerging field of transdisciplinarity as a novel mode of research and a new way of looking at the relationship between knowledge and society that are profoundly impacting and altering disciplinary epistemologies. It is clear that transdisciplinarity is changing the face of research and can lead to significant advances in producing more effective solutions for real-life problems. How well the libraries will respond to the undisputed growth of transdisciplinarity will have a direct impact on how effective transdisciplinary research will be performed in the future. Once again, libraries enter into an uncertain and demanding territory as they are faced with the challenges that impact multiple levels of library operations.

While transdisciplinarity presents these significant challenges for libraries, it also represents, in many ways, a continuation of librarians' traditional practice. As Knapp (2010) states, it is "a niche in academia that librarians are uniquely qualified to fill" (59). It is also an area that "should not be feared or avoided" (Ibid.) because supporting transdisciplinarity can be "a matter of simply identifying the obstacles [that] scholars face, and applying the principles of librarianship in order to remove those obstacles" (Knapp 2012, 209).

Transdisciplinarity also presents a transformation of librarians' traditional practice because it requires the cultivation of attitudes and habits of mind that are similar to those expected of transdisciplinary scholars themselves. These attitudes and habits of mind should be a required, rather than desirable, qualification in a transdisciplinary librarian's portfolio. While transdisciplinarity offers librarians an opportunity to elevate their status and profile beyond competent "helpers" into trusted partners in collaborative "researchship" (Maguire 2012), this can only be achieved if scholars and librarians work together as intellectual equals. Hopefully, this book has provided insights into this area that will help librarians create services that foster transdisciplinary research at their own institutions. In turn, enhanced research support for transdisciplinary efforts will provide librarians with a rich assortment of opportunities for collaboration that can forge a truly collegiate relationship between researchers and librarians. As Klein (2008) has predicted, "Ultimately, the challenge will be to advance the case of transdisciplinarity as both knowledge and action, not one or the other" (64).

Annotated Bibliography

While far from being exhaustive, this bibliography aims at making the discourse of transdisciplinarity more visible and more organized for interested readers who want to broaden their knowledge base in this area. This bibliography includes English-language monographs that can serve as the foundation for understanding the concept of transdisciplinarity. It also includes special issues of journals dedicated to the discussion of transdisciplinarity and key websites containing important resources that did not find a ready niche in more traditional publications.

This bibliography is organized into four sections:

1. Essential references
2. Selected publications on transdisciplinarity
3. Journal special issues with transdisciplinary themes
4. Key websites

Essential References

Apostel, Leo, et al. (editors). *Interdisciplinarity: Problems of Teaching and Research in Universities*. Paris: Organisation for Economic Co-operation and Development, 1972.

This seminal work is based on proceedings of the First International Seminar on Interdisciplinarity held in 1970 at the University of Nice, France, and jointly sponsored by the Organization of Economic Cooperation and Development (OECD) and the French Ministry of Higher Education. This seminar and the publication resulting from it became not only a widely cited authority on inter- and transdisciplinarity but also a major event in the history of transdisciplinarity. They provided a framework for new thinking about teaching and research beyond and across disciplinary boundaries and they stressed the need for researchers, and research and educational organizations to modify their approach to knowledge production. The term "transdisciplinarity" was introduced at this seminar in order to distinguish transdisciplinarity from multidisciplinarity and interdisciplinarity.

Freitas, Lima, Basarab Nicolescu, and Edgar Morin. *Charter of Transdisciplinarity*. http://inters.org/Freitas-Morin-Nicolescu-Transdisciplinarity (accessed June 12, 2016).

The *Charter of Transdisciplinarity* was produced during the First World Congress of Transdisciplinarity held in 1994 in Convento da Arrabida, Portugal. The *Charter* was drafted and signed by the Congress's editorial committee, which included an artist Lima de Freitas, a quantum physicist Basarab Nicolescu, and a philosopher and sociologist Edgar Morin. This *Charter* contains 14 articles that describe "the fundamental principles of the community of transdisciplinary researchers" and refer to the notions of multiple levels of reality and the Hidden Third, Logic of the included middle, and the complexity of the world, which were further developed by Nicolescu in his *Manifesto of Transdisciplinarity* (2002) and in his later works.

Gibbons, Michael, Camille Limoges, Helga Nowotny, Simon Schwartzman, Peter Scott, and Martin Trow. *The New Production of Knowledge: The Dynamics of Science and Research in Contemporary Societies*. Los Angeles, CA: Sage, 1994.

Written in the form of reflective essays, this book is still one of the key references of transdisciplinarity discourse. Co-authored by an international team of scholars, whose professional and academic backgrounds were in the social and policy sciences, this book presents an innovative approach to research that works across the barriers between science and society. The authors point to the need for a new approach to knowledge production that should not be limited to the sciences, technology, and medicine but should also involve experts from government, industry, and the private sector and also extend to the humanities and arts. They argued that besides the traditional disciplinary production of knowledge (which they called Mode 1) that has little need for collaboration with nonscientists, there is another form of knowledge production (which they called Mode 2) that transcends the boundaries between science and society, integrates disciplinary paradigms, and is strongly sensible to societal needs. The ideas presented in this book were further developed by the same authors in their second joint publication *Re-thinking Science: Knowledge and the Public in an Age of Uncertainty* (2001).

Nicolescu, Basarab. *Manifesto of Transdisciplinarity*. Albany, NY: SUNY Press, 2002.

In his *Manifesto,* Nicolescu presented a new visionary way of thinking about knowledge and inquiry and promoted prescriptive ideas for making revolutionary changes in knowledge creation. He stated the goal of transdisciplinarity as "the understanding of the present world, of which one of the imperatives is the unity of knowledge" (44) and stressed that the transdisciplinary methodology did not replace disciplinary methodologies, nor did it strive to master multiple disciplines but rather complemented and enriched them with "new and indispensable insights" (122). The *Manifesto* encapsulated Nicolescu's methodology of transdisciplinarity into three axioms (or three "pillars"): multiple levels of reality and the Hidden Third; the logic of the included middle; and the complexity of the world. For Nicolescu, these three "pillars" of transdisciplinarity revealed coherence among the different levels of reality, accounted for inconsistencies and contradictions, and enabled a more comprehensive understanding of complexity. Originally published in France in 1996, the *Manifesto* was later republished in Romania, Portugal, Brazil, Syria, Mexico, and the United States.

Nowotny, Helga, Peter Scott, and Michael Gibbons. *Re-thinking Science: Knowledge and the Public in an Age of Uncertainty.* Cambridge, UK: Polity, 2001.

In this book, the authors continued developing an idea presented in their earlier book, *The New Production of Knowledge* (Gibbons et al. 1994), the idea about the need for a much closer relationship between knowledge production and society. They argued that despite the evidence that a more dynamic interaction between science and society leads to a more contextualized, more socially relevant knowledge production, the view about a one-way communication flow from science to society still persists. They proposed an open dynamic framework for rethinking science that they base on four conceptual pillars: (1) the nature of Mode-2 knowledge production, which was the focus of the authors' previous work; (2) the development of conditions that are more conducive to the production of "socially robust knowledge," which is influenced by social knowledge and continuously tested; (3) the incorporation of science into the *agora*, a new public space, which consists of "highly-articulated, well-educated population"; and (4) the emergence of socially distributed expertise, in which authority is more widely "diffused through society" and includes knowledge and expertise not only of scientists and researchers but also of individuals from other parts of society. The authors described these emergent trends during the last half-century and pursued a hypothesis (a "conclusion," in their words) about a new kind of science (which they called "contextualized science") that was emerging due to the continuing process of coevolution of science and society, which is characterized by their closer, more dynamic interaction.

Selected Publications on Transdisciplinarity

Bergmann, Matthias, Thomas Jahn, Tobias Knobloch, Wolfgang Krohn, Christian Pohl, Engelbert Schramm, and Ronald C. Faust. *Methods for Transdisciplinary Research: A Primer for Practice*. Frankfurt/New York: Campus Verlag, 2012.

This book is the result of many years of transdisciplinary research work during which methods and tools for knowledge integration, quality standards, and evaluation criteria were analyzed for several transdisciplinary projects. The book describes and compares methods of knowledge integration and provides researchers with theoretical knowledge for conceptualizing and executing transdisciplinary research as well as practical examples of carrying out actual problem-oriented research tasks. First published in 2010 in Germany and later translated into English in 2012, this book is now considered an indispensable guide for transdisciplinary scholars and educators.

Brown, Valerie A., John Alfred Harris, and Jacqueline Y. Russell. *Tackling Wicked Problems through the Transdisciplinary Imagination*. London, UK: Earthscan, 2010.

This book emerged through a series of informal seminars conducted under the auspices of the Australian National University in Canberra. Twenty-one scholars from diverse fields and disciplines proposed a framework for transdisciplinary inquiries into complex societal and environmental problems and provided a strong set of practical examples for tackling "wicked problems" that the editors define as "complex issue[s] that [defy] complete definition, for which there can be no final solution, since any resolution generates further issues, and where solutions are not true or false or good or bad, but the best that can be done at the time" (4). Even though the authors of this fascinating volume come from different backgrounds, all demonstrate a shared commitment to the idea of "transdisciplinary imagination," which they believe is essential in decision-making with regard to "wicked problems" as well as in dealing with "paradox, uncertainty and complexity" (5) and overcoming "the current cultural limitations in the way that we think" (Ibid.).

Gibbs, Paul (editor). *Transdisciplinary Professional Learning and Practice*. Cham, Switzerland: Springer International Publishing, 2015.

This book brings together the voices of 17 scholars from 3 continents and a wide range of disciplinary backgrounds and practices who offer their unique perspectives on the application of transdisciplinarity in professional practice, pedagogy, and research. The purpose of this book is to present transdisciplinarity as an educative process and to demonstrate that disciplinarity and transdisciplinarity are not in opposition to each other but rather are complementary aspects of routine scholarly work. A unique feature of the book is an examination of key issues and concepts in the context of the "lived experiences" of transdisciplinarity.

Hadorn, Gertrude Hirsch, Holger Hoffmann-Riem, Susette Biber-Klemm, Walter Grossenbacher-Mansuy, Dominique Joye, Christian Pohl, Urs Wiesmann, and Elisabeth Zemp (editors). *Handbook of Transdisciplinary Research.* Dordrecht, London: Springer Science + Business Media B.V., 2008.

This handbook assembles contributions of scholars from around the world on crucial topics in transdisciplinary research. It presents a collection of research projects in a wide range of fields, including rural development and natural resources, urban development, biodiversity issues, and emerging sciences and technologies, in order to illustrate the broad applicability of transdisciplinarity for tackling persistent, complex problems faced by society. The handbook is structured according to the three phases of a transdisciplinary research process: (1) problem identification and structuring, (2) problem analysis, and (3) bringing results to fruition. It describes the unique requirements and opportunities of this type of research and multifaceted challenges faced by transdisciplinary researchers. It also provides a wealth of specific recommendations for conducting transdisciplinary research emanating from the projects that have already been conducted. The handbook includes easy-to-understand explanations of the core terms used in transdisciplinary research and a summary of the handbook's content in 15 propositions for enhancing transdisciplinary research.

Klein, J. Thompson, Walter Grossenbacher-Mansuy, Rudolf Häberli, Alain Bill, Roland W. Scholz, and Myrtha Welti (editors). *Transdisciplinarity: Joint Problem Solving among Science, Technology, and Society: An Effective Way for Managing Complexity.* Basel, Switzerland: Birkhäuser Verlag, 2001.

This volume includes proceedings from the International Transdisciplinary Conference, held from February 27 to March 1, 2000, in Zurich, Switzerland, the focus of which was on sustainability research. The conference brought together representatives from science and technology, government agencies, and private corporations. At this conference, transdisciplinarity was presented as not replacing more traditional approaches to research but rather as a demand-driven collaborative research that involves participants both from within and outside academia. This post-conference volume includes 29 papers that explore the possibilities of transdisciplinarity for managing effective relations between science, technology, and society.

Leavy, Patricia. *Essentials of Transdisciplinary Research: Using Problem-Centered Methodologies.* Walnut Creek, CA: Left Coast Press, 2011.

This book emphasizes the idea of "social justice and moral underpinning to transdisciplinary research" (9) and describes key principles and methods for conducting transdisciplinary projects. It provides numerous examples from various research sectors on how a transdisciplinary approach to research can produce more effective results for addressing societal problems and fostering social justice. The book can serve as a user-friendly guide for students and researchers in designing transdisciplinary research projects as well as an introductory text for educators who teach problem-based courses.

McGregor, Sue L. T., and Russ Volckmann (editors). *Transversity: Transdisciplinary Approaches in Higher Education*. Tucson, AZ: Integral Publishers, 2011.

This book provides a clear and concise introduction to the concept of transdisciplinarity, applies this concept to higher education, and examines transdisciplinary approaches and issues in higher education institutions. The authors lay out a vision for a new institution of higher education that would provide transformational university education. They suggest a new label for such an institution—the Transversity—that they define as "seeking the truth by moving back and forth among [and] between disciplines and between the academy and civil society" (19–20). They describe several transdisciplinary educational initiatives in the United States, the European Union, Brazil, Mexico, Austria, Romania, and Australia (and alluding to one in India and another one in South Africa). The authors also discuss their current practices, guiding principles, and intended future developments, and provide valuable material from interviews with the initiators of these programs.

Montuori, Alfonso (editor). *Journeys in Complexity: Autobiographical Accounts by Leading Systems and Complexity Thinkers*. New York: Routledge, 2015.

Originally published as a series of articles in the special issue of *World Futures: The Journal of New Paradigm Research*, the chapters in this book present a rich variety of autobiographical accounts by renowned scholars from different fields and disciplines who discuss systems and complexity theories and who interpret these theories in different ways. The authors discuss how their interest in systems and complexity thinking developed, how it relates to transdisciplinarity, and what key figures, major works, and personal experiences shaped their views.

Nicolescu, Basarab, editor, with foreword by Alfonso Montuori. *Transdisciplinarity: Theory and Practice*. Cresskill, NJ: Hampton Press, 2008.

An international team of authors covers a wide variety of topics related to transdisciplinarity, ranging from education, theology, experimentation, epistemological awareness, and transdisciplinary learning. The authors include some of the key theorists in the field such as Basarab Nicolescu, Edgar Morin, and Alfonso Montuori, among others. Montuori's foreword provides a captivating overview of transdisciplinarity, which he defines as "a new way of thinking about, and engaging in, inquiry" (ix), and it serves as an excellent introduction to this compelling volume.

Somerville, Margaret A., and David J. Rapport (editors). *Transdisciplinarity: Recreating Integrated Knowledge*. Montréal, Canada: McGill-Queen's Press-MQUP, 2000.

This volume comprises the papers originally presented at the Colloquium on Transdisciplinarity, held in 1998 at Royaumont Abbey, Asnières-sur-Oise in Val-d'Oise, France. These papers map out the conceptual development and practice of transdisciplinarity from the perspectives of an international team of scholars who came from diverse disciplinary and intellectual cultures.

Journal Special Issues

Futures: The Journal of Policy, Planning and Futures Studies 36, no. 4 (2004). Special issue "Transdisciplinarity," edited by Roderick J. Lawrence and Carole Després.

The nine articles in this special issue are contributed by scholars from Canada, France, Germany, Switzerland, the United Kingdom, and the United States who came from different disciplinary backgrounds but who share professional interests in the study of human-environment relations. The authors offer their perspectives on the origins, goals, methods, and principles of transdisciplinary research as well as on the differences between multi-, inter-, and transdisciplinary approaches.

Futures: The Journal of Policy, Planning and Futures Studies 65 (January 2015). Special issue "Advances in Transdisciplinarity 2004–2014," edited by Roderick J. Lawrence.

The 18 articles in this special issue are contributed by researchers from Australia, Austria, Belgium, Italy, Japan, Germany, Sweden, Switzerland, the United Kingdom, and the United States. It revisits what has been accomplished in transdisciplinary education and research during the period from 2004 to 2014.

Systema: Connecting Matter, Life, Culture and Technology 4, no. 1 (2016). Special issue "General Systems Transdisciplinarity," with Guest Editor Debora Hammond.

The collection of papers in this special issue presents "a comprehensive framework for a research agenda to establish a fully developed general theory of systems" (1) and includes "Manifesto for General Systems Transdisciplinarity," which was launched at the 59th annual conference of the International Society for the Systems Sciences held in Berlin, Germany, in August of 2015.

World Futures: The Journal of New Paradigm Research 70, no. 3–4 (2014). Special issue "Transdisciplinarity," with the introduction by Sue L. T. McGregor.

This special issue features five themes: (1) transleadership, which is concerned with bringing together diverse teams of people involved in transdisciplinary initiatives, (2) transdisciplinarity as a new methodology for knowledge creation, (3) transdisciplinary conceptual change ("mental shift") that takes place when people transition from multi- and interdisciplinarity to transdisciplinarity, (4) the characteristics of individuals involved in the process of transdisciplinary knowledge creation, and (5) transdisciplinary generativity that refers to initiatives that work toward improvement of society for the next generation.

Key Websites

The Academy of Transdisciplinary Learning & Advanced Studies (TheATLAS) http://www.theatlas.org.

Founded in 2000, TheATLAS is a nonprofit organization committed to sustainable development through the integration of skills and knowledge from the disciplines in complex systems and engineering. TheAtlas funds and supports transdisciplinary research and educational activities around the world. It hosts biannual meetings on transdisciplinary and transcultural problems and provides a wide range of services to higher education institutions, including the provision of free educational materials and textbooks to students and faculty through its digital library. It publishes the *Transdisciplinary Journal of Engineering & Science (TJES)*, a peer-reviewed, open access journal promoting transdisciplinarity and its applications in the natural and social sciences, humanities, and engineering. Basarab Nicolescu serves as editor-in-chief for this journal.

The International Center for Transdisciplinary Research (in French: Centre International de Recherches et Études Transdisciplinaires—CIRET) http://ciret-transdisciplinarity.org/index_en.php.

Cofounded by Basarab Nicolescu in 1987, CIRET is a worldwide nonprofit organization located in Paris, France. CIRET serves as a virtual meeting space for transdisciplinary researchers from 26 countries, offers multilingual forums, reports on transdisciplinary projects from around the world, and publishes an online journal and the results of UNESCO-sponsored international colloquia. One of the major achievements of CIRET was the CIRET-UNESCO project "The Transdisciplinary Evolution of the University," which resulted in the organization of the International Congress "What University for Tomorrow? Towards a Transdisciplinary Evolution of the University" (1997), in a declaration and a set of recommendations later applied in a number of transdisciplinary programs around the world.

td-net: Network for Transdisciplinary Research http://transdisciplinarity.ch/en/td-net/Aktuell.html.

Emanated from a new research approach emphasized at a benchmark International Conference on Transdisciplinarity held in 2000 in Zurich, Switzerland, td-net is the Swiss-based network that serves as a communication and collaboration platform for researchers, educators, and stakeholders in society who are involved in inter- and transdisciplinary research and teaching. td-net also contributes to the further conceptualization of transdisciplinarity through the publication of books, organization of conferences, and the upkeep of "the toolbox for co-producing knowledge" that contains an overview of methods, practical experiences, and criteria for addressing the challenges of coproducing knowledge.

Notable Theorists, Educators, and Advocates

This chapter highlights some of the key contributors to the development and promotion of the transdisciplinary approach for use in research and education.

de Freitas, Lima (1927–1998)

A Portuguese artist. De Freitas coauthored and cosigned (with Basarab Nicolescu and Edgar Morin) the *Charter of Transdisciplinarity* (1994) and created the original logo for the International Center for Transdisciplinary Research and Studies (CIRET).

Dewey, John (1859–1952)

An American philosopher and educational reformer. Dewey advocated for use-value education that is intended for solving real-world problems. He developed the idea of participatory engagement of citizens and proposed a mutually beneficial partnership between scientists and those individuals who are affected by the consequences of scientific research. To illustrate his idea, he used shoemaking as an example: "The man who wears the shoe knows best that it pinches and where it pinches, even if the expert shoemaker is the best judge of how the trouble is to be remedied" (1927/2012, 154).

Ertas, Atila (1944–)

Professor and director of Academy for Transdisciplinary Studies, Department of Mechanical Engineering, Texas Tech University, USA. Ertas has been recognized as one of the major driving forces behind the development of the transdisciplinary model for education. He is a founding Fellow of TheATLAS, a nonprofit organization that funds and supports transdisciplinary research and educational activities around the world.

Hadorn, Gertrude Hirsch (1953–)

Professor at the Department of Environmental Systems Science, Swiss Federal Institute of Technology, Zurich, Switzerland. Hadorn has contributed to development of the methodology of transdisciplinary research through her numerous publications on philosophy of science and on transdisciplinary research. She was a lead editor of the *Handbook of Transdisciplinary Research* (2008) that provides theoretical basics, practical examples, and tools for collaborative knowledge production.

Jantsch, Erich (1929–1980)

An Austrian-born American astrophysicist and systems scientist. Jantsch conceptualized transdisciplinarity as "the organizational principle" (1972, 100). He proposed that knowledge should be organized into a multilevel cross-disciplinary hierarchy, which he called a knowledge pyramid. In this knowledge pyramid, Jantsch placed multidisciplinarity on the bottom, interdisciplinarity in the middle, and transdisciplinarity at the top. Jantsch imbued transdisciplinarity with a strong sense of social purpose initiated by unsolved societal problems and proclaimed the urgent need for a new kind of research organization—the "transdisciplinary university."

Klein, Julie Thompson (1944–)

Professor of humanities and faculty fellow for interdisciplinary development in the Division of Research at Wayne State University. Klein has written extensively on inter- and transdisciplinary research and education and consulted widely on the design and evaluation of cross-disciplinary projects and programs.

Kockelmans, Joseph (1923–2008)

A Dutch-born American philosopher. Kockelmans offered a philosophical perspective on transdisciplinarity as an all-encompassing philosophy of science that concerns itself with fundamental aspects of all disciplines. For Kockelmans, the goal of transdisciplinarity was not so much to solve concrete problems of the world as to develop a unifying, overarching theoretical framework for scientific work. Kockelmans was among the first theorists who called for a transdisciplinary "attitude" oriented toward comprehending and appreciating contributions of all disciplines in the form of philosophical "supra-scientific" reflection.

Lichnerowicz, André (1915–1998)

A French differential geometer and mathematical physicist. Lichnerowicz approached transdisciplinarity from a mathematical perspective relating it to set theory and logic. He promoted transdisciplinarity as a tool of thought capable of creating interlanguages and advocated mathematics as a universal interlanguage. He believed that only a mathematical approach could describe "the homogeneity of the theoretical activity in different sciences and techniques, independently of the field where this activity is effectuated" (1972, 130–131).

Montuori, Alfonso (1960–)

A professor in the Tansformative Iquiry Department at the California Institute of Integral Studies, USA, an artist, and a musician. Montuori is well known for his transdisciplinary research on complexity, leadership, creative inquiry, future studies, and cultural pluralism. Montuori has published widely on transdisciplinarity and designed two transdisciplinary graduate programs at the California Institute of Integral Studies, one of which includes a semester-long course titled "Transdisciplinarity: Complex Thought and the Pattern That Connects."

Morin, Edgar (1921–)

A French philosopher and sociologist, coauthor of the *Charter of Transdisciplinarity* (1994). Morin developed the concept of complexity as a fundamental aspect of transdisciplinarity. His concept of complexity drew upon a plurality of disciplines and was discussed in his writings on the evolution of disciplines, including six volumes of *The Method* (1977–2004) and his book *On Complexity* (2008).

Nicolescu, Basarab (1942–)

A Romanian-born French quantum physicist. Nicolescu is considered one of the major proponents of transdisciplinarity. He is known for advocating the idea of transdisciplinarity as a methodology in its own right that he encapsulates into three axioms (or three "pillars"): multiple levels of reality and the Hidden Third; the logic of the included middle; and the complexity of the world.[1] Nicolescu is an author of numerous publications on transdisciplinarity, including his visionary work *Manifesto of Transdisciplinarity* (2002). He is the cofounder of the International Centre of Transdisciplinary Research and Studies (CIRET), a worldwide organization, founded in 1987 and located in Paris, France, that aims to promote and advance transdisciplinarity around the world.[2]

Piaget, Jean (1896–1980)

A Swiss biologist, philosopher, and psychologist. It is generally believed that Piaget coined the term "transdisciplinarity" at the First International Seminar on Interdisciplinarity held in 1970 at the University of Nice, France.[3] In his post-seminar essay "The Epistemology of Interdisciplinary Relationships," Piaget envisioned transdisciplinarity as a higher stage in the epistemology of interdisciplinary relationships based on reciprocal assimilations capable of producing a truly "general" science.

Pohl, Christian (1966–)

Co-executive-director of td-net at the Swiss Academies of Arts and Sciences in Bern, Switzerland, and core member of TdLab of the Department of Environmental Systems Science at ETH Zurich, Switzerland. Pohl's research focuses on the collaboration between social and natural sciences in environmental research and the design and methodology of transdisciplinary research, particularly in the field of the sustainability sciences. He coedited the *Principles for Designing Transdisciplinary Research* (2007) and the *Handbook of Transdisciplinary Research* (2008).

Stokols, Daniel (1948–)

Professor at the School of Social Ecology, University of California, USA, who has made a significant contribution to research on the "science of team science," including his research on the factors affecting the collaborative success of transdisciplinary research and training programs.

Notes

1. Nicolescu's ideas are discussed in more detail in Chapter 3 of this book.

2. Nicolescu's complete biography and bibliography can be found at http://basarab-nicolescu.fr/.

3. According to other sources, it was Erich Jantsch, an Austrian-born American astrophysicist and systems scientist, who coined the term "transdisciplinarity" at the same seminar (Leavy 2011; Newell 2000; Weingart 2010).

Glossary

The following definitions are based on how specific terms are used in the context of transdisciplinary research. These definitions are intended to guide readers who are unfamiliar with transdisciplinarity, or confused by the diversity of meanings assigned to some of these terms.

actors
Individuals, groups of individuals, or institutions who are involved in a *problem field* and who are actively participating in working out solutions to concrete *real-world problems*.

disciplinarity
Acting within the bounds of a discipline or maintaining the characteristics of a discipline.

discipline
A specific organized field of knowledge, the defining characteristics of which distinguish it from other fields of knowledge. See Chapter 5 for a list of defining characteristics of a discipline.

holistic
Encompassing the study of a complex system as a whole rather than focusing on the study of a system's individual components in isolation from one another.

interdisciplinarity
A problem-oriented integrative research approach, in which two or more disciplines apply their knowledge and methods needed to solve a specific research problem.

knowledge integration
A process in which various bodies and types of knowledge and know-how from diverse sources are brought together to form a new understanding of the problem under investigation, create new conceptualizations and methodological approaches, and expand or transform knowledge within participating disciplines.

life-world
The everyday human world, a social reality prior to scientific knowledge.

Mode 1 knowledge production
A form of traditional disciplinary knowledge production, which is characterized by primarily homogeneous and hierarchical approaches to research and which has little need for collaboration with nonacademic participants.

Mode 2 knowledge production
A nonhierarchical heterogeneous form of knowledge production which transcends disciplinary boundaries, is strongly sensible to societal needs, and is characterized by a close interaction among academic and nonacademic participants.

monodisciplinarity
A process, in which researchers from a single established discipline or a research field work individually or collaboratively to study a research object or address a research question or problem.

multidisciplinarity
A nonintegrative research approach, in which researchers from two or more established disciplines work collaboratively on the same theme *without* integrating the concepts, methodologies, or epistemologies from their respective disciplines.

normal science
A concept introduced by Thomas Kuhn in *The Structure of Scientific Revolutions* (1961) who explained "normal science" (versus revolutionary science) as the one being practiced routinely by researchers within a settled ("normal") single paradigm in accordance with an established broad theory and without questioning or challenging the previous assumptions of that theory.

post-normal science
A concept developed by Silvio Funtowicz and Jerome Ravetz in the 1990s that focuses on the aspects of complex science-related issues, such as uncertainty and conflicting values that are often neglected in more dogmatic ("normal") scientific practice.

problem field
A specific area, in which the need for knowledge arises within society.

problems
Specific, identified, and structured research questions within *a problem field*, which are formulated in such a way that they can be investigated and addressed.

real-world problems
Large-scale, difficult-to-solve problems that reflect the complexity of real-world systems (such as human society and environment) and that typically have negative impact on these systems.

recursiveness

An approach to the research process, in which concepts and methods are continuously tested and in which underlying assumptions are modified if they are proved to be inadequate.

reductionism

A research approach to explaining the nature of complex entities and interactions by "reducing" them to the sum of their simpler or more fundamental constituent parts.

reflexivity

The process, in which researchers reflect critically both on themselves as researchers and on their research experiences, assumptions, and decisions.

rhizome

An underground root-like plant stem capable of producing from its nodes the roots and shoots of a new plant. When applied to transdisciplinarity, the metaphor of rhizome implies a nonhierarchical multiplicity and interconnectedness between all aspects of knowledge and society.

social inclusion

The involvement of marginalized social groups and ordinary citizens as valuable contributors to the research process.

transdisciplinarity

A new mode of knowledge production, which is driven by the need to solve *real-world problems*.

transdisciplinary research

A new way of conducting research, in which multiple *actors*, both from within and from outside academia, are collaboratively working on identifying specific *real-world problems* and on finding solutions to these problems.

unity of knowledge

The idea of unifying all areas of knowledge in order to understand the underlying unity of the world.

wicked problems

Extremely complex, difficult to define problems, which cannot be addressed using existing research modes and for which a final resolution cannot be found since any resolution generates new problems.

References

AAAS. *Science for All Americans: A Project 2061*. Washington, DC: American Association for the Advancement of Science, 1989.

Abbott, Andrew. "Things of Boundaries." *Social Research* (1995): 857–882. http://www.jstor.org/stable/40971127.

Ackerson, Linda G. "Challenges for Engineering Libraries: Supporting Research and Teaching in a Cross-Disciplinary Environment." *Science & Technology Libraries* 21, no. 1–2 (2001): 43–52. http://dx.doi.org/10.1300/J122v 21n01_05.

ACRL. *Framework for Information Literacy for Higher Education*. Association of College and Research Libraries, 2015. http://www.ala.org/acrl/standards/ ilframework (accessed July 3, 2016).

ACRL. *Information Literacy Competency Standards for Higher Education*, 2000. http://www.ala.org/acrl/standards/informationliteracycompetency (accessed June 28, 2016).

Ally, Mohamed. "Foundations of Educational Theory for Online Learning." In *Theory and Practice of Online Learning*, edited by Terry Anderson, 15–44. Edmonton, AB: AU Press, 2004.

Amselle, Jean-Loup. *Mestizo Logics: Anthropology of Identity in Africa and Elsewhere*. Stanford, CA: Stanford University Press, 1998.

Anderson, Rick. "Collections 2021: The Future of the Library Collection is not a Collection." *Serials* 24, no. 3 (2011): 211–215.

Apostel, Leo, Guy Berger, Asa Briggs, and Guy Michaud (editors). *Interdisciplinarity Problems of Teaching and Research in Universities*. Paris: Organisation for Economic Co-operation and Development, 1972.

Aslin, Heather J., and Kirsty L. Blackstock. " 'Now I'm not an Expert in Anything': Challenges in Undertaking Transdisciplinary Inquiries across the Social and Biophysical Sciences." In *Tackling Wicked Problems: Through the Transdisciplinary Imagination*, edited by Valerie A. Brown, John Alfred Harris, and Jacqueline Y. Russell, 117–129. London: Earthsca, 2010.

Association of American Colleges & Universities. *A Statement on Integrative Learning.* 2004. http://evergreen.edu/washingtoncenter/docs/intlearning/statementintlearning.pdf (accessed October 31, 2015).

Association of University Leaders for a Sustainable Future (AULSF). *The Talloires Declaration: 10 Point Action Plan,* 1990. http://www.ulsf.org/pdf/TD.pdf (accessed May 10, 2016).

Augsburg, Tanya. *Becoming Interdisciplinary: An Introduction to Interdisciplinary Studies.* Dubuque, IA: Kendall Hunt, 2006.

Augsburg, Tanya. "Becoming Transdisciplinary: The Emergence of the Transdisciplinary Individual." *World Futures* 70, no. 3–4 (2014): 233–247. http://dx.doi.org/10.1080/02604027.2014.934639.

Balsamo, Anne, and Carl Mitcham. "Interdisciplinarity in Ethics and the Ethics of Interdisciplinarity." In *The Oxford Handbook of Interdisciplinarity,* edited by Robert Froderman, Julie Thompson Klein, and Carl Mitcham, 259–272. Oxford, NY: Oxford University Press, 2010.

Balsiger, Jörg. "Transdisciplinarity in the Class Room? Simulating the Co-Production of Sustainability Knowledge." *Futures* 65 (2015): 185–194. http://dx.doi.org/10.1016/j.futures.2014.08.005.

Barbieri, Masini Eleonora. "Transdisciplinarity, Futures Studies, and Empirical Research." In *Transdisciplinarity: Recreating Integrated Knowledge,* edited by Margaret A. Somerville and David J. Rapport, 117–124. Montréal, Canada: McGill-Queen's Press-MQUP, 2000.

Bardwell, Lisa V. "Problem-Framing: A Perspective on Environmental Problem-Solving." *Environmental Management* 15, no. 5 (1991): 603–612. http://dx.doi.org/10.1007/BF02589620.

Bartolo, Laura M., and Timothy D. Smith. "Interdisciplinary Work and the Information Search Process: A Comparison of Manual and Online Searching." *College & Research Libraries* 54, no. 4 (1993): 344–353. http://crl.acrl.org/content/54/4/344.full.pdf (accessed September 15, 2016).

Bates, Marcia J. "The Design of Browsing and Berrypicking Techniques for the Online Search Interface." *Online Review* 13, no. 5 (1989): 407–424. http://dx.doi.org/10.1108/eb024320.

Bates, Marcia J. "Learning about the Information Seeking of Interdisciplinary Scholars and Students." *Library Trends* 45, no. 2 (1996): 155–164.

Bateson, Gregory. *Steps to an Ecology of Mind: Collected Essays in Anthropology, Psychiatry, Evolution, and Epistemology.* Chicago, IL: University of Chicago Press, 1972.

Becher, Tony. *Academic Tribes and Territories: Intellectual Enquiry and the Culture of the Disciplines.* Milton Keynes: Open University Press, 1989.

Becher, Tony. "The Significance of Disciplinary Differences." *Studies in Higher Education* 19, no. 2 (1994): 151–161. http://dx.doi.org/10.1080/03075079412331382007.

Becher, Tony. "Towards a Definition of Disciplinary Cultures." *Studies in Higher Education* 6, no. 2 (1981): 109–122. http://dx.doi.org/10.1080/03075078112331379362.

Becher, Tony, and Paul Trowler. *Academic Tribes and Territories: Intellectual Enquiry and the Culture of Disciplines*, 2nd edition. Buckingham, UK: Society for Research into Higher Education & Open University Press, 2001.

Becker, Egon, Thomas Jahn, Immanuel Stiess, and Peter Wehling. *Sustainability: A Cross-Disciplinary Concept for Social Transformations*. Paris: UNESCO, 1997.

Beghtol, Clare. "Facets as Undiscovered Public Knowledge: S. R. Ranganathan in India and S. Guttman in Israel." *Journal of Documentation* 51, no. 3 (1995): 194–224. http://dx.doi.org/10.1108/eb026948.

Benatar, Solomon. "Transdisciplinarity: A Personal Odyssey." In *Transdisciplinarity: Recreating Integrated Knowledge*, edited by Margaret A. Somerville and David J. Rapport, 171–178. Montréal, Canada: McGill-Queen's Press-MQUP, 2000.

Bergmann, Matthias, Thomas Jahn, Tobias Knobloch, Wolfgang Krohn, Christian Pohl, Engelbert Schramm, and Ronald C. Faust. *Methods for Transdisciplinary Research: A Primer for Practice*. Frankfurt/New York: Campus Verlag, 2012.

Bernstein, Jay Hillel. "Transdisciplinarity: A Review of Its Origins, Development, and Current Issues." *Journal of Research Practice* 11, no. 1, Article R1 (2015). http://jrp.icaap.org/index.php/jrp/article/view/510/412 (accessed August 23, 2016).

Bollen, Johan, Herbert Van de Sompel, Aric Hagberg, Luis Bettencourt, Ryan Chute, Marko A. Rodriguez, and Lyudmila Balakireva. "Clickstream Data Yields High-Resolution Maps of Science." *PLoS One* 4, no. 3 (2009): e4803. http://dx.doi.org/10.1371/journal.pone.0004803.

Bowonder, B. "Integrating Perspectives in Environmental Management." *Environmental Management* 11, no. 3 (1987): 305–315. http://dx.doi.org/10.1007/BF01867158.

Bradford, Samuel C. *Documentation*. London, UK: Crosby Lockwood, 1948.

Brandt, Patric, Anna Ernst, Fabienne Gralla, Christopher Luederitz, Daniel J. Lang, Jens Newig, Florian Reinert, David J. Abson, and Henrik von Wehrden. "A Review of Transdisciplinary Research in Sustainability Science." *Ecological Economics* 92 (2013): 1–15. http://dx.doi.org/10.1016/j.ecolecon.2013.04.008.

Braudel, Fernand. *A History of Civilizations*. Harmondsworth, UK: Penguin Books, 1995.

Brown, Valerie A., John Alfred Harris, and Jacqueline Y. Russell (editors). *Tackling Wicked Problems through the Transdisciplinary Imagination*. London, UK: Earthscan, 2010.

Bruce, Ann, Catherine Lyall, Joyce Tait, and Robin Williams. "Interdisciplinary Integration in Europe: The Case of the Fifth Framework Programme." *Futures* 36, no. 4 (2004): 457–470. http://dx.doi.org/10.1016/j.futures.2003.10.003.

Bruce, Christine S. "Information Literacy as a Catalyst for Educational Change. A Background Paper." In *Lifelong Learning: Whose Responsibility and What*

Is Your Contribution? Refereed papers from the 3rd International Lifelong Learning Conference Yeppoon, Central Queensland, Australia 13–16 June 2004, edited by Danaher, Patrick Alan, Colin Macpherson, Fons Nouwens, and Debbie Orr, 8–19. Rockhampton, Australia: Central Queensland University Press, 2004.

Brundiers, Katja, Arnim Wiek, and Charles L. Redman. "Real-World Learning Opportunities in Sustainability: From Classroom into the Real World." *International Journal of Sustainability in Higher Education* 11, no. 4 (2010): 308–324. http://dx.doi.org/10.1108/14676371011077540.

Burggren, Warren, Kent Chapman, Bradley Keller, Michael Monticino, and John Torday. "Biological Sciences." In *The Oxford Handbook of Interdisciplinarity*, edited by Robert Froderman, Julie Thompson Klein, and Carl Mitcham, 119–132. Oxford, NY: Oxford University Press, 2010.

Bush, Christopher. "The Lost Samurai: Researching Across and Between" (panel presentation, ALA Annual Conference, Chicago, July 9–15, 2009), as quoted in "ACRL in Chicago: ACRL programs at the ALA Annual Conference." *College and Research Libraries News* 70, no. 8 (2009): 449.

Canepi, Kitti. "Fund Allocation Formula Analysis: Determining Elements for Best Practices in Libraries." *Library Collections, Acquisitions, and Technical Services* 31, no. 1 (2007): 12–24.

Cannata, Nicola, Emanuela Merelli, and Russ B. Altman. "Time to Organize the Bioinformatics Resourceome." *PLoS Computational Biology* 1, no. 7 (2005): e76. http://dx.doi.org/10.1371/journal.pcbi.0010076.

Caper, Robert. "Play, Experimentation and Creativity." *The International Journal of Psychoanalysis* 77, no. 5 (1996): 859–869.

Carroll, Leigh, Mohammed K. Ali, Patricia Cuff, Mark D. Huffman, Bridget B. Kelly, Sandeep P. Kishore, K. M. Narayan, Karen R. Siegel, and Rajesh Vedanthan. "Envisioning a Transdisciplinary University." *The Journal of Law, Medicine & Ethics* 42, no. s2 (2014): 17–25. http://dx.doi.org/10.1111/jlme.12183.

Case, Donald A. and Lisa M. Given. *Looking for Information: A Survey of Research on Information Seeking, Needs and Behavior*, 4th edition. Bingley, UK: Emerald Group Publishing, 2016.

Choi, Bernard, and Anita Pak. "Multidisciplinarity, Interdisciplinarity, and Transdisciplinarity in Health Research, Services, Education, and Policy." *Clinical Investigative Medicine* 29, no. 6 (2006): 351–364.

Chubin, Daryl E. "State of the Field: The Conceptualization of Scientific Specialties." *The Sociological Quarterly* 17, no. 4 (1976): 448–476. http://dx.doi.org/10.1111/j.1533-8525.1976.tb01715.x.

Clark, Burton R. *Places of Inquiry: Research and Advanced Education in Modern Universities*. Berkeley, CA: University of California Press, 1995.

Classification Research Group. "The Need for a Faceted Classification as the Basis for All Methods of Information Retrieval." *Library Association Record* 57, no. 7 (1955): 262–268. http://dx.doi.org/10.1108/00012530610648671.

Claverie, Bernard. La Transdisciplinarité: À Travers les Réseaux de Savoir, 2009. http://hdl.handle.net/2042/28893 (accessed August 14, 2016).

Cobbledick, Susie. "The Information-Seeking Behavior of Artists: Exploratory Interviews." *The Library Quarterly* (1996): 343–372. http://www.jstor.org/stable/4309154.

Cohen, Jon. "Balancing the Collaboration Equation." *Science* 288, no. 5474 (2000): 2155–2159. http://dx.doi.org/10.1126/science.288.5474.2155.

Cohen, Susan G., and Diane E. Bailey. "What Makes Teams Work: Group Effectiveness Research from the Shop Floor to the Executive Suite." *Journal of Management* 23, no. 3 (1997): 239–290. http://dx.doi.org/10.1177/014920 639702300303.

Convergence: Facilitating Transdisciplinary Integration of Life Sciences, Physical Sciences, Engineering, and Beyond. Committee on Key Challenge Areas for Convergence and Health, Board on Life Sciences, Division on Earth and Life Studies. Washington, DC: National Academies Press, 2014.

Copeland, Ann. "Managing the Interdisciplinary Information Universe: Artisan Activities in a Machine Environment." In *Interdisciplinarity and Academic Libraries*, edited by Daniel C. Mack and Craig Gibson, 79–95. Chicago, IL: Association of College and Research Libraries, 2012.

Cormier, Dave. "Rhizomatic Education: Community as Curriculum." *Innovate: Journal of Online Education* 4, no. 5, Article 2 (2008).

Costa, Arthur L., and Bena Kallick. *Habits of Mind across the Curriculum: Practical and Creative Strategies for Teachers.* Alexandria, VA: Association for Supervision and Curriculum Development, 2009.

Crane, Diana. *Invisible Colleges: Diffusion of Knowledge in Scientific Communities.* Chicago, IL: University of Chicago Press, 1972.

Cronin, Blaise. "Invisible Colleges and Information Transfer a Review and Commentary with Particular Reference to the Social Sciences." *Journal of Documentation* 38, no. 3 (1982): 212–236. http://dx.doi.org/10.1108/eb026730.

Cummings, Jonathon N., and Sara Kiesler. "Collaborative Research across Disciplinary and Organizational Boundaries." *Social Studies of Science* 35, no. 5 (2005): 703–722.

Cummings, Jonathon N., and Sara Kiesler. "Coordination Costs and Project Outcomes in Multi-University Collaborations." *Research Policy* 36, no. 10 (2007): 1620–1634. http://dx.doi.org/10.1016/j.respol.2007.09.001.

D'Agostino, Fred. "Disciplinarity and the Growth of Knowledge." *Social Epistemology* 26, no. 3–4 (2012): 331–350. http://dx.doi.org/10.1080/02691728 .2012.727192.

Davies, Darron. *Curriculum Is a Construct. In Clued—Ed*, 2009. http://www .inclueded.net/writing/curriculum.html (accessed July 12, 2016).

Deleuze, Gilles, and Félix Guattari. *A Thousand Plateaus: Capitalism and Schizophrenia.* Minneapolis, MN: University of Minnesota Press, 1987.

Delgadillo, Roberto, and Beverly P. Lynch. "Future Historians: Their Quest for Information." *College & Research Libraries* 60, no. 3 (1999): 245–259. http://crl.acrl.org/content/60/3/245.full.pdf (accessed August 1, 2016).

Delors, Jacques, In'am Al Mufti, Isao Amagi, Roberto Carneiro, Fay Chung, Bronislaw Geremek, William Gorham, Aleksandra Kornhauser, Michael

Manley, Marisela Padrón Quero, Marie-Angélique Savané, Karan Singh, Rodolfo Stavenhagen, Myong Won Suhr, and Zhou Nanzhao. *Learning: The Treasure Within.* Paris: UNESCO, 1996. http://unesdoc.unesco.org/images/0010/001095/109590eo.pdf (accessed May 15, 2016).

Denda, Kayo. "Beyond Subject Headings: A Structured Information Retrieval Tool for Interdisciplinary Fields." *Library Resources & Technical Services* 49, no. 4 (2005): 266–275.

Derry, Sharon J., and Gerhard Fischer. "Transdisciplinary Graduate Education." Paper based on the symposium *Socio-Technical Design for Lifelong Learning: A Crucial Role for Graduate Education* presented at the meeting of the American Educational Research Association, Montreal, Canada, 2005. http://l3d.cs.colorado.edu/~gerhard/papers/transdisciplinary-sharon.pdf (accessed August 20, 2015).

Descartes, René. *Philosophical Writings.* Translated and edited by Elizabeth Anscombe, and Peter Thomas Geach, with introduction by Alexander Koyré. Nelson: Thomas Nelson & Sons, 1647/1954.

Dewey, John, edited and with introduction by Melvin L. Rogers. *The Public and Its Problems: An Essay in Political Inquiry.* University Park, PA: Pennsylvania State University Press, 1927/2012.

DeZure, Deborah. "Interdisciplinary Pedagogies in Higher Education." In *The Oxford Handbook of Interdisciplinarity*, edited by Robert Froderman, Julie Thompson Klein, and Carl Mitcham, 372–386. Oxford, NY: Oxford University Press, 2010.

Disis, Mary L., and John T. Slattery. "The Road We Must Take: Multidisciplinary Team Science." *Science Translational Medicine* 2, no. 22 (2010): 22cm9–22cm9. http://dx.doi.org/10.1126/scitranslmed.3000421.

Dold, Claudia J. "Critical Information Literacy: A Model for Transdisciplinary Research in Behavioral Sciences." *The Journal of Academic Librarianship* 40, no. 2 (2014): 179–184. http://dx.doi.org/10.1016/j.acalib.2014.03.002.

Du Plessis, Hester, Jeffrey Sehume, and Leonard Martin. *Concept and Application of Transdisciplinarity in Intellectual Discourse and Research.* Johannesburg: Real African Publishers, 2014.

During, Simon. "Is Cultural Studies a Discipline? And Does It Make Any Political Difference?" *Cultural Politics* 2, no. 3 (2006): 265–281. http://dx.doi.org/10.2752/174321906778531673.

Eagleman, David. *Incognito: The Secret Lives of the Brain.* New York: Pantheon, 2011.

Eco, Umberto. "Between La Mancha and Babel." *Variaciones Borges: Revista del Centro de Estudios y Documentación Jorge Luis Borges* 4 (1997): 51–61.

Ecosystem Health Program. http://www.uwo.ca/research/excellence/docs/Ecosystem Health.pdf (accessed May 17, 2016).

Eisenberg, Leon, and Terry C. Pellmar (editors). *Bridging Disciplines in the Brain, Behavioral, and Clinical Sciences.* Washington, DC: National Academies Press, 2000.

Ellis, David. "Modeling the Information-Seeking Patterns of Academic Researchers: A Grounded Theory Approach." *The Library Quarterly* 63, no. 4 (1993): 469–486. http://www.jstor.org/stable/4308867.

Ertas, Atila, Timothy Maxwell, Vicki P. Rainey, and Murat M. Tanik. "Transformation of Higher Education: The Transdisciplinary Approach in Engineering." *Education, IEEE Transactions on* 46, no. 2 (2003): 289–295. http://dx.doi.org/10.1109/TE.2002.808232.

Ertas, Atila, Murat M. Tanik, and T. T. Maxwell. "Transdisciplinary Engineering Education and Research Model." *Journal of Integrated Design and Process Science* 4, no. 4 (2000): 1–11.

Farkas, Meredith G. *Social Software in Libraries: Building Collaboration, Communication, and Community Online.* Medford, NJ: Information Today, 2007.

Feinstein, Jonathan. *The Nature of Creative Development.* Stanford, CA: Stanford University Press, 2006.

Filbert, Nathan W. "Framing the Framework: The Rigorous Responsibilities of Library and Information Science." *Reference & User Services Quarterly* 55, no. 3 (2016): 199–202. https://journals.ala.org/rusq/article/view/5929/7517 (accessed September 1, 2016).

Fink, Deborah, and Abigail Loomis. "Meta-Learning for Professional Development." In *Teaching Electronic Information Literacy: A How-to-Do-It Manual*, edited by Donald Barclay, 3–21. New York: Neal-Schuman, 1995.

Fish, Stanley. "Being Interdisciplinary Is So Very Hard to Do." *Profession* (1989): 15–22. http://www.jstor.org/stable/25595433.

Flexner, Hans. "The Curriculum, the Disciplines, and Interdisciplinarity in Higher Education: Historical Perspective." In *Interdisciplinarity and Higher Education*, edited by Joseph J. Kockelmans, 93–122. University Park, PA: Pennsylvania State University Press, 1979.

Flyvbjerg, Bent. *Rationality and Power: Democracy in Practice.* Chicago, IL: University of Chicago Press, 1998.

Foster, Allen. "A Nonlinear Model of Information-Seeking Behavior." *Journal of the American Society for Information Science and Technology* 55, no. 3 (2004): 228–237. http://dx.doi.org/ 10.1002/asi.10359.

Foster, Allen, and Nigel Ford. "Serendipity and Information Seeking: An Empirical Study." *Journal of Documentation* 59, no. 3 (2003): 321–340. http://dx.doi.org/10.1108/00220410310472518.

Foster, Allen, and Christine Urquhart. "Modelling Nonlinear Information Behaviour: Transferability and Progression." *Journal of Documentation* 68, no. 6 (2012): 784–805. http://dx.doi.org/10.1108/00220411211277046.

Foster, Allen, Christine Urquhart, and Janet Turner. "Validating Coding for a Theoretical Model of Information Behaviour." *Information Research* 13, no. 4, paper 358 (2008). http://InformationR.net/ir/13-4/paper358.html (accessed September 6, 2016).

Foucault, Michel. *The Archeology of Knowledge.* New York: Pantheon, 1972.

Foucault, Michel. *Discipline and Punish: The Birth of the Prison.* New York: Pantheon, 1978.

Foucault, Michel. "The Order of Discourse." In *Untying the Text: A Post-Structuralist Reader,* edited by Robert Young. Boston, MA: Routledge & Kegan Paul, 1981.

Fowler, Henry Watson, Francis George Fowler, and David Crystal. *The Concise Oxford Dictionary: The Classic First Edition.* Oxford, UK: Oxford University Press, 2011.

Freitas, Lima, Basarab Nicolescu, and Edgar Morin. "Charter of Transdisciplinarity." In *First World Congress on Transdisciplinarity. Convento de Arrabida, Portugal,* 1994. http://inters.org/Freitas-Morin-Nicolescu-Transdisciplinarity (accessed June 12, 2016).

Frescoln, Laura M., and J. G. Arbuckle Jr. "Changes in Perceptions of Transdisciplinary Science Over Time." *Futures* 73 (2015): 136–150. http://dx.doi.org/10.1016/j.futures.2015.08.008.

Fry, Gary L. A. "Multifunctional Landscapes—Towards Transdisciplinary Research." *Landscape and Urban Planning* 57, no. 3 (2001): 159–168. http://dx.doi.org/10.1016/S0169-2046(01)00201–8.

Fuller, Steve. *Knowledge Management Foundations.* Boston, MA: Butterworth-Heinemann, 2002.

Funtowicz, Silvio O., and Jerome R. Ravetz. "A New Scientific Methodology for Global Environmental Issues." In *Ecological Economics: The Science and Management of Sustainability,* edited by Robert Costanza, 137–152. New York: Columbia University Press, 1991.

Funtowicz, Silvio O., and Jerome R. Ravetz. "Science for the Post-Normal Age." *Futures* 25, no. 7 (1993): 739–755. http://dx.doi.org/10.1016/0016-3287(93)90022-L.

Funtowicz, Silvio O., and Jerome R. Ravetz. *Uncertainty and Quality in Science for Policy.* Dordrecht, The Netherlands: Springer, 1990.

Funtowicz, Silvio O., and Jerome R. Ravetz. "Values and Uncertainties." In *Handbook of Transdisciplinary Research,* edited by Gertrude Hirsch Hadorn, Holger Hoffmann-Riem, Susette Biber-Klemm, Walter Grossenbacher-Mansuy, Dominique Joye, Christian Pohl, Urs Wiesmann, and Elisabeth Zemp, 361–368. Dordrecht, London: Springer Science + Business Media B.V., 2008.

Galison, Peter. *Image and Logic: A Material Culture of Microphysics.* Chicago, IL: University of Chicago Press, 1997.

Geiger, Roger L. *To Advance Knowledge: The Growth of American Research Universities, 1900–1940.* New York: Oxford University Press, 1986.

Gibbons, Michael, Camille Limoges, Helga Nowotny, Simon Schwartzman, Peter Scott, and Martin Trow. *The New Production of Knowledge: The Dynamics of Science and Research in Contemporary Societies.* Los Angeles, CA: Sage Publications, 1994.

Gibbs, Paul. "Coda." In *Transdisciplinary Professional Learning and Practice,* edited by Paul Gibbs, 197–204. Cham, Switzerland: Springer International Publishing, 2015.

Gibbs, Paul. "Introduction." In *Transdisciplinary Professional Learning and Practice*, edited by Paul Gibbs, 1–8. Cham, Switzerland: Springer International Publishing, 2015.

Gieryn, Thomas F. "Boundary-Work and the Demarcation of Science from Non-Science: Strains and Interests in Professional Ideologies of Scientists." *American Sociological Review* (1983): 781–795. http://www.jstor.org/stable/2095325.

Gilmore, Norbert. "Experiences with Transdisciplinarity: From Neologism to Worldview." In *Transdisciplinarity: Recreating Integrated Knowledge*, edited by Margaret A. Somerville and David J. Rapport, 185–192. Montréal, Canada: McGill-Queen's Press-MQUwP, 2000.

Giri, Ananta Kumar. "The Calling of a Creative Transdisciplinarity." *Futures* 34, no. 1 (2002): 103–115. http://dx.doi.org/10.1016/S0016-3287(01)00038-6.

Gnoli, Claudio. "Classification Transcends Library Business." *Knowledge Organization* 37, no. 3 (2010): 223–229. http://mate.unipv.it/gnoli/gnoli2010.pdf (accessed July 5, 2016).

Godemann, Jasmin. "Knowledge Integration: A Key Challenge for Transdisciplinary Cooperation." *Environmental Education Research* 14, no. 6 (2008): 625–641. http://dx.doi.org/10.1080/13504620802469188.

Gutiérrez, Antonio García. *Desclasificados*: Pluralismo Lógico y Violencia de la Clasificación. Barcelona: Anthropos, 2007.

García Gutiérrez, Antonio. "Declassification in Knowledge Organization: A Post-Epistemological Essay." *Transinformaçao* 23, no. 1 (2011): 5–14.

García Gutiérrez, Antonio. "Declassifying Knowledge Organization." *Knowledge Organization* 41, no. 5 (2014): 393–409.

Häberli, R., A. Bill, W. Grossenbacher-Mansuy, J. Thompson Klein, R. W. Scholz and M. Welti. "Synthesis: Inter- and Transdisciplinary Research Methods." In *Transdisciplinarity: Joint Problem Solving among Science, Technology, and Society: An Effective Way for Managing Complexity*, edited by Julie Thomson Klein, 6–22. Basel: Birkhäuser, 2001.

Hadorn, Gertrude Hirsch, Christian Pohl, and Gabriele Bammer. "Solving Problems through Transdisciplinary Research." In *The Oxford Handbook of Interdisciplinarity*, edited by Robert Froderman, Julie Thompson Klein, and Carl Mitcham, 431–452. Oxford, NY: Oxford University Press, 2010.

Hadorn, Gertrude Hirsch, Susette Biber-Klemm, Walter Grossenbacher-Mansuy, Holger Hoffmann-Riem, Dominique Joye, Christian Pohl, Urs Wiesmann, and Elisabeth Zemp. "The Emergence of Transdisciplinarity as a Form of Research." In *Handbook of Transdisciplinary Research*, edited by Gertrude Hirsch Hadorn, Holger Hoffmann-Riem, Susette Biber-Klemm, Walter Grossenbacher-Mansuy, Dominique Joye, Christian Pohl, Urs Wiesmann, and Elisabeth Zemp. Dordrecht, London: Springer Science + Business Media B.V., 2008.

Hall, Kara L., Daniel Stokols, Richard P. Moser, et al. "The Collaboration Readiness of Transdisciplinary Research Teams and Centers: Findings from the National Cancer Institute's TREC Year-One Evaluation Study." *American Journal of Preventive Medicine* 35, no. 2 (2008): S161–S172.

Hall, Kara L., Daniel Stokols, Brooke A. Stipelman, Amanda L. Vogel, Annie Feng, Beth Masimore, Glen Morgan, Richard P. Moser, Stephen E. Marcus, and David Berrigan. "Assessing the Value of Team Science: A Study Comparing Center- and Investigator-Initiated Grants." *American Journal of Preventive Medicine* 42, no. 2 (2012): 157–163. http://dx.doi.org/10.1016/j.amepre.2011.10.011.

Hammer, M., and Söderqvist, T. "Enhancing Transdisciplinary Dialogue in Curricula Development." *Ecological Economics* 38, no. 1 (2001): 1–5. http://dx.doi.org/10.1016/S0921-8009(01)00168-9.

Harley, Diane, Sophia Krzys Acord, Sarah Earl-Novell, Shannon Lawrence, and C. Judson King. "Assessing the Future Landscape of Scholarly Communication: An Exploration of Faculty Values and Needs in Seven Disciplines." Center for Studies in Higher Education, Berkeley, CA. (2010). https://escholarship.org/uc/item/15x7385g (accessed February 26, 2014).

Harris, Frances, and Fergus Lyon. "Transdisciplinary Environmental Research: Building Trust across Professional Cultures." *Environmental Science & Policy* 31 (2013): 109–119. http://dx.doi.org/10.1016/j.envsci.2013.02.006.

Harrison, David A., Susan Mohammed, Joseph E. McGrath, Anna T. Florey, and Scott W. Vanderstoep. "Time Matters in Team Performance: Effects of Member Familiarity, Entrainment, and Task Discontinuity on Speed and Quality." *Personnel Psychology* 56, no. 3 (2003): 633–669. http://dx.doi.org/10.1111/j.1744-6570.2003.tb00753.x.

Haynes, Caroline (editor). *Innovations in Interdisciplinary Teaching.* ACE Series on Higher Education. Westport, CT: Oryx Press, 2002.

Heider, Karl G. "The Rashomon Effect: When Ethnographers Disagree." *American Anthropologist* 90 (1988): 73–81.

Henriksen, Danah, and Punya Mishra. "We Teach Who We Are: Creativity in the Lives and Practices of Accomplished Teachers." *Teachers College Record* 117, no. 7 (2015): 1–46.

Henriksen, Danah, Punya Mishra, and Petra Fisser. "Infusing Creativity and Technology in 21st Century Education: A Systemic View for Change." *Journal of Educational Technology & Society* 19, no. 3 (2016): 27–37. http://www.jstor.org/stable/jeductechsoci.19.3.27.

Henriksen, Danah, Punya Mishra, and the Deep-Play Research Group. "Twisting Knobs and Connecting Things: Rethinking Technology & Creativity in the 21st Century." *TechTrends* 58, no. 1 (2014): 15–19.

Hickey, David, and Shelley Arlen. "Falling Through the Cracks: Just How Much 'History' Is History?" *Library Collections, Acquisitions, and Technical Services* 26, no. 2 (2002): 97–106.

Holbrook, J. Britt. "Peer Review." In *The Oxford Handbook of Interdisciplinarity*, edited by Robert Froderman, Julie Thompson Klein, and Carl Mitcham, 321–332. Oxford, NY: Oxford University Press, 2010a.

Holbrook, J. Britt. "The Use of Societal Impacts Considerations in Grant Proposal Peer Review: A Comparison of Five Models." *Technology & Innovation* 12, no. 3 (2010b): 213–224. http://dx.doi.org/10.3727/194982410X12895 770314078.

Hollaender, Kristen, and P. Leroy. "Reflections on the Interactive Sessions—From Skepticism to Good Practices." In *Transdisciplinarity: Joint Problem Solving among Science, Technology, and Society: An Effective Way for Managing Complexity*, edited by Julie Thomson Klein, 217–235. Basel: Birkhäuser, 2001.

Hong, Lu, and Scott E. Page. "Groups of Diverse Problem Solvers Can Outperform Groups of High-Ability Problem Solvers." *Proceedings of the National Academy of Sciences of the United States of America 101*, no. 46 (2004): 16385–16389. http://www.pnas.org/content/101/46/16385.full.pdf (accessed June 15, 2016).

Horwitz, Sujin K., and Irwin B. Horwitz. "The Effects of Team Diversity on Team Outcomes: A Meta-Analytic Review of Team Demography." *Journal of Management* 33, no. 6 (2007): 987–1015. http://dx.doi.org/10.1177/0149206 307308587.

Hoskin, Keith W., and Richard H. Macve. "Accounting and the Examination: A Genealogy of Disciplinary Power." *Accounting, Organizations and Society* 11, no. 2 (1986): 105–136. http://dx.doi.org/10.1016/0361-3682 (86)90027-9.

Hugill, Andrew, and Sophy Smith. "Digital Creativity and Transdisciplinarity at Postgraduate Level: The Design and Implementation of a Transdisciplinary Masters Programme and Its Implications for Creative Practice." *Digital Creativity* 24, no. 3 (2013): 191–207. http://dx.doi.org/10.1080/146 26268.2013.827099.

Hunt, Lynn. "The Virtues of Disciplinarity." *Eighteenth-Century Studies* 28, no. 1 (1994): 1–7. http://www.jstor.org/stable/2739218.

Hurd, Julie M. "Interdisciplinary Research in the Sciences: Implications for Library Organization." *College & Research Libraries* 53, no. 4 (1992): 283–297.

Hutchins, W. John. "The Concept of 'Aboutness' in Subject Indexing." *Aslib Proceedings* 30, no. 5 (1978): 172–181. http://dx.doi.org/10.1108/eb050629.

Huuotoniemi, Katri. "Evaluating Interdisciplinary Research." In *The Oxford Handbook of Interdisciplinarity*, edited by Robert Froderman, Julie Thompson Klein, and Carl Mitcham, 309–320. Oxford, NY: Oxford University Press, 2010.

Ipri, Tom. "Introducing Transliteracy: What Does It Mean to Academic Libraries?" *College & Research Libraries News* 71, no. 10 (2010): 532–567. http://crln.acrl.org/content/71/10/532.full.pdf (accessed August 1, 2016).

Jackson, Susan E., Karen E. May, and Kristina Whitney. "Understanding the Dynamics of Diversity in Decision-Making Teams." In *Team Effectiveness and Decision Making in Organizations*, edited by Richard Guzzo and Eduardo Salas, 204–261. San Francisco, CA: Jossey-Bass, 1995.

Jacobs, I. M., and S. Nienaber. "Waters without Borders: Transboundary Water Governance and the Role of the 'Transdisciplinary Individual' in Southern Africa." *Water SA* 37, no. 5 (2011): 665–678.

Jahn, Thomas, Matthias Bergmann, and Florian Keil. "Transdisciplinarity: Between Mainstreaming and Marginalization." *Ecological Economics* 79 (2012): 1–10. http://dx.doi.org/10.1016/j.ecolecon.2012.04.017.

Jakobsen, Christine Haugaard, Tove Hels, and William J. McLaughlin. "Barriers and Facilitators to Integration among Scientists in Transdisciplinary Landscape Analyses: A Cross-Country Comparison." *Forest Policy and Economics* 6, no. 1 (2004): 15–31. http://dx.doi.org/10.1016/S1389-9341 (02)00080-1.

Jantsch, Erich. "Towards Interdisciplinarity and Transdisciplinarity in Education and Innovation." In *Interdisciplinarity: Problems of Teaching and Research in Universities*, edited by Leo Apostel, Guy Berger, Asa Briggs, and Guy Michaud, 97–121. Paris: OECD, Centre for Educational Research and Innovation, 1972.

Jasanoff, Sheila S. "Contested Boundaries in Policy-Relevant Science." *Social Studies of Science* 17, no. 2 (1987): 195–230. http://dx.doi.org/10.1177/030631287017002001.

Jarvenpaa, Sirkka L., and Dorothy E. Leidner. "Communication and Trust in Global Virtual Teams." *Organizational Science* 10 (1999): 791–815. http://dx.doi.org/10.1111/j.1083-6101.1998.tb00080.x.

Jeffrey, Paul. "Smoothing the Waters Observations on the Process of Cross-disciplinary Research Collaboration." *Social Studies of Science* 33, no. 4 (2003): 539–562.

Jencks, Christopher, and David Riesman. *The Academic Revolution*. Garden City, NY: Doubleday, 1968.

Jones, Maralyn. "Teaching Research across Disciplines: Interdisciplinarity and Information Literacy." In *Interdisciplinarity and Academic Libraries*, edited by Daniel C. Mack and Craig Gibson, 167–181. Chicago, IL: Association of College and Research Libraries, 2012.

Katz, J. Sylvan, and Ben R. Martin. "What Is Research Collaboration?" *Research Policy* 26, no. 1 (1997): 1–18. http://dx.doi.org/10.1016/S0048-7333 (96)00917-1.

Kerr, Norbert L., and R. Scott Tindale. "Group Performance and Decision Making." *Annual Review of Psychology* 55 (2004): 623–655. http://dx.doi.org/10.1146/annurev.psych.55.090902.142009.

Klein, Julie Thompson. "A Conceptual Vocabulary of Interdisciplinary Science." In *Practising Interdisciplinarity*, edited by Weingart, Peter and Nico Stehr, 3–24. Toronto, Canada: University of Toronto Press, 2000a.

Klein, Julie Thompson. *Crossing Boundaries: Knowledge, Disciplinarities, and Interdisciplinarities*. Charlottesville, VA: University of Virginia Press, 1996.

Klein, Julie Thompson. "Discourses of Transdisciplinarity: Looking Back to the Future." *Futures* 63 (2014): 68–74. http://dx.doi.org/10.1016/j.futures.2014.08.008.

Klein, Julie Thompson. "Education." In *Handbook of Transdisciplinary Research*, edited by Gertrude Hirsch Hadorn, Holger Hoffmann-Riem, Susette Biber-Klemm, Walter Grossenbacher-Mansuy, Dominique Joye, Christian Pohl, Urs Wiesmann, and Elisabeth Zemp, 399–410. Dordrecht, London: Springer Science + Business Media B.V., 2008.

Klein, Julie Thompson. "Finding Interdisciplinary Knowledge and Information." In *Interdisciplinary Studies Today* (*New Directions for Teaching and Learning*, vol. 58), edited by Julie Thompson Klein and William G. Doty, 7–33. San Francisco, CA: Jossey-Bass, 1994.

Klein, Julie Thompson. "Integration, Evaluation, and Disciplinarity." In *Transdisciplinarity: Recreating Integrated Knowledge*, edited by Margaret A. Somerville and David J. Rapport, 49–59. Montréal, Canada: McGill-Queen's Press-MQUP, 2000b.

Klein, Julie Thompson. *Interdisciplinarity: History, Theory, and Practice*. Detroit: Wayne State University Press, 1990.

Klein, Julie Thompson. "Interdisciplinary Needs: The Current Context." *Library Trends* 45, no. 2 (1996a): 134–154.

Klein, Julie Thompson. "The Interdisciplinary Process." In *International Research Management: Studies in Interdisciplinary Methods from Business, Government, and Academia*, edited by Philip H. Birnbaum, Frederick A. Rossini, and Donald R. Baldwin, 20–30. New York: Oxford University Press, 1990a.

Klein, Julie Thompson. "A Platform for a Shared Discourse of Interdisciplinary Education." *JSSE-Journal of Social Science Education* 5, no. 4 (2006): 10–18. http://dx.doi.org/10.4119/UNIBI/jsse-v5-i4-1026.

Klein, Julie Thompson. "Prospects for Transdisciplinarity." *Futures* 36, no. 4 (2004): 515–526. http://dx.doi.org/10.1016/j.futures.2003.10.007.

Klein, Julie Thompson. "A Taxonomy of Interdisciplinarity." In *The Oxford Handbook of Interdisciplinarity*, edited by Robert Froderman, Julie Thompson Klein, and Carl Mitcham, 15–30. Oxford, NY: Oxford University Press, 2010.

Klein, Julie Thompson. "Unity of Knowledge and Transdisciplinarity: Contexts of Definition, Theory and the New Discourse of Problem Solving." In *Unity of Knowledge in Transdisciplinary Research for Sustainability*, edited by Hirsch G. Hadorn, 35–69. *Encyclopedia of Life Support System (EOLSS)*, 2009.

Klein, Julie Thompson. "Voices of Royaumont." In *Transdisciplinarity: Recreating Integrated Knowledge*, edited by Margaret A. Somerville and David J. Rapport, 3–13. Montréal, Canada: McGill-Queen's Press-MQUP, 2000c.

Klein, Julie Thompson, Walter Grossenbacher-Mansuy, Rudolf Häberli, Alain Bill, Roland W. Scholz, and Myrtha Welti (editors). *Transdisciplinarity: Joint Problem Solving among Science, Technology, and Society: An Effective Way for Managing Complexity*. Basel: Springer, 2012.

Klein, Julie Thomson, and Roderick Macdonald. "Exploring Transdisciplinarity." In *Transdisciplinarity: Recreating Integrated Knowledge*, edited by Margaret A. Somerville and David J. Rapport, 215–217. Montréal, Canada: McGill-Queen's Press-MQUP, 2000.

Kleineberg, Michael. "The Blind Men and the Elephant: Towards an Organization of Epistemic Contexts." *Knowledge Organization* 40, no. 5 (2013): 340–362.

Knapp, Jeffrey A. "Plugging the 'Whole': Librarians as Interdisciplinary Facilitators." *Library Review* 61, no. 3 (2012): 199–214. http://dx.doi.org/10.1108/00242531211259328.

Knapp, Jeffrey A. "Walls Tumbling Down: Opportunities for Librarians in Interdisciplinary Research." In *Social Science Libraries: Interdisciplinary Collections, Services, Networks*, edited by Steven W. Witt and Lynne M. Rudasill, 53–61. New York: De Gruyter Saur, 2010.

Kockelmans, Joseph J. "Why Interdisciplinarity?" In *Interdisciplinarity and Higher Education*, edited by Joseph J. Kockelmans, 123–160. University Park, PA: Pennsylvania State University Press, 1979.

Krimsky, Sheldon. "Transdisciplinarity for Problems at the Interstices of Disciplines." In *Transdisciplinarity: Recreating Integrated Knowledge*, edited by Margaret A. Somerville and David J. Rapport, 109–114. Montréal, Canada: McGill-Queen's Press-MQUP, 2000.

Krohn, Wolfgang. "Interdisciplinary Cases and Disciplinary Knowledge." In *The Oxford Handbook of Interdisciplinarity*, edited by Robert Frodeman, Julie Thompson Klein, and Carl Mitcham, 39–49. Oxford, NY: Oxford University Press, 2010.

Krott, Max. "Evaluation of Transdisciplinary Research." *Encyclopedia of Life Support Systems (EOLSS)* 3 (2002).

Kueffer, Christoph, G. Hirsch Hadorn, Gabriele Bammer, Lorrae van Kerkhoff, and Christian Pohl. "Towards a Publication Culture in Transdisciplinary Research." *Gaia* 16, no. 1 (2007): 22–26.

Kuhn, Thomas S. *The Structure of Scientific Revolutions*. Chicago, IL: University of Chicago Press, 1962.

Kutner, Laurie A. "Library Instruction in an Interdisciplinary Environmental Studies Program: Challenges, Opportunities, and Reflections." *Issues in Science & Technology Librarianship* 28 (2000). http://www.istl.org/00-fall/article2.html. Accessed August 12, 2016.

Lattuca, Lisa R. *Creating Interdisciplinarity: Interdisciplinary Research and Teaching among College and University Faculty*. Nashville, TN: Vanderbilt University Press, 2001.

Lave, Jean, and Etienne Wenger. *Situated Learning: Legitimate Peripheral Participation*. Cambridge, MA: Cambridge Press, 1991.

Lawlor, Edward F., Matthew W. Kreuter, Anne K. Sebert-Kuhlmann, and Timothy D. McBride. "Methodological Innovations in Public Health Education: Transdisciplinary Problem Solving." *American Journal of Public Health* 105, no. S1 (2015): S99–S103. http://dx.doi.org/10.2105/AJPH.2014.302462.

Lawrence, Roderick J. "Advances in Transdisciplinarity: Epistemologies, Methodologies and Processes." *Futures* 65 (2015): 1–9. http://dx.doi.org/10.1016/j.futures.2014.11.007.

Leavy, Patricia. *Essentials of Transdisciplinary Research: Using Problem-Centered Methodologies*. Walnut Creek, CA: Left Coast Press, 2011.

Levitan, Karen B. "Applying a Holistic Framework to Synthesize Information Science Research." In *Progress in Communication Sciences*, edited by Brenda Dervin and Melvin J. Voigt, Volume II, 241–273. Norwood, NJ: Ablex, 1980.

Lewis, J. David, and Andrew Weigert. "Trust as a Social Reality." *Social Forces* 63, no. 4 (1985): 967–985. http://dx.doi.org/10.1093/sf/63.4.967.

Lichnerowicz, André. "Mathematic and Transdisciplinarity." In *Interdisciplinarity Problems of Teaching and Research in Universities*, edited by Leo Apostel, Guy Berger, Asa Briggs, and Guy Michaud, 121–127. Paris: Organisation for Economic Co-operation and Development, 1972.

Lindholm-Romantschuk, Ylva. *Scholarly Book Reviewing in the Social Sciences and Humanities: The Flow of Ideas within and among Disciplines*. New York: Greenwood Publishing Group, 1998.

Lloyd, Annemaree. "Information Literacy Landscapes: An Emerging Picture." *Journal of Documentation* 62, no. 5 (2006): 570–583. http://dx.doi.org/10.1108/00220410610688723.

Lloyd, Annemaree, and Margaret Somerville. "Working Information." *Journal of Workplace Learning* 18, no. 3 (2006): 186–198. http://dx.doi.org/10.1108/13665620610654603.

Loibl, Marie Céline. "Integrating Perspectives in the Practice of Transdisciplinary Research." In *Reflexive Governance for Sustainable Development*, edited by Voss, Jan-Peter, and Dierk Bauknecht, 294–309. Cheltenham, UK: Edward Elgar Publishing, 2006.

López-Huertas, María. "Reflexions on Multidimensional Knowledge: Its Influence on the Foundation of Knowledge Organization." *Knowledge organization* 40, no. 6 (2013): 400–407.

Lyons, John. *Introduction to Theoretical Linguistics*. Cambridge, UK: Cambridge University Press, 1968.

Maasen, Sabine, and Olivier Lieven. "Transdisciplinarity: A New Mode of Governing Science?" *Science and Public Policy* 33, no. 6 (2006): 399–410. http://dx.doi.org/10.3152/147154306781778803.

Macdonald, Roderick. "Practicing Transdisciplinarity. The Education Sector." In *Transdisciplinarity: Recreating Integrated Knowledge*, edited by Margaret A. Somerville and David J. Rapport, 241–244. Montréal, Canada: McGill-Queen's Press-MQUP, 2000a.

Macdonald, Roderick. "Transdisciplinarity and Trust." In *Transdisciplinarity: Recreating Integrated Knowledge*, edited by Margaret A. Somerville and David J. Rapport, 61–76. Montréal, Canada: McGill-Queen's Press-MQUP, 2000b.

Mack, Daniel C., and Craig Gibson. *Interdisciplinarity and Academic Libraries*. Chicago, IL: Association of College and Research Libraries, 2012.

Maguire, Kate. "Perspectives 2: Transdisciplinarity and Professional Doctorates: Facilitating Metanoia through the Art of Translation." In *Doctorate in*

Professional Studies by Public Works Candidate Handbook, 64–68. London, UK: Middlesex University, 2012.

Maguire, Kate. "Transdisciplinarity as Translation." In *Transdisciplinary Professional Learning and Practice,* edited by Paul Gibbs, 165–177. Cham, Switzerland: Springer International Publishing, 2015.

Makkreel, Rudolf A. "Gadamer and the Problem of How to Relate Kant and Hegel to Hermeneutics." *Laval Théologique et Philosophique* 53, no. 1 (1997): 151–166. http://www.erudit.org/revue/ltp/1997/v53/n1/401046ar.pdf (accessed June 21, 2016).

Manderson, Desmond. "Some Considerations about Transdisciplinarity: A New Metaphysics?" In *Transdisciplinarity: Recreating Integrated Knowledge,* edited by Margaret A. Somerville and David J. Rapport, 86–93. Montréal, Canada: McGill-Queen's Press-MQUP, 2000.

Mansilla, Veronica Boix. "Assessing Student Work at Disciplinary Crossroads." *Change: The Magazine of Higher Learning* 37, no. 1 (2005): 14–21. http://dx.doi.org/10.3200/CHNG.37.1.14-21.

Maron, M. E. "On Indexing, Retrieval and the Meaning of About." *Journal of the American Society for Information Science* 28, no. 1 (1977): 38–43. http://dx.doi.org/10.1002/asi.4630280107.

Martin, Victoria. *Demystifying eResearch: A Primer for Librarians.* Santa Barbara, CA: ABC-CLIO, 2014.

Massey, Claire, Fiona Alpass, Ross Flett, Kate Lewis, Stuart Morriss, and Frank Sligo. "Crossing Fields: The Case of a Multi-Disciplinary Research Team." *Qualitative Research* 6, no. 2 (2006): 131–147. http://dx.doi.org/10.1177/1468794106062706.

Max-Neef, Manfred A. "Foundations of Transdisciplinarity." *Ecological Economics* 53, no. 1 (2005): 5–16. http://dx.doi.org/10.1016/j.ecolecon.2005.01.014.

Mayer, Roger C., James H. Davis, and F. David Schoorman. "An Integrative Model of Organizational Trust." *Academy of Management Review* 20, no. 3 (1995): 709–734. http://dx.doi.org/10.5465/AMR.1995.9508080335.

McCain, Katherine W. "Cross-Disciplinary Citation Patterns in the History of Technology." In *Proceedings of the American Society for Information Science,* Chicago, Illinois, September 28–October 2, 1986, 194–198. Medford, NJ: Learned Information, 1986.

McClam, Sherie, and Emma M. Flores-Scott. "Transdisciplinary Teaching and Research: What Is Possible in Higher Education?" *Teaching in Higher Education* 17, no. 3 (2012): 231–243. http://dx.doi.org/10.1080/13562517.2011.611866.

McGregor, Sue L. T. "Enriching Responsible Living Curricula with Transdisciplinarity." In *Responsible Living,* edited by Robert Didham, Declan Doyle, Jørgen Klein, and Victoria W. Thoresen, 97–111. New York: Springer International Publishing, 2015c.

McGregor, Sue L. T. "The Nicolescuian and Zurich Approaches to Transdisciplinarity." *Integral Leadership Review* 15, no. 2 (2015a). http://integralleader

shipreview.com/13135-616-the-nicolescuian-and-zurich-approaches-to-transdisciplinarity/ (accessed August 23, 2016).

McGregor, Sue L. T. "Transdisciplinary Knowledge Creation." In *Transdisciplinary Professional Learning and Practice*, edited by Paul Gibbs, 9–24. Cham, Switzerland: Springer International Publishing, 2015b.

McMichael, Anthony J. "Transdisciplinarity in Science." In *Transdisciplinarity: Recreating Integrated Knowledge*, edited by Margaret A. Somerville and David J. Rapport, 203–209. Montréal, Canada: McGill-Queen's Press-MQUP, 2000b.

Melin, Göran. "Pragmatism and Self-Organization: Research Collaboration on the Individual Level." *Research Policy* 29, no. 1 (2000): 31–40. http://dx.doi.org/10.1016/S0048-7333(99)00031-1.

Merriam-Webster's Collegiate Dictionary. Springfield, MA: Merriam-Webster Inc., 2004.

Messerli, Bruno, and Paul Messerli. "From Local Projects in the Alps to Global Change Programmes in the Mountains of the World: Milestones in Transdisciplinary Research." In *Handbook of Transdisciplinary Research*, edited by Gertrude Hirsch Hadorn, Holger Hoffmann-Riem, Susette Biber-Klemm, Walter Grossenbacher-Mansuy, Dominique Joye, Christian Pohl, Urs Wiesmann, and Elisabeth Zemp, 43–62. Dordrecht, London: Springer Science + Business Media B.V., 2008.

Metz, Paul, and Béla Foltin. "A Social History of Madness; Or, Who's Buying This Round? Anticipating and Avoiding Gaps in Collection Development." *College and Research Libraries* 51, no. 1 (1990): 33–39. http://crl.acrl.org/content/51/1/33.full.pdf (accessed July 3, 2016).

Michener, William K., Thomas J. Baerwald, Penelope Firth, Margaret A. Palmer, James L. Rosenberger, Elizabeth A. Sandlin, and Herman Zimmerman. "Defining and Unraveling Biocomplexity." *BioScience* 51, no. 12 (2001): 1018–1023.

Miller, Clark A. "Policy Challenges and University Reform." In *The Oxford Handbook of Interdisciplinarity*, edited by Robert Frodeman, Julie Thompson Klein, and Carl Mitcham, 333–44. Oxford, NY: Oxford University Press, 2010.

Miller, Raymond C. "Varieties of Interdisciplinary Approaches in the Social Sciences: A 1981 Overview." *Issues in Integrative Studies* 1 (1982): 1–37.

Miller, Rebecca K. *Individual Adaptation: Interdisciplinary Perspectives on Personal Identity and Learning during Organizational Change*. Paper presented at ACRL 2015, Portland, OR. In ACRL Proceedings. Chicago: American Library Association, 2015. http://www.ala.org/acrl/sites/ala.org.acrl/files/content/conferences/confsandpreconfs/2015/Miller.pdf (accessed July 2, 2016).

Miller, Robin E. "Reference Communities: Applying the Community of Practice Concept to Development of Reference Knowledge." *Public Services Quarterly* 7, no. 1–2 (2011): 18–26. http://dx.doi.org/10.1080/15228959.2011.572772.

Miller, William Cox. *Flash of Brilliance: Inspiring Creativity Where You Work.* New York: Perseus Books, 1998.

Miller, Thaddeus R., Timothy D. Baird, Caitlin M. Littlefield, Gary Kofinas, F. Stuart Chapin III, and Charles L. Redman. "Epistemological Pluralism: Reorganizing Interdisciplinary Research." *Ecology and Society* 13, no. 2 (2008). http://www.ecologyandsociety.org/vol13/iss2/art46/ (accessed March 1, 2016).

Milliken, Frances J., and Luis L. Martins. "Searching for Common Threads: Understanding the Multiple Effects of Diversity in Organizational Groups." *Academy of Management Review* 21, no. 2 (1996): 402–433. http://dx.doi.org/10.5465/AMR.1996.9605060217.

Milstead, Jessica L. "Needs for Research in Indexing." *Journal of the American Society for Information Science (1986–1998)* 45, no. 8 (1994): 577–582.

Mishra, Punya, Matthew J. Koehler, and Danah Henriksen. "The 7 Transdisciplinary Habits of Mind: Extending the TPACK Framework towards 21st Century Learning." *Educational Technology* 51, no. 2 (2010): 22–28.

Mittelmark, Maurice B., Michaela Bitarello Do Amaral-Sabadini, Peter Anderson, Antoni Gual, Fleur Braddick, Silvia Matrai, and Tamyko Ysa. "Computer-Mediated Communication in Alice Rap: A Methodology to Enhance the Quality of Large-Scale Transdisciplinary Research." *The Innovation Journal* 17, no. 3 (2012): 1–13.

Mobjörk, Malin. "Consulting versus Participatory Transdisciplinarity: A Refined Classification of Transdisciplinary Research." *Futures* 42, no. 8 (2010): 866–873. http://dx.doi.org/10.1016/j.futures.2010.03.003.

Montuori, Alfonso. "Five Dimensions of Applied Transdisciplinarity." *Integral Leadership Review* (2012). http://integralleadershipreview.com/7518-transdisciplinary-reflections-2/ (accessed August 23, 2016).

Montuori, Alfonso. "Foreword: Transdisciplinarity." In *Transdisciplinarity: Theory and Practice*, edited by Basarab Nicolescu, ix-xvii. Creskill, NJ: Hampton Press, 2008.

Montuori, Alfonso. "Gregory Bateson and the Promise of Transdisciplinarity." *Cybernetics & Human Knowing* 12, no. 1–2 (2005): 147–158.

Montuori, Alfonso. "The Joy of Inquiry." *Journal of Transformative Education* 6, no. 1 (2008a): 8–26. http://dx.doi.org/10.1177/1541344608317041.

Montuori, Alfonso. "Transformative Leadership for the 21st Century: Reflections on the Design of a Graduate Leadership Curriculum." *ReVision* 30 (2010): 4–14.

Morgan, Glen D., Kimberly Kobus, Karen K. Gerlach, Charles Neighbors, Caryn Lerman, David B. Abrams, and Barbara K. Rimer. "Facilitating Transdisciplinary Research: The Experience of the Transdisciplinary Tobacco Use Research Centers." *Nicotine & Tobacco Research* 5, no. Suppl 1 (2003): S11–S19. http://dx.doi.org/10.1080/14622200310001625537.

Morgan, Howard. "Open Letter to NIH. Review of Cross-Disciplinary Applications." *The Physiologist* 31, no. 2 (1988): 17–19.

Morgan, Nicole. "Notions of Transdisciplinarity." In *Transdisciplinarity: Recreating Integrated Knowledge*, edited by Margaret A. Somerville and David J. Rapport, 38–41. Montréal, Canada: McGill-Queen's Press-MQUP, 2000.

Moseley, Eva Steiner. *Women, Information and the Future. Collecting and Sharing Resources Worldwide*. Fort Atkinson, WI: Highsmith Press, 1995.

Moss, David M., Terry A. Osborn, and Douglas Kaufman. "Going Beyond the Boundaries." In *Beyond the Boundaries: A Transdisciplinary Approach to Learning and Teaching*, edited by Douglas Kaufman, Terry A. Osborn, and David M. Moss, 1–11. Westport, CT: Praeger Publishers, 2003.

Mote, L.J.B. "Reasons for the Variations in the Information Needs of Scientists." *Journal of Documentation* 18, no. 4 (1962): 169–175. http://dx.doi.org/10.1108/eb026319.

Moulaert, Frank. "Social Innovation and Community Development: Concepts, Theories, and Challenges." In *Can Neighbourhoods Save the City?: Community Development and Social Innovation*, edited by Frank Moulaert, Erik Swyngedouw, Flavia Martinelli, and Sara Gonzalez, 4–16. London: Routledge, 2010.

Moulaert, Frank, Flavia Martinelli, Erik Swyngedouw, and Sara Gonzalez. "Towards Alternative Model (s) of Local Innovation." *Urban Studies* 42, no. 11 (2005): 1969–1990. http://dx.doi.org/10.1080/00420980500279893.

Müller, Daniel B., Sybrand P. Tjallingii, and Kees J. Canters. "A Transdisciplinary Learning Approach to Foster Convergence of Design, Science and Deliberation in Urban and Regional Planning." *Systems Research and Behavioral Science* 22, no. 3 (2005): 193–208. http://dx.doi.org/10.1002/sres.655.

National Academies of Sciences. *Facilitating Interdisciplinary Research, Report from Committee on Facilitating Interdisciplinary Research Committee on Science, Engineering, and Public Policy*. Washington, DC: The National Academies Press, 2005. http://www.nap.edu/catalog/11153/facilitating-interdisciplinary-research (accessed April 2, 2016).

National Science Foundation. *Globalization of Science and Engineering Research*. 2010. http://www.nsf.gov/statistics/nsb1003/ (accessed July 22, 2015).

National Science Foundation. Merit Review Broader Impacts Criterion: Representative Activities. 2002. https://www.nsf.gov/pubs/2002/nsf022/bicexamples.pdf (accessed August 30, 2016).

Neuhauser, Linda, and Christian Pohl. "Integrating Transdisciplinarity and Translational Concepts and Methods into Graduate Education." In *Transdisciplinary Professional Learning and Practice*, edited by Paul Gibbs, 99–120. Cham, Switzerland: Springer International Publishing, 2015.

Newby, Jill. "Entering Unfamiliar Territory: Building an Information Literacy Course for Graduate Students in Interdisciplinary Areas." *Reference & User Services Quarterly* 50, no. 3 (2011): 224–229. http://www.jstor.org/stable/41241167.

Newell, William H. "Distinctive Challenges of Library-Based Interdisciplinary Research and Writing: A Guide." *Issues in Integrative Studies* 25 (2007): 84–110.

Newell William H. "Transdisciplinarity Reconsidered." In *Transdisciplinarity: Recreating Integrated Knowledge*, edited by Margaret A. Somerville and David J. Rapport, 42–48. Montréal, Canada: McGill-Queen's Press-MQUP, 2000.

Newell, William H. "Undergraduate General Education." In *The Oxford Handbook of Interdisciplinarity*, edited by Robert Frodeman, Julie Thompson Klein, and Carl Mitcham, 360–371. Oxford, NY: Oxford University Press, 2010.

Nicolescu, Basarab. *Transdisciplinarity: Past, Present and Future.* In *Palestra apresentada no II Congresso Mundial de Transdisciplinaridade 06 a 12 de setembro de 2005 Vila Velha/Vitória-SC—Brasil*, 2005. http://cetrans.com.br/textos/transdisciplinarity-past-present-and-future.pdf (accessed August 23, 2016)

Nicolescu, Basarab (editor) *Transdisciplinarity: Theory and Practice.* With foreword by Alfonso Montuori. Cresskill, NJ: Hampton Press, 2008.

Nicolescu, Basarab. "Disciplinary Boundaries—What Are They and How They Can Be Transgressed." In *International Symposium on Research across Boundaries.* 2010a. http://basarab-nicolescu.fr/Docs_articles/Disciplinary_Boundaries.htm (accessed January 27, 2016).

Nicolescu, Basarab. *Manifesto of Transdisciplinarity.* Albany, NY: SUNY Press, 2002.

Nicolescu, Basarab. "Methodology of Transdisciplinarity." *Transdisciplinary Journal of Engineering and Science* 1, no. 1 (2010b): 19–38. http://www.basarab-nicolescu.fr/Docs_Notice/TJESNo_1_12_2010.pdf (accessed August 27, 2016).

Nicolescu, Basarab. "Transdisciplinarity as Methodological Framework for Going beyond the Science-Religion Debate." *Transdisciplinarity in Science and Religion* 2 (2007): 35–60.

Nicolescu, Basarab. "Transdisciplinarity: Past, Present and Future." In *Palestra apresentada no II Congresso Mundial de Transdisciplinaridade 06 a 12 de setembro de 2005 Vila Velha/Vitória—SC—Brasil*, 2005. http://cetrans.com.br/textos/transdisciplinarity-past-present-and-future.pdf (accessed August 23, 2016).

Nicolescu, Basarab. *The Transdisciplinary Evolution of Learning: Condition for Sustainable Development.* Talk at the International Congress "Universities' Responsibilities to Society," International Association of Universities, Chulalongkorn University, Bangkok, Thailand, November 12–14, 1997. http://ciret-transdisciplinarity.org/bulletin/b12c8.php (accessed February 8, 2016).

Novy, Andreas, Sarah Habersack, and Barbara Schaller. "Innovative Forms of Knowledge Production: Transdisciplinarity and Knowledge Alliances." In *The International Handbook on Social Innovation: Collective Action, Social*

Learning and Transdisciplinary Research, edited by Frank Moulaert, 430–441. Cheltenham, UK: Edward Elgar Publishing, 2013.

Nowotny, Helga. "The Potential of Transdisciplinarity." In *Discussing Transdisciplinarity: Making Professions and the New Mode of Knowledge Production, the Nordic Reader*, edited by Halina Dunin-Woyseth and M. Nielsen, 10–19. Oslo, Norway: Oslo School of Architecture, 2004.

Nowotny, Helga, Peter Scott, and Michael Gibbons. *Re-Thinking Science: Knowledge and the Public in an Age of Uncertainty*. Cambridge, UK: Polity, 2001.

Novy, Andreas, Sarah Habersack, and Barbara Schaller. "Innovative Forms of Knowledge Production: Transdisciplinarity and Knowledge Alliances." In *The International Handbook on Social Innovation: Collective Action, Social Learning and Transdisciplinary Research*, edited by Frank Moulaert, 430–441. Cheltenham, UK: Edward Elgar Publishing, 2013.

O'Donnell, Angela M., Lori Adams DuRussel, and Sharon J. Derry. *Cognitive Processes in Interdisciplinary Groups: Problems and Possibilities (Research Monograph No. 5)*.Madison, WI: University of Wisconsin-Madison, National Institute for Science Education, 1997.

OECD. *The University and the Community: The Problems of Changing Relationships*. Paris: Organisation for Economic Co-operation and Development, 1982.

Olson, Gary M., and Judith S. Olson. "Distance Matters." *Human-Computer Interaction* 15, no. 2 (2000): 139–178. http://dx.doi.org/10.1207/S15327051HCI1523_4.

Ortega, Lina, and Karen Antell. "Tracking Cross-Disciplinary Information Use by Author Affiliation: Demonstration of a Method." *College & Research Libraries* 67, no. 5 (2006): 446–462. http://dx.doi.org/10.5860/crl.67.5.446.

Ouspensky, Peter Demianovich. *In Search of the Miraculous: Fragments of an Unknown Teaching*. San Diego, CA: Houghton Mifflin Harcourt, 2001.

Oxford English Dictionary, edited by John Simpson and Edmund Weiner. New York: Oxford University Press, 1989.

Pahre, Robert. "Patterns of Knowledge Communities in the Social Sciences." *Library Trends* 44, no. 2 (1996): 204–226.

Palmer, Carole L. "Information Research on Interdisciplinarity." In *The Oxford Handbook of Interdisciplinarity*, edited by Robert Frodeman, Julie Thompson Klein, and Carl Mitcham, 174–188. Oxford, NY: Oxford University Press, 2010.

Palmer, Carole L. "Information Work at the Boundaries of Science: Linking Library Services to Research Practices." *Library Trends* 45, no. 2 (1996): 165–191.

Palmer, Carole L. "Scholarly Work and the Shaping of Digital Access." *Journal of the American Society for Information Science and Technology* 56, no. 11 (2005): 1140–1153. http://dx.doi.org/10.1002/asi.20204.

Palmer, Carole L. "Structures and Strategies of Interdisciplinary Science." *Journal of the Association for Information Science and Technology* 50, no. 3 (1999): 242–253.

Palmer, Carole L. *Work at the Boundaries of Science: Information and the Interdisciplinary Research Process*. Dordrecht, The Netherlands:Springer Science & Business Media, 2001.

Palmer, Carole L., and Melissa H. Cragin. "Scholarship and Disciplinary Practices." *Annual Review of Information Science and Technology* 42, no. 1 (2008): 163–212. http://dx.doi.org/10.1002/aris.2008.1440420112.

Palmer, Carole L., and Laura J. Neumann. "The Information Work of Interdisciplinary Humanities Scholars: Exploration and Translation." *The Library Quarterly* (2002): 85–117.

Palmer, Carole L., Lauren C. Teffeau, and Carrie M. Pirmann. *Scholarly Information Practices in the Online Environment. Report Commissioned by OCLC Research (2009)*. http://www.conference-center.oclc.org/content/dam/research/publi cations/library/2009/2009-02.pdf (accessed August 1, 2016).

Park, Ji-Yong, and Jeong-Bae Son. "Transitioning toward Transdisciplinary Learning in a Multidisciplinary Environment." *International Journal of Pedagogies and Learning* 6, no. 1 (2010): 82–93. http://dx.doi.org/10.5172/ijpl.6.1.82.

Pasler, Jann. "Round Table III: Directions in Musicology." *Acta Musicologica* 69, Fasc. 1 (1997): 16–21. http://www.jstor.org/stable/932796.

Patell, Shireen R. K. "Disciplinarity." *Social Text* 27, no. 3 (2009): 104–111. http://dx.doi.org/10.1215/01642472-2009-018.

Piaget, Jean. "The Epistemology of Interdisciplinary Relationships." In *Interdisciplinarity: Problems of Teaching and Research in Universities*, 127–139. Paris: OECD, Centre for Educational Research and Innovation, 1972.

Pierce, Sydney J. "Boundary Crossing in Research Literatures as a Means of Interdisciplinary Information Transfer." *Journal of the Association for Information Science and Technology* 50, no. 3 (1999): 271–279.

Pink, Daniel H. *A Whole New Mind: Why Right-Brainers Will Rule the Future*. New York: Riverhead Books, 2006.

Plucker, Jonathan, and Ronald Beghetto. "Why Creativity is Domain General, Why It Looks Domain Specific, and Why the Distinction Does Not Matter." In *Creativity: From Potential to Realization*, edited by Robert J. Sternberg, Elena L. Grigorenko, and Jerome L. Singer, 153–167. Washington, DC: American Psychological Association, 2004.

Plucker, Jonathan, and Dasha Zabelina. "Creativity and Interdisciplinarity: One Creativity or Many Creativities?" *ZDM: The International Journal on Mathematics Education* 41, no. 1–2 (2009): 5–11. http://dx.doi.org/10.1007/s11858-008-0155-3.

Pohl, Christian. "What Is Progress in Transdisciplinary Research?" *Futures* 43, no. 6 (2011): 618–626. http://dx.doi.org/10.1016/j.futures.2011.03.001.

Pohl, Christian, and Gertrude Hirsch Hadorn. *Principles for Designing Transdisciplinary Research*. Munich: Oekom, 2007.

Popova, Maria. "Combinatorial Creativity and the Myth of Originality: The Power of the Synthesizing Mind and the Building Blocks of Combinatorial

Creativity." *Smithsonian.com*, June 6, 2012. http://www.smithsonianmag.com/innovation/combinatorial-creativity-and-the-myth-of-originality-114843098/?no-ist (accessed September 10, 2016).

Porter, Alan L., and Daryl E. Chubin. "An Indicator of Cross-Disciplinary Research." *Scientometrics* 8, no. 3–4 (1985): 161–176. http://dx.doi.org/10.1007/BF02016934.

Powell, Walter. "Neither Market nor Hierarchy." In *The Sociology of Organizations: Classic, Contemporary, and Critical Readings*, edited by Michael J. Handel, 315–330. Thousand Oaks, CA: Sage Publications, 2003.

Price, Derek J. de Solla. *Little Science, Big Science.* New York: Columbia University Press, 1963.

Price, Derek J. de Solla. *Science since Babylon.* New Haven, Yale University Press, 1961.

Prokopy, Linda S., Chad E. Hart, Raymond Massey, et al. "Using a Team Survey to Improve Team Communication For Enhanced Delivery of Agro-Climate Decision Support Tools." *Agricultural Systems* 138 (2015): 31–37. http://dx.doi.org/10.1016/j.agsy.2015.05.002.

Qiu, Liwen. "A Study of Interdisciplinary Research Collaboration." *Research Evaluation* 2, no. 3 (1992): 169–175.

Ramadier, Thierry. "Transdisciplinarity and Its Challenges: The Case of Urban Studies." *Futures* 36, no. 4 (2004): 423–439. http://dx.doi.org/10.1016/j.futures.2003.10.009.

Ranganathan, Shiyali Ramamrita. *Reference Service*, 2nd edition. Bombay, India: Asia Publishing House, 1961.

Rapport, David J. "Transdisciplinarity: An Approach to Problem-solving in a Complex World." In *Transdisciplinarity: Recreating Integrated Knowledge*, edited by Margaret A. Somerville and David J. Rapport, 135–144. Montréal, Canada: McGill-Queen's Press-MQUP, 2000.

Repko, Allen F., Rick Szostak, and Michelle Phillips Buchberger. *Introduction to Interdisciplinary Studies.* Thousand Oaks, CA: Sage Publications, 2013.

Reynolds, Sally Jo. "In Theory There Is No Solution: The Impediments to a Subject Cataloging Code." *The Library Quarterly* (1989): 223–238. http://www.jstor.org/stable/4308378.

Reynolds, Gretchen E., Cynthia Holt, and John Walsh. "Collection Development: Acquiring Content Across and Beyond Disciplines." In *Interdisciplinarity and Academic Libraries*, edited by Daniel C. Mack and Craig Gibson, 97–113. Chicago, IL: Association of College and Research Libraries, 2012.

Rittel, Horst W. J., and Melvin M. Webber. "Dilemmas in a General Theory of Planning." *Policy Sciences* 4, no. 2 (1973): 155–169. http://dx.doi.org/10.1007/BF01405730.

Robb, Margaret. "Disciplinary Boundaries in an Interdisciplinary World." In *Social Science Libraries: Interdisciplinary Collections, Services, Networks*, edited by Steve W. Witt and Lynne M. Rudasill, 40–52. New York: De Gruyter Saur, 2010.

Robinson, Lyn, and Mike Maguire. "The Rhizome and the Tree: Changing Metaphors for Information Organisation." *Journal of Documentation* 66, no. 4 (2010): 604–613. http://dx.doi.org/10.1108/00220411011052975.

Root-Bernstein, Robert S. "The Sciences and Arts Share a Common Creative Aesthetic." In *The Elusive Synthesis: Aesthetics and Science*, edited by Alfred I. Tauber, 49–82. Amsterdam, The Netherlands: Kluwer Academic Publishers, 1996.

Root-Bernstein, Robert S., and Michele M. Root-Bernstein. *Sparks of Genius: The Thirteen Thinking Tools of the World's Most Creative People*. New York: Houghton Mifflin, 1999.

Rosenfield, Patricia L. "The Potential of Transdisciplinary Research for Sustaining and Extending Linkages between the Health and Social Sciences." *Social Science & Medicine* 35, no. 11 (1992): 1343–1357. http://dx.doi .org/10.1016/0277-9536(92)90038-R.

Roux, Dirk J., Kevin H. Rogers, Harry Biggs, Peter J. Ashton, and Anne Sergeant. "Bridging the Science-Management Divide: Moving from Unidirectional Knowledge Transfer to Knowledge Interfacing and Sharing." *Ecology and Society* 11, no. 1 (2006): 4. http://www.ecologyandsociety.org/vol11/iss1/ art4/ (accessed August 23, 2016).

Roux, Dirk J., Richard J. Stirzaker, Charles M. Breen, E. C. Lefroy, and Hamish P. Cresswell. "Framework for Participative Reflection on the Accomplishment of Transdisciplinary Research Programs." *Environmental Science & Policy* 13, no. 8 (2010): 733–741. http://dx.doi.org/10.1016/j.envsci.2010.08.002.

Rowlands, Ian, David Nicholas, Peter Williams, Paul Huntington, Maggie Fieldhouse, Barrie Gunter, Richard Withey, Hamid R. Jamali, Tom Dobrowolski, and Carol Tenopir. "The Google Generation: The Information Behaviour of the Researcher of the Future." *Aslib Proceedings* 60, no. 4 (2008): 290–310. http://dx.doi.org/10.1108/00012530810887953.

Roy, Rustum. "Interdisciplinary Science on Campus—The Elusive Dream." *Chemical and Engineering News* 55, no. 35 (1977): 28–30.

Rubio, Doris McGartland, Ellie E. Schoenbaum, Linda S. Lee, et al. "Defining Translational Research: Implications for Training." *Academic Medicine: Journal of the Association of American Medical Colleges* 85, no. 3 (2010): 470–475. http://dx.doi.org/10.1097/ACM.0b013e3181ccd618.

Russell, A. Wendy, Fern Wickson, and Anna L. Carew. "Transdisciplinarity: Context, Contradictions and Capacity." *Futures* 40, no. 5 (2008): 460–472. http://dx.doi.org/10.1016/j.futures.2007.10.005.

Ryan, Marianne. Editor's note for "Framing the Framework: The Rigorous Responsibilities of Library and Information Science" by Nathan Filbert. *Reference & User Services Quarterly* 55, no. 3 (2016): 199. https://journals. ala.org/rusq/article/view/5929/7517 (accessed September 1, 2016).

Sage, Andrew. "Transdisciplinarity Perspectives in Systems Engineering and Management." In *Transdisciplinarity: Recreating Integrated Knowledge*, edited by Margaret A. Somerville and David J. Rapport, 158–169. Montréal, Canada: McGill-Queen's Press-MQUP, 2000.

Saint-Exupéry, Antoine de. *The Little Prince*. New York: Harcourt, Brace and World, 2000.

Salter, Liora. *Mandated Science: Science and Scientists in the Making of Standards (Environmental Ethics and Science Policy)*. Norwell, MA: Kluwer Academic Publishers, 1988.

Salter, Liora, and Alison Hearn. *Outside the Lines: Issues in Interdisciplinary Research*. Montreal: McGill-Queen's University Press, 1997.

Sandstrom, Pamela Effrein. "An Optimal Foraging Approach to Information Seeking and Use." *The Library Quarterly* (1994): 414–449. http://www.jstor.org/stable/4308969.

Sarewitz, Daniel. "Against Holism." In *The Oxford Handbook of Interdisciplinarity*, edited by Robert Frodeman, Julie Thompson Klein, and Carl Mitcham, 65–75. Oxford, NY: Oxford University Press, 2010.

Schmitt, Nola A. "Moving towards Transdisciplinary Learning for Graduate Nursing Students." Paper presented at the 18th International Nursing Research Congress. Vienna, Austria, July 11–14, 2007.

Scholz, Roland W., Daniel J. Lang, Arnim Wiek, Alexander I. Walter, and Michael Stauffacher. "Transdisciplinary Case Studies as a Means of Sustainability Learning: Historical Framework and Theory." *International Journal of Sustainability in Higher Education* 7, no. 3 (2006): 226–251. http://dx.doi.org/10.1108/14676370610677829.

Schön, Donald. *Beyond the Stable State: Public and Private Learning in a Changing Society*. Harmondsworth: Penguin, 1973.

Schön, Donald A. "Knowing-in-Action: The New Scholarship Requires a New Epistemology." *Change: The Magazine of Higher Learning* 27, no. 6 (1995): 27–34. http://dx.doi.org/10.1080/00091383.1995.10544673.

Schön, Donald A. *The Reflective Practitioner: How Professionals Think in Action*. New York: Basic Books, 1983.

Schummer, Joachim. "Multidisciplinarity, Interdisciplinarity, and Patterns of Research Collaboration in Nanoscience and Nanotechnology." *Scientometrics* 59, no. 3 (2004): 425–465. http://dx.doi.org/10.1023/B:SCIE.0000018542.71314.38.

Schwartz, Meredith. "Top Skills for Tomorrow's Librarians." *Library Journal* (March 9, 2016). http://lj.libraryjournal.com/2016/03/careers/top-skills-for-tomorrows-librarians-careers-2016/#_ (accessed September 8, 2016).

Science. Special issue: Grand Challenges in Science Education, April 19, 2013.

Scimeca, Ross, and Robert V. Labaree. "Synoptic Reference: Introducing a Polymathic Approach to Reference Services." *Library Trends* 63, no. 3 (2015): 464–486. http://dx.doi.org/10.1353/lib.2015.0005.

Searing, Susan E. "How Libraries Cope with Interdisciplinarity: The Case of Women's Studies." *Issues in Integrative Studies* 10 (1992): 7–25.

Searing, Susan E. "Meeting the Information Needs of Interdisciplinary Scholars: Issues for Administrators of Large University Libraries." *Library Trends* 45, no. 2 (1996): 315–342.

Segalàs, J., and G. Tejedor. "Transdiciplinarity: A Must for Sustainable Education." Keynote address at the 41st SEFI Conference, Leuven, Belgium, September 16–20, 2013. http://www.sefi.be/conference-2013/images/keynote_segalas.pdf (accessed August 23, 2016).

Sexton, John. "A Measure of the Creativity of a Nation Is How Well It Works with Those Beyond Its Borders." *Scientific American* 307, no. 4 (2012): 36.

Shenton, Andrew K., and Naomi V. Hay-Gibson. "Information Behaviour and Information Literacy: The Ultimate in Transdisciplinary Phenomena?" *Journal of Librarianship and Information Science* 43, no. 3 (2011): 166–175. http://dx.doi.org/10.1177/0961000611410767.

Shumway, David R., and Ellen Messer-Davidow. "Disciplinarity: An Introduction." *Poetics Today* 12, no 2 (1991): 201–225. http://www.jstor.org/stable/1772850.

Simonton, Dean Keith. "The Continued Evolution of Creative Darwinism." *Psychological Inquiry* 10, no. 4 (1999): 362–367. http://www.jstor.org/stable/1449466.

Simonton, Dean Keith. "Creative Development as Acquired Expertise: Theoretical Issues and an Empirical Test." *Developmental Review* 20, no. 2 (2000): 283–318. http://dx.doi.org/10.1006/drev.1999.0504.

Simonton, Dean Keith. *Creativity in Science: Chance, Logic, Genius, and Zeitgeist.* Cambridge: Cambridge University Press, 2004.

Simonton, Dean Keith. "Expertise, Competence, and Creative Ability. The Perplexing Complexities." In *Perspectives on the Psychology of Abilities, Competencies, and Expertise*, edited by Robert J. Sternberg and Elena L. Grigorenko, 213–239. New York: Cambridge University Press, 2003.

Smith, Liberty, Heather J. Martin, Jason Burrage, Megan E. Standridge, Sarah Ragland, and Martina Bailey. "Service-Learning and Interdisciplinarity." In *Creating Our Identities in Service-Learning and Community Engagement*, edited by Barbara E. Moely, Shelley Billig, and Barbara A. Holland, 215–235. Charlotte, NC: Information Age Publishing, 2009.

Somerville, Margaret A. "Transdisciplinarity: Structuring Creative Tension." In *Transdisciplinarity: Recreating Integrated Knowledge*, edited by Margaret A. Somerville and David J. Rapport, 94–107. Montréal, Canada: McGill-Queen's Press-MQUP, 2000.

Somerville, Margaret A., and David J. Rapport (editors). *Transdisciplinarity: Recreating Integrated Knowledge*. Montréal, Canada: McGill-Queen's Press-MQUP, 2000.

Sonnenwald, Diane H. "Scientific Collaboration: A Synthesis of Challenges and Strategies." In *Annual Review of Information Science and Technology*, vol. 41, edited by Blaise Cronin, 643–681. Medford, NJ: Information Today, 2007. http://dx.doi.org/ 10.1002/aris.2007.1440410121.

Spanner, Don. "Border Crossings: Understanding the Cultural and Informational Dilemmas of Interdisciplinary Scholars." *The Journal of Academic Librarianship* 27, no. 5 (2001): 352–336. http://dx.doi.org/10.1016/S0099-1333(01)00220-8.

Stock, Paul, and Rob J. F. Burton. "Defining Terms for Integrated (Multi-Inter-Trans-Disciplinary) Sustainability Research." *Sustainability* 3, no. 8 (2011): 1090–1113.

Stokols, Daniel. "Toward a Science of Transdisciplinary Action Research." *American Journal of Community Psychology* 38, no. 1–2 (2006): 79–93. http://dx.doi.org/10.1007/s10464-006-9060-5.

Stokols, Daniel, Juliana Fuqua, Jennifer Gress, et al. "Evaluating Transdisciplinary Science." *Nicotine & Tobacco Research* 5, no. Suppl 1 (2003): S21–S39. http://dx.doi.org/10.1080/14622200310001625555.

Stokols, Daniel, Kara L. Hall, Richard P. Moser, Annie X. Feng, Shalini Misra, and Brandie K. Taylor. "Cross-disciplinary Team Science Initiatives: Research, Training, and Translation." In *The Oxford Handbook of Interdisciplinarity*, edited by Robert Froderman, Julie Thompson Klein, and Carl Mitcham, 471–493. Oxford, NY: Oxford University Press, 2010.

Stokols, Daniel, Richard Harvey, Jennifer Gress, Juliana Fuqua, and Kimari Phillips. "In Vivo Studies of Transdisciplinary Scientific Collaboration: Lessons Learned and Implications for Active Living Research." *American Journal of Preventive Medicine* 28, no. 2 (2005): 202–213. http://dx.doi.org/10.1016/j.amepre.2004.10.016.

Stokols, Daniel, Shalini Misra, Richard P. Moser, Kara L. Hall, and Brandie K. Taylor. "The Ecology of Team Science: Understanding Contextual Influences on Transdisciplinary Collaboration." *American Journal of Preventive Medicine* 35, no. 2 (2008): S96–S115. http://dx.doi.org/10.1016/j.amepre.2008.05.003.

Swanson, Don R. "Fish Oil, Raynaud's Syndrome, and Undiscovered Public Knowledge." *Perspectives in Biology and Medicine* 30, no. 1 (1986): 7–18. http://dx.doi.org/10.1353/pbm.1986.0087.

Swanson, Don R. "Undiscovered Public Knowledge." *The Library Quarterly* (1986): 103–118. http://www.jstor.org/stable/4307965.

Swanson, Don R., and Neil R. Smalheiser. "Undiscovered Public Knowledge: A Ten-Year Update." *KDD-96 Proceedings*, 1996: 295–298. http://www.aaai.org/Papers/KDD/1996/KDD96-051.pdf (accessed July 8, 2016).

Syme, Geoff. "Integration Initiatives at CSIRO: Reflections of an Insider." *Journal of Research Practice* 1, no. 2, Article M3 (2005). http://jrp.icaap.org/index.php/jrp/article/view/17/26 (accessed March 19, 2016).

Szostak, Rick. "The Basic Concepts Classification as a Bottom-Up Strategy for the Semantic Web." *International Journal of Knowledge Content Development and Technology* 4, no. 1 (2014): 39–51. http://dx.doi.org/10.5865/IJKCT.2014.4.1.039.

Szostak, Rick. "Classification, Interdisciplinarity, and the Study of Science." *Journal of Documentation* 64, no. 3 (2008): 319–332. http://dx.doi.org/10.1108/00220410810867551.

Szostak, Rick. "Complex Concepts into Basic Concepts." *Journal of the American Society for Information Science and Technology* 62, no. 11 (2011): 2247–2265. http://dx.doi.org/10.1002/asi.21635.

Szostak, Rick, Claudio Gnoli, and María López-Huertas. *Interdisciplinary Knowledge Organization*. Switzerland: Springer International Publishing, 2016.

Tachibana, Chris. "Navigating Collaborative Grant Research." *Science* (September 13, 2013). doi: 10.1126/science.opms.r1300136.

Tress, Bärbel, Gunther Tress, and Gary Fry. "Defining Concepts and the Process of Knowledge Production in Integrative Research." In *From Landscape Research to Landscape Planning: Aspects of Integration, Education and Application*, edited by Bärbel Tress, Gunther Tress, Gary Fry, and Paul Opdam, 13–26. Dordrecht, The Netherlands: Springer, 2005.

21st Century Skills and the Workplace: A 2013 Microsoft Partners in Learning and Pearson Foundation Study (May 28, 2013). https://www.gyli.org/wp-content/uploads/2014/02/21st_century_skills_Gallup.pdf (accessed October 10, 2015).

UNESCO. *Beacons of the Information Society. Alexandria Proclamation on Information Literacy and Lifelong Learning.* 2005. http://portal.unesco.org/ci/en/ev.php-URL_ID=20891&URL_DO=DO_TOPIC&URL_SECTION=201.html (accessed August 23, 2016).

van Kerkhoff, Lorrae. "Global Inequalities in Research: A Transdisciplinary Exploration of Causes and Consequences." In *Tackling Wicked Problems: Through the Transdisciplinary Imagination*, edited by Valerie A. Brown, John Alfred Harris, and Jacqueline Y. Russell, 130–138. London: Earthsca, 2010.

Vasbinder, Jan W., Bertil Andersson, W. Brian Arthur, et al. "Transdisciplinary EU Science Institute Needs Funds Urgently." *Nature* 463, no. 7283 (2010): 876–876. http://dx.doi.org/10.1038/463876a.

Veld, Roeland Jaap. *Knowledge Democracy: Consequences for Science, Politics, and Media*. New York: Springer, 2010.

Vickery, Brian C. "The Structure of Subject Classifications for Document Retrieval." In *Integrative Levels Classification*, 2008–2009. http://www.iskoi.org/ilc/vickery.php (accessed July 14, 2016).

Vieira, Ricardo. "Life Stories, Cultural Métissage, and Personal Identities." *SAGE Open* 4, no. 1 (2014): 1–12. http://dx.doi.org/10.1177/2158244013517241.

Wall, Sarah, and Irene Shankar. "Adventures in Transdisciplinary Learning." *Studies in Higher Education* 33, no. 5 (2008): 551–565. http://dx.doi.org/10.1080/03075070802373008.

Ware, Mark, and Michael Mabe. *The STM Report: An Overview of Scientific and Scholarly Journal Publishing.* The Hague, The Netherlands: The International Association of Scientific, Technical and Medical Publishers, 2015. http://digitalcommons.unl.edu/scholcom/9/ (accessed August 28, 2016).

Weinberg, Bella Hass. "Why Indexing Fails the Researcher." *The Indexer* 16, no. 1 (1988): 3–6. http://www.theindexer.org/files/16-1/16-1_003.pdf (accessed July 11, 2016).

Weingart, Peter. "A Short History of Knowledge Formations." In *The Oxford Handbook of Interdisciplinarity*, edited by Robert Frodeman, Julie Thompson Klein, and Carl Mitcham, 3–14. Oxford; New York: Oxford University Press, 2010.

Weingart, Peter, and Nico Stehr (editors). *Practising Interdisciplinarity*. Toronto, Canada: University of Toronto Press, 2000.

Weller, Martin. *The Digital Scholar: How Technology Is Transforming Scholarly Practice*. London, UK: Bloomsbury, 2011.

Wenger, Etienne, Richard Arnold McDermott, and William Snyder. *Cultivating Communities of Practice: A Guide to Managing Knowledge*. Boston, MA: Harvard Business School Press, 2002.

Westbrook, Lynn. "Information Needs and Experiences of Scholars in Women's Studies: Problems and Solutions." *College & Research Libraries* 64, no. 3 (2003): 192–209. http://dx.doi.org/10.5860/crl.64.3.192.

Westbrook, Lynn. *Interdisciplinary Information Seeking in Women's Studies*. Jefferson, NC: McFarland, 1999.

White, Howard D. "Literature Retrieval for Interdisciplinary Syntheses." *Library Trends* 45, no. 2 (1996): 239–264.

White, James Boyd. "Intellectual Integration." *Northwestern University Law Review* 82, no.1 (1987): 1–18.

Wickson, Fern, Anna L. Carew, and A. W. Russell. "Transdisciplinary Research: Characteristics, Quandaries and Quality." *Futures* 38, no. 9 (2006): 1046–1059. http://dx.doi.org/10.1016/j.futures.2006.02.011.

Wilson, Edward O. "Back from Chaos." *Atlantic Monthly* 281, no. 3 (1998a): 41–62.

Wilson, Edward O. *Consilience: The Unity of Knowledge*. New York: Knopf, 1998b.

Wilson, Patrick. "Interdisciplinary Research and Information Overload." *Library Trends* 44, no. 2 (1996): 192–204.

Wilson, Myoung Chung, and Hendrik Edelman. "Collection Development in an Interdisciplinary Context." *The Journal of Academic Librarianship* 22, no. 3 (1996): 195–200. http://dx.doi.org/10.1016/S0099-1333(96)90058-0.

Windelband, Wilhelm. *A History of Philosophy*. New York: Macmillan, 1901.

Windelband, Wilhelm. "Rectorial Address, Strasbourg, 1894." *History and Theory* 19, no. 2 (1980): 169–185. http://www.jstor.org/stable/2504798.

Wolf, Gary. "Steve Jobs: The Next Insanely Great Thing." *Wired*, February 1995. http://www.wired.com/wired/archive/4.02/jobs_pr.html (accessed September 10, 2016).

Wray, K. Brad. "Scientific Authorship in the Age of Collaborative Research." *Studies in History and Philosophy of Science Part A* 37, no. 3 (2006): 505–514. http://dx.doi.org/10.1016/j.shpsa.2005.07.011.

Wu, Ling-Ling, Mu-Hsuan Huang, and Ching-Yi Chen. "Citation Patterns of the Pre-Web and Web-Prevalent Environments: The Moderating Effects of

Domain Knowledge." *Journal of the American Society for Information Science and Technology* 63, no. 11 (2012): 2182–2194. http://dx.doi.org/10.1002/asi.22710.

Young, Katherine. "Transdisciplinarity: Postmodern Buzz Word or New Methods for New Problems?" In *Transdisciplinarity: Recreating Integrated Knowledge*, edited by Margaret A. Somerville and David J. Rapport, 125–134. Montréal, Canada: McGill-Queen's Press-MQUP, 2000.

Zhou, Chunfang (editor). *Handbook of Research on Creative Problem-Solving Skill Development in Higher Education*. Hershey, PA: IGI Global, 2016.

Ziman, John. "Disciplinarity and Interdisciplinarity in Research." In *Interdisciplinarity and the Organization of Knowledge in Europe. A Conference Organized by the Academia Europaea. Cambridge, 24–26 September 1997*, edited by Richard Cunningham, 24–26. Luxembourg: Office for Official Publications of the European Communities, 1999.

Index

About the Author

Victoria Martin is the Scholarly Communications Librarian at Salisbury University Libraries in Maryland. She previously worked as the Life Sciences Librarian at the University Libraries of George Mason University in Virginia. She holds a Master of Library Science degree from Texas Woman's University and a Master of Fine Arts degree in creative writing from George Mason University. She is the author of journal articles, reviews, a book chapter, and the book *Demystifying eResearch: A Primer for Librarians*, which, according to *Library Journal*, "belongs in most academic libraries . . . and would make a great text for LIS students."